Walking the Streets of Eighteenth-Century London

John Gay's *Trivia* (1716)

EDITED BY CLARE BRANT AND SUSAN E. WHYMAN

OXFORD
UNIVERSITY PRESS

OXFORD
UNIVERSITY PRESS

Great Clarendon Street, Oxford OX2 6DP

Oxford University Press is a department of the University of Oxford.
It furthers the University's objective of excellence in research, scholarship,
and education by publishing worldwide in

Oxford New York

Auckland Cape Town Dar es Salaam Hong Kong Karachi
Kuala Lumpur Madrid Melbourne Mexico City Nairobi
New Delhi Shanghai Taipei Toronto

With offices in

Argentina Austria Brazil Chile Czech Republic France Greece
Guatemala Hungary Italy Japan Poland Portugal Singapore
South Korea Switzerland Thailand Turkey Ukraine Vietnam

Oxford is a registered trade mark of Oxford University Press
in the UK and in certain other countries

Published in the United States
by Oxford University Press Inc., New York

British Library Cataloguing in Publication Data
Data available

Library of Congress Cataloging in Publication Data
Data available

Typeset by Graphicraft Ltd., Hong Kong
Printed on acid-free paper
by the MPG Books Group
in the UK

ISBN 978-0-19-928049-0 (Hbk.)
ISBN 978-0-19-928072-8 (Pbk.)

1 3 5 7 9 10 8 6 4 2

Acknowledgements

The editors thank the helpful editorial staff at Oxford University Press, especially Rupert Cousens, Anne Gelling, Ruth Parr, and Timothy Saunders.

The editors also thank Penelope J. Corfield for chairing the North American Conference of British Studies conference panel, which was the genesis of this book and for continued support. Tim Hitchcock and Margaret Hunt also participated in this panel and gave valuable encouragement to the project. Both editors are grateful to all of the contributors for their enthusiasm, commitment, and imagination. For help with illustrations, special thanks go to Mark Jenner and Aileen Ribiero.

Clare would like to thank her family and close friends, who listened patiently to Trivial matters. Special thanks to James Waterfield for computer help, to Adrian Arbib for photographic expertise, and to Elizabeth Eger and Neil Vickers for creative conversations about the eighteenth century.

Susan also thanks Scott Wilcox, Elizabeth Fairman, and Melissa Gold Fournier for assistance at the Yale Center for British Art.

Susan wishes to thank Natalie Zemon Davis for her Folger Library seminar during which she contributed ideas towards this project.

Susan thanks her husband Frank and her children Jennifer and Bill for their constant loyalty and understanding.

Contents

List of Illustrations

Notes on Contributors

Clare Brant is a Senior Lecturer in the Department of English, King's College London. She is the author of *Eighteenth-Century Letters and British Culture* (2006) and numerous articles on literature, culture, and gender; she has also co-edited two essay collections. She is writing a book on eighteenth-century ballooning.

Susanna Braund is Professor of Classics at Stanford University. Her publications on Latin literature and Roman culture include an edition of Juvenal's first book of Satires (1996) and the Loeb Classical Library edition of the Satires of Persius and Juvenal (2004); a translation of Lucan's epic poem Civil War (1992); co-edited volumes on the passions in Roman thought and on ancient anger, and an introductory book called *Latin Literature* (2002). The reception of Latin literature in later eras will form her next major project.

Philip Carter is Publication Editor at the *Oxford Dictionary of National Biography*, University of Oxford. He is the author of *Men and the Emergence of Polite Society, Britain 1660–1800* (2001).

Tim Hitchcock is Professor of Eighteenth-Century History at the University of Hertfordshire. He has published widely on the histories of eighteenth-century poverty, sexuality, and masculinity. His most recent book is *Down and Out in Eighteenth-Century London* (2004). With Professor Robert Shoemaker he has also created 'The Old Bailey Online' (**www.oldbaileyonline.org**), a searchable edition of the 100,000 trial transcripts published between 1674 and 1834 as *The Old Bailey Proceedings*.

Margaret Hunt is Professor of History and Women's and Gender Studies at Amherst College in Massachusetts. She is the author of *The Middling Sort: Commerce, Gender, and the Family in England, 1680–1780* (1996) and has written articles on women and the law, family violence, and gender and the military.

Mark Jenner is a Senior Lecturer in the Department of History, University of York. He has published widely on the history of early modern London and on early modern medicine and hygiene. His publications include *Londinopolis* (co-edited with Paul Griffiths, 2000) and *Medicine and the Market in Premodern England and its Colonies* (co-edited with Patrick Wallis, 2007).

Aileen Ribeiro is Professor in the History of Art at the University of London , and lectures in the History of Dress at the Courtauld Instiue of Art. She has acted as costume consultant to a number of major portrait exhibitions in the UK and the

USA, and is the author of numerous articles and books, the most recent of which is *Fashion and Fiction: Dress in Art and Literature in Stuart England* (2005).

Alison Stenton recently completed a Ph.D. on Eighteenth-Century Home Tours and Discourses of Travel. She is a Teaching Fellow at King's College London, where she teaches writing skills and eighteenth-century literature to students on the Extended Medical Degree Programme.

Susan E. Whyman, formerly of Princeton University, is an independent historian who divides her time between Oxford and Princeton. She is the author of *Sociability and Power: The Cultural Worlds of the Verneys* (1999, 2001). Her current project is a cultural history of letter writing, literacy, and literature in the long eighteenth century.

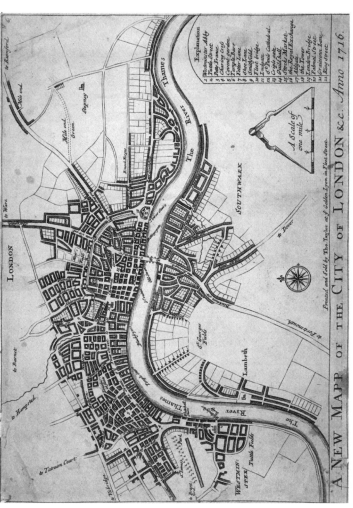

'The busy City asks instructive Song.'

Map of the City of London, Westminster, River Thames, Lambeth, Southwark and surrounding areas, anonymous (1716).

Introduction

This book offers an exciting opportunity to achieve four goals. It provides a window into the world of eighteenth-century London for all who are interested in history, literature, and the city. It invites students and teachers to take a walk along the dirty, crowded, but fascinating streets of London. It gives acknowledged experts a chance to write accessibly and imaginatively across the disciplines. Finally, it recovers one of the most lively, funny, and thought-provoking statements about urban life: John Gay's poem *Trivia: or, the Art of Walking the Streets of London* (1716). It does all of these things by linking a passionate conviction about scholarship to a very simple idea.

Our idea is that the best way to connect people with different points of view is to read the same text—in our case, John Gay's *Trivia*. We offer nine different interpretations of the poem from nine writers who are specialists in the eighteenth century. Their work ranges widely across the humanities in the fields of literature, history, classics, biography, geography, costume, and gender. Though the chapters have distinct points of view, they are united in their focus upon the poem, the period, and the place. Together they make the heat, grime, and smells of the underbelly of London come alive in new ways.

We hope that the book will help all readers to probe an intellectual topic from a variety of points of view—to take ideas apart, look at them from different angles, and put them back together again. The sum of our readings, we believe, is greater than its individual parts. We offer multiple approaches to the city—literary and historical, visual and spatial, past and present. Readers will find a spectrum of ways to think about history, and distinct ways to read a literary text.

Our book has four subjects—a poem, London, readings of the poem, and reflections on ways of reading that poem. Like compass points, these four subjects may draw readers differently through the book. Some may wish to go to the poem first to discover Gay's wit and poetic skill. The poem notes offer many surprises about eighteenth-century London and help the reader to understand ways of speaking in Gay's city—its slang, allusions, stories, and rhymes. Those most interested in London and readings of the poem can go straight to the essays. Some readers may prefer to dip in and out of the poem and essays. The route taken will itself be a way of reading, one that participates in our project of learning more about why we take the paths we do.

LONDON IN 1716

At the dawn of the eighteenth century, William King described the streets of London ' "pestered with Hackney Coaches and insolent carmen, shops and taverns, noise and such a cloud of sea coals that if there be a resemblance of Hell upon earth it is this volcano in a foggy day" '.[1] Yet in 1709 a country gentleman thought the city and its thoroughfares were a sunlit 'paradise'. For the ladies, he remarked, the city was 'women's heaven'.[2] Which view was right, we may ask, and why did Gay choose to write poetry about London's streets? Of course, there were as many views about the city's streets as the number of people who strode through them. It is not at all surprising that Gay found London street life a compelling topic or that it still captivates present-day writers.[3] Without a coach for most of his life, Gay would have learned to walk in a streetwise manner. This was a significant activity with considerable ramifications. In the simple act of being a pedestrian, Gay was participating in a metropolitan experiment that was creating a new urban way of life, particular to London. This development prefigured the urbanization that would spread throughout Britain later in the century. It captivated the attention of residents, country folk, and foreigners alike.

London's urban way of life was heady and intense, exhilarating and exasperating, but never dull. One could hate it or love it or do both at the same time. But it was not to be ignored or relegated into the background. Guidebooks, diaries, parish records, and literary works like *Trivia* confirm that all human experience was to be found on the streets of London. This hackneyed saying expressed a deep-seated truth that had special resonance in 1716—fifty years after fire had swept away lanes inside the old City walls. Now new streets and squares in outlying areas were lined with buildings and pulsating with life. They created a dense web of humanity to the east, north, and west of the old city, where fields had lain vacant in the seventeenth century.

We see a fragment of this rebuilt London in our cover painting of Covent Garden (*c*.1726) by Pieter Angillis (1685–1734).[4] It depicts a place outside the City walls that was central to the lives of people who spent their days on the street. Angillis shows individuals of every rank and age mingling together in the market. They buy, sell, and carry goods, some of which are falling off a porter's head to the consternation of passers-by. An aged crone offers vegetables, whilst children play at cards or have their fortunes told. A poor man sleeps on a basket lid, while a gallant dallies with two handsome women. Wheelbarrows filled with onions, heavily laden carts, and flying coaches in the background inject movement into a panorama that radiates energy and vitality.

Yet above, behind, and around the bustle and disorder, classical colonnades shelter Inigo Jones's piazza and church. Polite customers with money in their pockets have come to buy goods and enjoy the playhouses, alehouses, coffee houses, brothels, and retailers of every kind. As buyers leave to roam the streets, however, they are forced to become part of a remarkably mixed crowd. They must literally rub shoulders with the fops, gamblers, whores, mendicants, pickpockets, vendors, and spectators who populate the pages of *Trivia*. They must also suffer the traffic jams, open sewers, and air pollution that Gay carefully describes.

Yet they appear to be free. The lowest and the highest move at will as they play out their lives on the streets. London's thoroughfares are still open, public places of ritual, exchange, and above all conflict.[5] Angillis and Gay offer representations of a fluid city in movement—a place of social, economic, and geographic mobility filled with opportunity as well as peril. Freedom of movement was not always available to this degree, and after the mid-eighteenth century, it would become less so. In 1716, however, codes of street conduct were still evolving, and Gay was quick to offer his own in *Trivia*. Successful attempts at paving, lighting, and the Bow Street police would come later.

It was these vibrant places of intersection that inspired Gay. The crowd gave the street structure and constructed its own codes, manners, rituals, and views of what London was all about. The threat of disorder always lay just below the surface, as the surging mass of humanity pushed and shoved against each other. Indeed, the crowd might be considered an emblem of London in 1716—a product of the urbanization that drew people together in the first place and a symbol that shaped ideas about the city in real and imagined ways. The brief description of London that follows is intended to help readers understand the poem and the essays. Like Angellis's painting, it envisions London as a marketplace of competing goods, people, and ideas—a city of many contrasts in a fluid time of transition. This is not to deny London's inherent stability and the continuing influence of the old physical and cultural foundations that gave the capital its strength. Our goal is to bring to life the slice of street life that was accessible to people from every rank of society.

Londoners could be excused for thinking their city was the centre of the world. Unlike any other European city, London was at once the legal, administrative, political, social, and economic centre of an emerging empire. In 1500 there were ten European cities that were larger than London; in 1600 there were only two, and by 1716, none. The capital's huge population dwarfed all other English towns, surging from 200,000 in 1600 to over 575,000 in 1700, or 11 per cent of the nation—the largest percentage of any country's inhabitants.[6] There was not only growth in numbers but also a stunning spatial expansion of buildings outside the City walls. As the built-up core extended in every direction, especially to Westminster and fields to the west, a new urban region marked by uncontrolled growth was being formed. This expansion upset traditional patterns of government as old medieval parishes and corporate governing bodies lost control over inhabitants.

The new areas, now under the jurisdiction of magistrates and local vestries, contained 75 per cent of London's population.[7] In some cases, authorities created to govern rural communities were overseeing urban parishes of more than 10,000 inhabitants.[8] Yet the rigid distinctions between the east and west ends had not yet come into being. Boundaries were blurred as tradesmen, workmen, and those who served the propertied class occupied back alleys and lanes in all parts of the capital. Gay and Angillis would have noticed that London was changing from a compact traditional city to a rambling heterogeneous metropolis.[9] A perambulation of its thoroughfares might now cover some 250 miles and include 2,175 streets.[10]

To garner the fruits of this relentless expansion, over 8,000 people migrated annually to the capital. They were needed to offset soaring death rates and to provide servants and manpower for burgeoning industries. Many of the newcomers were youths, women, and unskilled workers who were vulnerable to economic change. About a third of them laboured in the manufacturing sector whilst the port and docks spawned their own employment. London had always been the commercial centre for a community of merchants and retailers. But this period saw unprecedented growth in London's trade and industry, whose effects stimulated a national market that required a wide range of skills.

The workers who came to provide them settled in densely packed neighbourhoods marked by open sewers, decaying rubbish, virulent disease, and overflowing graveyards.[11] The poorest neighbourhoods lay outside the City walls, where building codes were less applied and side streets were not set at right angles. Gay often mentioned sites located within a three-sided area bounded by St Martin's Lane on the west, the Strand on the south, and Drury Lane on the east. The notorious Seven Dials lay near the apex of the triangle at St Giles-in-the-Fields church, while the base joined Charing Cross and St Clement Danes. Inside this triangle one could indulge in gambling, sex, and crime as well as commercial activities and theatrical pursuits.[12] There was a high turnover in all parts of the city, for lodgers were the norm in London. Unlike in Paris, the elite did not live in grand town houses. Instead they poured their money and possessions into country estates. Whilst the old mansions along the Strand had been demolished or converted, there was a brisk demand for and supply of housing for the prosperous middling sort. New residences were erected with lighting, water, and sewerage services as well as short-term leases. The contrast between housing for rich and poor was one by-product of rapid urbanization.

For those who could afford the fashionable new houses, London was the most civilized, beautiful, and modern city, far superior to Paris and other capitals.[13] Bookshops, theatres, art exhibitions, operas, and concerts beckoned those in search of culture and entertainment. A huge outpouring of printed material included newspapers, periodicals, poetry, and pamphlets on every topic. Some of them addressed the risks and benefits of living in London. They exposed the snares and corruption of urban life but also its joys and pleasures. Gay would have known this literature and seen the maps and guides to London that flooded the market.[14] The number of his potential city readers was also growing. By 1700, the national literacy rate was at least 45 per cent for men and 25 per cent for women, though for London women it was nearer 48 per cent.[15] Even the poor might read his poem, Gay suggested, and he called on his publisher in *Trivia* to display it on the streets.[16]

But poems and goods cost money and the working people on the street struggled just to stay alive. As Gay shows us in *Trivia*, gender and class relations were dramatically visible on the streets, as all sorts of people interacted with each other, often with bodily contact. The streets were filled with the most vulnerable part of the population, who plied their wares, begged for alms, and hovered on the edge of poverty. In good times, the streets gave them a livelihood, but often this was not the case and death came early. Women were especially at risk and they dominated the poverty rolls when pregnancy, ill health, or old age struck them. The fragile makeshift economy of both men and women meant that they dropped in and out of what work was available—both legal and illegal.[17]

In *Trivia* Gay, like many polite writers, is carefully selective about representing the seamier sides of the city. Yet less exalted literature on this subject poured into the marketplace. This should not surprise us, for the London underworld was a topic of intense public concern. Press coverage of trials and executions told stories of how men and women were corrupted by London's vice and sin. Pamphlets of the Society for the Reformation of Manners and reports of lurid crimes caused concerns about safety on the streets. By the eighteenth century it had become clear that traditional public punishments were not only disruptive, they were unequal to the task of preventing offences, especially petty crime. Prostitution and theft were visible parts of street life. Recent statistics show that women accounted for more than half the property offences in City of London cases at the Old Bailey from 1690 to 1713—a fact that indicates women's difficulties in making a living. Fears about crime were highest in the 1690s with its bad harvests, high food prices, and coinage crisis. Worries mounted again after 1713, when troops returned home after more than a quarter-century of wars with France (1680–1713).[18] They finally ended with the Peace of Utrecht in 1713, an event with which Gay was associated as a minor diplomat.

Hard economic conditions and worries about war and peace were but two of the anxieties that troubled early eighteenth-century Londoners. Gay, a Tory who failed to win government patronage, lived in a time and a place marked by deep ideological divisions. Like everyone in the capital, Gay was a member of what has been called a 'fractured society'.[19] After years of Civil War, Charles II was restored to the throne. Yet fears for the Church of England and representative government through Parliament mounted in the 1670s and 80s, in response to James II's Catholicism and repressive policies. The Glorious Revolution of 1688 that placed William III on the throne was intended to resolve political and religious problems. Yet this did not happen. Whigs and Tories engaged in a violent rage of party that reached a crescendo during Queen Anne's reign (1710–14). Voters on both sides were actively involved. Between 1689 and 1715 there were more general elections than in the rest of the century and an astonishing growth in popular participation in politics. In the City of London, the electorate included the entire ratepaying adult male population.[20]

Trivia gives comic hints about the economic issues that inflamed party strife in the capital. The Whigs were supported by the City's 'monied interest'—stockbrokers, bankers, and financial men who had profited from the financial revolution that established the Bank of England, made public credit available, and funded William III's wars.[21] The Whigs also allied themselves with dissenters from the Church of England. This added a religious dimension to party conflict. Gay had little to say about religion in *Trivia* but there were about 100,000 nonconformists living in the capital.[22] Tory fears for the established Church ran deep. The accession of Queen Anne in 1710 led to a temporary restoration of the Tories to power, but the Elector of Hanover, the Queen's distant cousin, was due to ascend the throne. Tory crowds detested the City Whig establishment, which was sympathetic to the Hanoverian Succession.

This brief review of the political situation gives a backdrop to unrest on the streets in the years that preceded the publication of *Trivia*. In 1710 Tory riots in defence of clergyman William Sacheverell burst out to protect 'the church in danger'.[23] The destruction of property and violence of the mob made some thoroughfares seem dangerous. Street demonstrations in 1713 mocked the Hanoverian claimant. There was also concern about activities of Jacobites, who supported the return of the Stuart pretender in France. High churchmen mobilized popular sentiment that led to street demonstrations by what was perceived as a mob. The Whigs feared Tory populism in the streets, and not without reason. In 1715, a Riot Act was passed which gave the government repressive powers to deal with crowds.[24] The Jacobite rebellion of 1715–16 broke out soon after the main draft of *Trivia* was completed. This revolt was the final stage of deep party conflict that had been played out on the streets of London during Gay's lifetime.[25] The crowds that surged through *Trivia* were therefore a sensitive subject in 1716.

For inhabitants of London, the capital was indeed the centre of the world. Its residents were adapting to a dangerous, often thrilling, and multifaceted way of life. This style of living was a product of the urbanization that took place in London at this time. Subversive political ideas as well as luxury goods competed for attention in its metropolitan marketplace. The streets of London provide a perfect backdrop for the multifaceted poet who imagined the world of *Trivia*.

JOHN GAY'S LIFE AND LITERARY WORLD

Gay was born in 1685 in Barnstaple in Devon into a moderately prosperous family. He was educated at the town's grammar school but a dip in the family's fortunes saw him apprenticed in 1704 to John Willet, a silk mercer in London's New Exchange, a move that accounted for a knowledge of fabrics and clothes present in many of Gay's writings. He had literary ambitions from boyhood and shook off trade as soon as he could, by means of work for a literary magazine and a slowly established set of literary friendships. His first poem, *Wine*, was published in 1708. In 1711 he met the poet Alexander Pope and they began to collaborate on the satirical memoirs of Marin Scriblerus, a fictional figure representing all the pretensions of false learning. Pope took Gay under his wing, not always to Gay's benefit, but friendships thereafter with Jonathan Swift, Thomas Parnell, and Dr John Arbuthnot and the courtier Robert Harley, Earl of Oxford and Lord Treasurer, all participants in the Scriblerus Club, aligned Gay with Tory writers. They coexisted uneasily in London with a group of Whig writers of whom Joseph Addison and Richard Steele were the chief luminaries. Rivalries and conflicts between these groups structured personal friendships and literary productions, including poems and plays; theatrical success was often shaped and coloured by patronage and politics. Gay's play *The Wife of Bath* (1713) showed an interest in Chaucer that is easy to overlook in favour of his engagement with the classics. His interest in early English literature contributed to the reasonable success of *Rural Sports* (1713) and *The Shepherd's Week* (1714). They were pastorals which contributed to a lively debate about a genre normally associated with Arcadia and the ancients. By using a rustic English setting and Spenserian diction, Gay cleverly made his pastorals neither ancient nor modern.

Gay hoped for a post at court and in 1712 he was appointed domestic steward and secretary to the Duchess of Monmouth. In 1714 he left her household, helped by Swift, to take up an appointment as secretary to Lord Clarendon, the British envoy to the court of Hanover where the Elector was Queen Anne's nominated successor, the future George I. There Gay wrote part of *Trivia*. But the death of Queen Anne shortly afterwards spoilt his prospects and threw the Tories and their writers into disarray. The Scriblerian Club broke up—Arbuthnot lost his post as royal doctor; Swift and Parnell returned to Ireland; Harley was impeached for treason along with Lord Bolingbroke, to whom Gay had addressed the Prologue of *The Shepherd's Week*. Back in London, Gay was not without friends at court—Princess Caroline had enjoyed his poem *The Fan* (1714), he was friends with the rich collector Lord Burlington, and with Henrietta Howard, later Countess of Suffolk and mistress of Princess Caroline's husband the Prince of Wales. His literary friendships continued: he produced a comedy, *The What D'Ye Call It* (1715) with some help from Pope, and in 1717 another theatrical collaboration, with Pope and John Arbuthnot, *Three Hours after Marriage*. Possibly his advancement was prevented behind the scenes by Addison, whose very successful play *Cato* (1713) had been mocked by Gay; one story had it that on his deathbed Addison confessed he had injured Gay greatly.[26] After publishing *Trivia* in 1716, Gay translated parts of Ovid, imitated Chaucer, and published two epistles. In 1718 he produced a libretto for *Acis and Galatea*, with music by Handel. By 1720 he was in need of money. *Poems on Several Occasions*, published by Tonson and Lintot, had an impressive list of subscribers. It earned him £1,000 which he invested in stock in the South Sea Company, thought to be the most attractive investment opportunity of the moment. The Company had bought government debt in return for a joint stock issue, on the supposition that it would make immense profits from its exclusive trading rights in the South Seas. The company was incompetent and corrupt: its directors sold out, shares crashed from £1,000 to next to nothing, and thousands were ruined. Gay lost all his money. The event, known as the South Sea Bubble because share inflation was based on nothing of substance and because the surge in speculation burst, left Gay with considerable financial stress. Without remunerative employment and suffering from stomach trouble, Gay became more anxious, dependent, and prone to depression. In 1723 he accepted a somewhat disappointing post as a lottery commissioner and continued to ply the edges of the court in the hope of patronage. A play, *The Captives*, did well in 1724, helped by liberal amounts of brandy dispensed on the opening night. Nonetheless, advancement eluded him, despite Gay's persistence. As he put it after one hopeful visit, 'I . . . met with my usual success—a disappointment'.[27] Gay was promised a reward, according to Swift, for his 1727 volume of *Fables* which were dedicated to Princess Caroline's third son. All that materialized was an offer of a post as gentleman usher to Princess Louisa, aged 2. Gay refused it. Disenchantment with the world of courts and opposition to Sir Robert Walpole dampened his spirits but not his creativity: in 1728 appeared *The Beggar's Opera*, phenomenally successful in its high-low inversion of statesmen and highwaymen. Walpole managed to have the play's sequel, *Polly*, suppressed, though it made more than £1,000 for Gay. *The Beggar's Opera* allegedly made its producer John Rich £4,000—wittily it was said around town that it made Rich gay and Gay rich.

Financially secure at last, Gay spent his last years at work on various plays, operas, and poems, starting a second volume of *Fables* in 1731. After a bout of fever in 1728, he lived with the Duke and Duchess of Queensberry at Amesbury in Wiltshire, where they made rural virtue out of necessity, having been dismissed from court. After a visit to London in 1732, Gay caught fever again: on 4 December 1732, he died. He was buried on 23 December in Westminster Abbey, with an eloquent epitaph by Pope, and a monument erected by the Queensberrys inscribed with a couplet by Gay that had appeared in his *Poems* (1720): 'Life is a jest, and all things show it, / I thought so once, but now I know it.'

What sort of writer was Gay? He had a gift for taking traditional forms and applying them amusingly to topicalities. *The Beggar's Opera* shows Gay's satire is as much about things as against them—he is witty about moral values, Italian opera, and pastoral, comically and improbably relocated in a criminal underworld. It was a cliché of political satire at the time that corrupt politicians plundered the country, but it was Gay who gave the idea dramatic life. So with *Trivia*: analogies between London and Augustan Rome were old Whig, old wig, old hat, but an analogy between a Muse of the crossroads and musings about Charing Cross was fresh, original, and amusing. *Trivia's* proclamation of its usefulness becomes a joke about the purposiveness of literature—poetry reflects the world and also imaginatively transforms it. Gay makes no great claims for this enterprise, other than that one should be able to make a living out of it. The temperateness of that claim masked his deeper ambitions to be an established, recognized, and rewarded writer like Pope or Swift, even though Gay's personal amiability equipped him less well than they to deal with the combative world of wits. As a poet, Gay was less versatile than Pope and less trenchant than Swift, but he has contradictions and complexities that make him attractive to readers now, despite some of the fun of his parodies being hard to recover.

The major work of Gay's later life, the *Fables*, shows again his creative reworking of an existing form, the writer as artisan rather than artist. 'Gay's most characteristic literary persona is both self-effacing and self-mocking', says his biographer David Nokes;[28] although there is a self to be effaced and mocked, it creates a poetic voice that asserts genially. But for all his geniality Gay is sometimes a dark poet, alert to life's disappointments and evanescence, and his juxtapositions of high and low, English and classical, epic and trivial, can unfix certainties and with uncertainty. As Anne McWhir says of *Trivia*:

The poet challenges traditional generic distinctions, for the poet is at once pastoral singer, upstart epic poet, moral prophet, and self-proclaimed lover of trivia. There is no need to reconcile these roles, for absolute consistency would be a suspect stance in Gay's world of confusion and diversity. But the reader is left with the difficulty of determining the tone of particular passages in context.[29]

Later eighteenth-century readers seem to have warmed to Gay's story-telling skills—*Trivia's* episodes about the invention of pattens and the account of Cloacina were printed in anthologies. In his biography of Gay in *The Lives of the English Poets* (vol. ii, 1779), Samuel Johnson thought Gay's great achievement was the invention of ballad opera, 'a mode of comedy which at first was supposed to delight only by its novelty, but has now, by the experience of half a century, been found so well accommodated to the disposition of a popular audience, that it is likely to keep long possession of the stage.' That long possession has diverted attention away from Gay's poetry, which benefits from an understanding of the genre games of its time and how Gay plays them afresh. In the nineteenth century, critics thought highly of Gay's ballads, particularly 'Black-ey'd Susan' and ''Twas when the seas were roaring' (from *The What D'Ye Call It*, with music said to be by Handel): one biographer claimed 'In them he has broken through the conventional restraints of an age in which the Muse wore a full-bottomed wig and took snuff'.[30] In the twenty-first century, it may be that Gay's generic inventiveness will be revalued and his ironies appreciated, not least for how they comically suspend formalities, just as wigs in *Trivia* are lifted by thieving boys.

Gay's influence, appropriately, is musical and artistic as well as literary, thanks to the success of *The Threepenny Opera* (1928), in which Bertolt Brecht and composer Kurt Weill used some of the original's music. Their opening song was adopted by Louis Armstrong as 'Mack the Knife', made famous by Bobby Darin in 1958, and covered by numerous artists since including Ella Fitzgerald, Frank Sinatra, Nick Cave, Lyle Lovett, Sting, and Robbie Williams. *The Beggar's Opera* was also made into a film in 1953 starring a singing Laurence Olivier, directed by Peter Brook and co-scripted by the playwright Christopher Fry. Gay influenced William Hogarth directly by providing a subject from *The Beggar's Opera* which so fascinated Hogarth he painted it five times between 1728 and 1732. The highwayman Macheath, facing the gallows, stands between two women, Polly and Lucy, each of whom claims him in marriage. One version of that dramatic moment was engraved in 1790 by Blake, who also illustrated some of Gay's *Fables*. Gay also influenced Hogarth in how he represented London, for instance in *The Four Times of Day* (1738), four scenes of metropolitan comedy and cruelty. *Trivia's* influence may also be detected in other depictions of London by Hogarth, especially of Covent Garden. The snowy setting of *Morning* (reproduced in Fig. 2) includes details made resonant by *Trivia*, of icicles from penthouses, imprints of pattens in the snow, and shivering, huddled figures. Later poets who wrote of

London, like John Banks and Mary Robinson, may have known *Trivia* and drawn on its discourses of bustle and exchange. Influence can be hard to prove but *Trivia* certainly contributed to eighteenth-century discourses about urban life. Whether or not it can be called a landmark text, it was a landscape text, a poem that helped shape people's ideas of city life, and by means of its fanciful analogies as well as its truth-to-life. In prose too, although Boswell and Dickens tend to be instanced as archetypal London writers, Gay helped set patterns. So Hazlitt, writing in 1818 about the bewildering effect of London, followed up the lostness of Gay's Devon peasant: 'The same principle will also account for that feeling of littleness, vacuity, and perplexity, which a stranger feels on entering the streets of a populous city. Every individual he meets is a blow to his personal identity. Every new face is a teasing unanswered riddle.'[31] A modernist idea of 'street haunting', unexpectedly sociable, had precedents in *Trivia*: thus Virginia Woolf alluded to 'the greatest pleasure of town life in winter—rambling the streets of London.'[32] Writers who represent London seclusion may also have drawn on *Trivia*'s quiet passages. Thus a 1952 guidebook to London celebrated 'the almost secret places behind [great shopping streets]—the Georgian alleys, the intimate pubs, the little markets, the masked mews, the squares filled with great trees, the hidden "yards" covered in cobbles'.[33]

Gay's biographer proposes that 'the sense in which the London streets of *Trivia* are both topographically real, and literary metaphors, gives the poem an animation and vitality of reference which defiantly resists any simple reading.'[34] The reader can either now read the poem and test that theory by means of a single reading, or turn to the essays and see how different approaches to the poem offer lively readings. In both cases, we trust that *Trivia* continues to defy reduction to a simple reading.

A GUIDE TO THE POEM

Trivia plunges the reader into both a busy urban world and an intricate literary world. With so much happening, it benefits from a guide to the ground it covers, especially for readers not used to long poems. The following mini-map follows an itinerary through each of the poem's three books, taking its landmarks from Gay's side-headings to the poem, which act like signposts.

Book I, the shortest book of the poem, declares its terrain to be '*Of the Implements for walking the Streets, and Signs of the Weather.*' The poet announces his aim, to sing of how to walk aright, clean, and safe, which introduces a discussion of shoes, then coats, then canes. Equipment and accoutrements are defined humorously either through avoidance of wrong choices or selection of correct ones. The choice of stout shoes, proper coats, and strong canes depends on understanding how those objects protect against various threats and harms, in conditions particular to London. Real and allegorical figures mingle: London is a real place like other cities—Paris, Naples, Venice—and yet unlike them in its prosperity and security, expressed visibly on the streets through fashionable dress, which the poem sees ambivalently as signs of luxury. An idealized past in which ladies walk briskly on foot is unlike an indolent present in which lavishly dressed women are carried around. Then the poem discusses weather, whose signs—of cold, fair, rainy weather—also determine what clothes and behaviours should be adopted, including sex-specific implements, the umbrella and pattens. The contingency of weather and defences against it implies the material world and the behavioural world help define each other. Book I concerns itself with objects and interpretations, implements and signs, which are not confined to the material world of London—the umbrella comes from Persia, the patten is given a pastoral origin in Lincolnshire. London, in other words, appears in this first book as a place of flow, of commodities, ideas, impressions. There are a few actual locations—the Mall gets two mentions, but otherwise the geography is nearly all general—the Court, the Thames. People are generalized into groups, like the chairmen who gather at tavern doors (154–5), or types who are particularized loosely, like those who worry about fuel, represented by the dame who stays close to her fire in cold weather (138–42). In this book, the poet declares a purpose (at the start, 1–4), defines an audience ('honest Men', 119), and addresses a reader throughout, an indeterminate second-person (addressed poetically as thee and more prosaically as you).

Book II, the longest, '*Of Walking the Streets by Day*', declares its organizing principle to be time, but the side-headings spread more widely than times of day. In a world in which most business ran concurrently with daylight, daytime means working hours. The Muse ventures out from home (5); those who walk encounter people involved in trades, requiring negotiations—of space, of precedence, of purpose. Both the text and the side-headings feature the idea of usefulness—'useful Lays' (1), 'Useful Precepts' (91)—and the idea of time helps structure the encounters with different types, through terms such as 'Now', 'When', 'Sometimes' (21, 35, 53). Clothes in the first part of this book are materials vulnerable to stains, or showy signs of status, and there enters a sense of the city as confusing, possibly deceptive. Where Book I was confident about proper choices, Book II suggests one might be misled, literally and figuratively, like the peasant who gets lost at Seven Dials (73), a place as mythically confusing as Theseus's labyrinth. The poem sidesteps anxieties like open cellars before launching into an assured digression, a comic mythological account of the origin of shoe-cleaners (99–220). Added to the second edition, this section, about the amour of Cloacina, goddess of the sewer, with a mortal scavenger, makes vertical movements—between streets and sewers, city and heavens, beggars and gods—before Cloacina disappears back into the Fleet Ditch, leaving her son at Charing Cross to clean the shoes of the rich at the edge of Whitehall. The lad's shoe-cleaning materials—brush, tripod, oil, and soot allow him to dispense polish, literally, though he himself remains unpolished, figuratively. The poem then demonstrates its own metaphorical powers of polishing, as it glosses the ingenuity of the urban poor with mythic aspirations, turning the lowly origins of bootboys into a miniature mock-epic. Then the poem returns to its supposed business of instruction against dangers, represented by narrow streets, like smelly Watling Street, contrasted with perfumed Pall Mall, though the smarter location of the latter may also not be risk free. Reassuming a first-person persona, the poem tracks pleasurably through alleys and byways, quiet places harbouring reclusive types, before emerging again to busier streets like Ludgate Hill, and to inconveniencies, of cheats, of accidents, of stray threats like snowballs. *Trivia*'s wintry theme is made explicit (319) through snowballs and stoves and, via a game of football in Covent Garden, to an episode of the Great Frost (356) and a frost-fair scene on the Thames. A disturbing elegy for Doll the apple-seller, whose violent death echoes and inverts that of Orpheus, ushers in a scene of thaw (399–404) and a reversion to a world of commerce, where different commodities distinguish days of the week, cries of the town, and seasons like Christmas (437–50), a season for charity for which there are also year-round claimants like beggars (463). The importance of charity to Anglicans (adherents of the Church of England) provides the poem's only gesture to religion, though the practice of charity is also simply moral, as much a matter of benevolence as piety. A moral scene of a funeral touches fleetingly on concerns of the next world before the poem turns to the secular virtue of friendship, (475) represented by the person of F or Fortescue (475). As Gay strolls down the Strand with this friend, he steps out of persona, writing as himself. They pass the remains of grand houses of nobility with their artistic treasures belonging to munificent patrons like Burlington, also a friend of Gay. Celebrating the healthy happiness of walkers, the poem ranges over the solid pleasures of bookstalls, extolled in contrast to worldly and corrupt types of people. The poem then enfolds itself in a syllepsis, a rhetorical figure which links literal and figurative qualities: wrapping itself in virtue and a sturdy overcoat, the second book ends with a witty flourish.

Book III, '*Of Walking the Streets by Night*', starts out in moonlight with a traffic jam scene in narrow St Clement's. Pickpockets, ballad singers, tides of people flow to and fro, with dangers exacerbated by being hidden in darkness, requiring more 'Useful Precepts' (111) of avoidance. An explicitly night-time economy of thieves, footmen with flambeaux, and dangerous traffic merges into more figuratively black scenes—the sexually dangerous oyster wench, the dark story of Oedipus, and threats to virtue from 'petty Rapines of the Night' (248), epitomized by the night-walker or prostitute, and a tale of a Devon yeoman duped, robbed, and infected by a harlot (285–306). Watchmen and rakes and their shady tendencies are succeeded by scenes of fire and earthquake, before the poem ends self-consciously illuminatory, like a firework on a lamp-post.

The poem's side-headings have a descriptive function which is mostly uncomplicated, although there is a little more to 'Useful Precepts' than meets the eye. The most famous use of side-headings in English poetry is in Samuel Taylor Coleridge's *The Rime of the Ancient Mariner* (1798). Coleridge set up tensions and contradictions between his poem and its ostensibly explanatory apparatus: what appeared to be simple description turned out to be anything but. Gay's side-headings do not create as much ambiguity as Coleridge's marginal glosses, but in *Trivia* the relation between the poem and Gay's Index to the poem is not straightforward. The Index provides a map of the poem as negatives—'*Prentices not to be rely'd on*'—but also an unexpectedly negative map of the poem, in which positive lines in the poem are negatively described. Thus a cheerful account of gaily dressed ladies (I 149) becomes bluntly critical: '*Ladies dress neither by Reason nor Instinct*'. Avoidance is a key term. Gay joked in the Advertisement at the start of the poem about not being seen as the author of his own works; in the Index the Author appears as both writer and subject—'*Cheese not lov'd by the Author*'—a gloss quite surprising in relation to the section to which it is attached (II 254: 'how shall I / Pass, where in piles *Cornavian* Cheeses lye'). The poem's previous line, advising people passing animal wastes to hold their noses, semi-comically presents pungent smells as a danger; the following line gestures to Gay as a dependant in an aristocratic household, obliged like the chaplain to rise from the dinner table before the cheese course. The Index, then, appears to collect up signs to organize them, but it turns out to have as many gaps, twists, and pitfalls as the streets of *Trivia*. Even something as seemingly informative as an index shows readings of *Trivia* are not straightforward.

THE ESSAYS: CONNECTIONS, DIFFERENCES, AND DISCIPLINES

The nine essays in this book offer different readings of the same poem. These differences are an outgrowth of the varied training and experience of our contributors. They bring different methodologies, vocabularies, and writing styles to the project. Furthermore, the questions which contributors ask and the values that give meaning to their work are not the same. Yet they have much in common. They know a great deal about the eighteenth century and they are united in their desire to interpret a poem. The varied ways in which they do so may surprise the reader. In considering the essays we ask several questions: how do the writers engage with *Trivia*? What themes interest them? What are the connections between the chapters? Where do the differences lie? The fact that the essays are so varied but all have areas of overlap makes strict categorization both impossible and undesirable. We can however discuss the ways in which the essays engage with some of *Trivia*'s objects, characters, and concepts. Other categories and arrangements could be used to describe the essays, but we hope these will illustrate the richness and diversity of both the poem and the interpretations that it inspired.

An interest in material culture is demonstrated by Aileen Ribeiro in her essay: 'Street Style: Dress in John Gay's *Trivia*'. Ribiero uses the poem as a visual source. She shows how clothes were important in ways that were particular to the eighteenth century—ways that included the political concept of 'Englishness'. You might think costume history was a distinct discipline, and what the poem says about clothes requires specialist knowledge to understand it. Indeed it does. But the history of clothes includes their use, and several of the other essays engage with that: how differences in clothing help to construct gender and class; how the cleanliness of clothes involves histories of hygiene, labour, and transport; how investments in adornment and ornament connect people in periods as ostensibly different as eighteenth-century London and ancient Rome, not least through debates about luxury. Besides, 'dress' was an all-purpose verb in the early eighteenth century: it referred not only to clothes but also to many other kinds of transformation, including an idea of language as the dress of thought. From just one example you can see how subject boundaries invite dissolution and benefit from openness.

The mud that splatters onto the clothes that Ribiero describes fascinates Mark Jenner and Clare Brant. Though both focus on the literariness of the poem, they develop ideas about mire in different ways. In '"Nauceious and Abominable"? Pollution, Plague, and Poetics in John Gay's *Trivia*', Mark Jenner ranges boldly across a remarkable range of sources: Dorothy George's *London Life in the Eighteenth Century* (1925); Daniel Defoe's *Due Preparations for the Plague* (1722); pamphlets of the 1720s; classical accounts of plague; Virgil's *Georgics*; and Acts concerning sanitation. He compares their factual and fictional elements with those in *Trivia* and its engravings, and locates a shift in attitudes about passing through London's streets. His study of the language of pollution constructs a history of filth that flows through *Trivia*'s attitudes to streets and waterways—and vice versa, since the poem's language also flows into historical discourses of hygiene.

Clare Brant's 'Artless and Artful: John Gay's *Trivia*' also highlights mud. Brant helps us to understand the jokes, games, and witty play of language found in *Trivia*. At the same time, she illustrates how literary criticism can provide a capacious umbrella for different types of scholars. Brant uses psychoanalysis to track how mud works as comic and anxious stuff. In doing so she muddies the borders of genres and suggests that metaphor is one way in which material and imaginary relations are transacted. Brant's interest in urban theory causes her to reflect upon how Gay's poem may anticipate, or not, the nineteenth-century flâneur.

Objects like dress and mire have very direct effects upon people who walk along the streets. Tim Hitchcock, Margaret Hunt, and Philip Carter focus their gaze upon some of the characters who are staples of the London crowd. In '"All besides the Rail, rang'd Beggars lie": *Trivia* and the Public Poverty of Early Eighteenth-Century London', Tim Hitchcock graphically describes beggars and the urban poor through a web of complex stories about their lives. He observes the power of the poor to negotiate benefits with the authorities in sophisticated ways. Hitchcock sees an important gap between the representation of the poor in historical and in literary sources—a gap that enables literature to shape social policy in a dramatic way. His comparison of different kinds of sources illuminates Gay's poetic licence and reveals the need to think about how to handle the inventiveness of literature.

Margaret Hunt in 'The Walker Beset: Gender in the Early Eighteenth-Century City' is concerned with gender relations and brings ideological concerns and insights to the volume. She reads *Trivia* as a setting in which women are represented as emblems of corruption to be reviled and shunned. Their major use is to be read by males as 'useful natural feature[s] of the city, akin to street signs' who can help men negotiate urban time and space. Hunt uses the Bible and literature of the Society for the Reformation of Manners to contextualize the poem. She ends her story with multiple readings involving fire, gang-rape, falling towers, and engulfment, leaving the fate of male walkers to be concluded by the reader.

Philip Carter shines a spotlight on one specific male walker—the mysterious persona of *Trivia*, who imparts advice throughout the poem. In 'Faces and Crowds: Biography in the City', he offers a study of the walker and relates him to themes of eighteenth-century biography. Carter finds a self-absorbed unsociable man on the margin of urban society, very different from Addison and Steele's sociable spectator. He is interested in the self and society and how we can know others and ourselves in an urban environment. Ribiero and Hunt share Carter's concern in how individuals present themselves and are read by others. Other contributors give different readings of the walker's character. Carter's use of diaries, urban theory, periodicals, and life-writing adds textual variety to the chapter.

Characters and concepts are tightly interwoven in Gay's poem. Alison Stenton and Susan Whyman share many of Carter's concerns about a concept that is central to *Trivia*—the idea of urban space. But they look at how space is shared and negotiated from different points of view using different sources. In 'Spatial Stories: Movement in the City and Cultural Geography', Alison Stenton asks how a cultural geographer armed with theory and topographical maps confronts descriptions of an imagined space that is perpetually in motion? How can the study of specific places be reconciled to a city 'which will be forever viewed in different ways by a multitude of other walkers and writers?' Unlike Carter's walker, Stenton's is 'unable *not* to get involved' in the city's public life.

The concept of space is re-examined by Susan Whyman in 'Sharing Public Spaces'. Like Stenton and Carter, Whyman asks how individuals move through and interact in public arenas. She compares London street life in the poem to a wide range of personal manuscript letters that link *Trivia* to changes in eighteenth-century communication. Part literary, part historical, letters act as a bridge between the experiential world of the social historian and the textual world of the literary critic. Whyman finds permeable borders between the east and west ends of London, different types of genres, and disciplinary boundaries across the humanities. Carter, Stenton, and Whyman unite in seeing cultural forces informing bodily, geographic, and social movement. In these three essays, biography, topography, and sociability offer different views of inner and outer space.

Susanna Morton Braund in 'Gay's *Trivia*: Walking the Streets of Rome' stretches the scope of our book to include the sister concept of space: time. Time is most frequently thought of as the province of the historian who looks for change and continuity over various periods. Through her knowledge of literary theory and the classics, Braund takes us back in time to the streets of Rome. Though now a specialist academic knowledge, the classics were an eighteenth-century key to reading and knowing the world. Gay expected that many of his readers would catch his classical allusions. Braund helps us to experience that same pleasure, explaining how there's more than meets the eye in *Trivia*: citizens on the street and readers of the poem could see the streets of Rome beyond the streets of London. An original line by Gay can simultaneously be a reworking of a line from Juvenal: things are and are not what they seem. Braund ends with a footnote through which scholarly pathways converge with *Trivia* in a joke about genre. Clare and Susanna take us back and forth in time from the ancient world to the postmodern city via nineteenth-century Paris. Together the essays add a rich imaginative dimension to our knowledge of eighteenth-century London and Gay's poem.

As we reflect on how the essays fit together, we ask what if anything makes disciplines distinct from each other? Geographers, classicists, historians, and literary critics are organized by academia into distinct groups, though you might find biographers among any of them and all of them might meet under the banner of cultural studies. Both within and between disciplines, similarities and differences evolve, for instance via technology. Web-based resources, databases, and digitized texts encourage common research procedures. In searching by keywords, scholars share modes of enquiry in which disciplinary distinctions disappear.[35] Conversely, each group has its own taxonomy of subdivisions—thus historians can be further separated into, say, historians of art, of costume, of gender, of ideas, of particular cultures or periods or concepts. It would be interesting to repeat our experiment with an even wider line up: what might you find if you gave the same poem to, say, a physicist, an economist, or an anthropologist? And at what point might one come back to privilege some of the knowledge of literary criticism, because after all the poem is a poem, written in the language and metrics of its time, and with allusions and effects common to a particular period of literary history? Might one likewise argue for a special place for the geographer, because of the poem's location? Or the biographer, because the poem has an author?

Putting the essays under one book cover helped the contributors to see afresh that there is more diversity than is often imagined among people who practise what is usually thought of as one discipline. Most if not all subjects in the humanities have had internal battles and feuds, as fiercely debated as arguments between one discipline and another. When people with different training, experience, methodologies, and vocabularies try to talk to each other, learning and understanding become even more difficult. Open-mindedness has resistances; attempts to share and borrow are not always successful.

If so, why has interdisciplinarity become such a popular selling point in the intellectual marketplace? One reason may be that it functions as an ideal—a shorthand for expanded horizons. Yet in practice, interdisciplinarity can be elusive. Assembling a group of writers does not ensure their thought processes will interact; it may be the reader who takes on the role of cross-fertilizing different approaches. Documenting both processes is difficult. Our case study shows how one group of scholars explored and implemented the topic. Contributors met first on the page and then at a colloquium, where interdisciplinary identities and ideas were discussed. Attitudes and outcomes differed for each participant but some common themes emerged.

The first was pleasure in the intellectual adventure of 'multidisciplinarity', a term we preferred over 'interdisciplinarity' which suggests a conscious shift in one's methods and more active integration between fields. The second common theme was the challenge of self-definition in relation to a field of study. Who are we as scholars? How do we go about representing a subject? Is it possible to adopt the methods of another discipline? In hunting for answers to these questions, we acknowledged that multidisciplinarity increases self-consciousness about assumptions, priorities, and values, as well as methods. This book's use lies less in promoting any particular model of interdisciplinarity than in its invitation to readers to consider what values matter in scholarship, and why. Anything but pedestrian in the imaginative sense, the essays analyse the art of walking and also the art of reading. Without conceding an interpretative free-for-all, they show how a poem can support a variety of interpretations, and how one might use all the humanities to understand a subject conventionally confined to one.

Analysing what she calls 'discipline envy', Marjorie Garber argues that battles over disciplinary turf necessarily involve trespassing. She writes

There's a nice term that architectural planners use to describe the footpaths worn in the turf from one building or paved pathway to another, the shortcuts chosen by pedestrians and marked by their frequent traffic. The planners call them 'desire lines.' Often, when they are well worn, these 'lines' in the grass will themselves be paved over, transforming them from renegade or 'scofflaw' passages into new, officially sanctioned routes . . . 'Desire lines' are a feature of many public walking spaces, but they are especially noticeable on college campuses.[36]

Garber makes this term a metaphor for intellectual inquiry, noting that the medieval divisions of knowledge, the trivium and quadrium, take their names from the Latin terms for the place where three and then four roads meet. In discussing a poem about the art of walking, contributors have crossed familiar ground, taken disciplinary short cuts, and made new desire lines. Gay's *Trivia* serves as a meeting-point of subjects, a departure for discussion, and an intellectual crossroads.

NOTES

1. [William King], *A Journey to London, in the Year, 1698* (1699). Quoted in Norman G. Brett-James, *The Growth of Stuart London* (1935), 440, n. 50, 472.
2. Verney Letters, Princeton University Library microfilm edition, Reel 54, no. 112, Thomas Cave to John Verney, 19 July 1709.
3. Tim Hitchcock and Heather Shore (eds.), *The Streets of London from the Great Fire to the Great Stink* (2003). Interest in London may be seen in conferences, courses, museum exhibitions, and databases. The Museum of London (**www.museumoflondon.org.uk/archive/lbl**), the Guildhall Library (**http://collage.cityoflondon.gov.uk/collage/app**) and Old London Maps (**www.oldlondonmaps.com**) offer images. See Heather Creaton, *Bibliography of London History to 1939* (1994) and later supplements.
4. Malcolm Warner, *The Image of London: Views by Travelers and Emigres 1550–1920, Introduction and Catalogue* (1987), No. 60.
5. Robert Shoemaker, 'The Decline of Public Insult in London 1660–1800', *Past & Present*, 169 (2000), 97–131.
6. Vanessa Harding, 'The Population of London, 1550–1700: A Review of the Published Evidence', *London Journal*, 15 (1990), 111–28; Susan Whyman, *Sociability and Power: The Cultural Worlds of the Verneys 1660–1720* (Oxford, 1999), 55.

7. Vanessa Harding, 'New Types of Urbanism: Early Modern London 1550–1790', *Franco-British Studies*, 17 (1994), 87.

8. Robert Shoemaker, *The London Mob: Violence and Disorder in Eighteenth-Century London* (2004), 19.

9. Vanessa Harding, 'Recent Perspectives on Early Modern London', *Historical Journal*, 47 (2004), 435.

10. William Stow, *Remarks on London* (1722), preface. Quoted in J. F. Merritt (ed.), *Imagining Early Modern London: Perceptions and Portrayals of the City from Stow to Strype 1598–1720* (Cambridge, 2001), 2.

11. Maureen Waller, *1700: Scenes from London Life* (2000), 2.

12. Pat Rogers, 'Why *Trivia*? Myth, Etymology, and Topography', *Arion*, 3rd series, 12 (2005), 4–5.

13. Some travellers did think Paris was superior. Thus *c.*1718 Lady Mary Wortley Montagu wrote 'In general, I think Paris has the advantage of London in the neat pavement of the streets, and the regular lighting of them at night'. R. Halsband (ed.), *The Complete Letters of Lady Mary Wortley Montagu* (Oxford, 1968), 3 vols., i. 442.

14. For example: *A New View of London* (1708); E. Jones, *A Trip through London*, 5th edn. (1718); *The New Guide to London, or Directions to Strangers*, 2nd edn. (1726).

15. David Cressy, 'Literacy in Context: Meaning and Measurement in Early Modern England' in *Society and Culture in Early Modern England* (2003), 305–19. These statistics are low.

16. *Trivia*, III 415.

17. Tim Hitchcock, *Down and Out in Eighteenth-Century London* (2004).

18. J. M. Beattie, *Policing and Punishment in London, 1660–1750: Urban Crime and the Limits of Terror* (Oxford, 2001), 45–7, 65.

19. Gary De Krey, *A Fractured Society: The Politics of London in the First Age of Party 1688–1715* (Oxford, 1985).

20. Francis Sheppard, *London: A History* (Oxford, 1998), 250; De Krey, *Fractured Society*, 40.

21. P. G. M. Dickson, *The Financial Revolution in England: A Study of the Development of Public Credit, 1688–1756* (Aldershot, 1993).

22. Geoffrey Holmes, 'The Sacheverell Riots: The Crowd and the Church in Early Eighteenth-Century London', *Past and Present*, 72 (1976), 63.

23. Holmes, 'Sacheverell Riots', 55–85.

24. Nicholas Rogers, *Crowds, Culture, and Politics in Georgian Britain* (Oxford, 1998) and 'Popular Protest in Early Hanoverian London', *Past and Present*, 9 (1978), 74.

25. Daniel Szechi, *1715: The Great Jacobite Rebellion* (New Haven, 2006).

26. David Nokes, *John Gay: A Profession of Friendship* (Oxford, 1995), 190, citing Joseph Spence, *Observations, Anecdotes, and Characters of Men*, ed. J. M. Osborn (Oxford, 1966), 2 vols., i. 79–80.

27. John Gay, *Letters of John Gay*, ed. C. F. Burgess (Oxford, 1966), 51–2.
28. Nokes, *John Gay*, 3.
29. Anne McWhir, 'John Gay', *Dictionary of Literary Biography*, vol. xcv: *Eighteenth-Century British Poets*, ed. John Sitter, 1st Series (2000), 80–100 (93).
30. W. Clark Russell, *The Book of Authors* (n.d.), 187.
31. William Hazlitt, *Lectures on the English Poets, On Thomson and Cowper* (1951), 101–2.
32. Virginia Woolf, 'Street Haunting: A London Adventure', *The Death of the Moth and Other Essays* (1942), 19.
33. Sam Lambert (ed.) *London Night and Day* (1952), 5–6.
34. Nokes, *John Gay*, 212.
35. For instance, ESTC, or Eighteenth-Century Short Title Catalogue; ECCO, or Eighteenth Century Collections Online; LION, or LIterature ONline; EEBO, or Early English Books Online; The Proceedings of the Old Bailey, London 1674 to 1834, at **oldbaileyonline.org**.
36. Marjorie Garber, *Academic Instincts* (Princeton, 2001), 53–4.

THE ESSAYS

Faces and Crowds: Biography in the City

Philip Carter

Crossing the city in the winter of 1715/16, John Gay's walker followed hard on the heels of Mr Spectator, one of the period's most respected wanderers in and observers on London and its citizens. Addison's *Spectator* had begun his series in March 1711 'with my own History', since 'a Reader seldom pursues a Book with Pleasure 'till he knows whether the Writer of it be . . . of a mild or cholerick Disposition.'[1] Gay's walker, by contrast, offers no personal statement; indeed *Trivia*'s 'Advertisement' makes clear his (or Gay's) preference for anonymity, both as a commentator and a subject of possible censure from the critics: '*The World, I believe, will take so little Notice of me, that I need not take much of it.*' But interest in a narrator's identity, a 'Curiosity' which Mr Spectator thought 'so natural to a Reader', is not abated simply by the walker's unwillingness to provide his own character sketch—not least because the city through which he guides us is partly shaped by personal experience and interpretation. Denied a personal statement, any assessment of the walker's character must be a study of the man in action.

So what can *Trivia* tell us about its narrator? Physically he is a healthy and middle-aged man with a passion for walking and what he perceives to be a natural enthusiasm and ambition. In dress he is sensible and practical. In winter, the season of his walk, he favours warm over fashionable clothes, good shoes, and a sturdy cane chosen not 'for empty Show, but . . . for Use' (I 68). Such pragmatism is again evident in his ridicule of superstition and a rational preference for evidence, as in his observation of material clues to detect changes in the weather. Politically he appears sympathetic to a seventeenth-century model of classical republicanism which advocated acts of civic good along with a personal regime of honesty, moderation, and independence—qualities the walker associates with pedestrianism and denies to those corrupted by modern luxury. In keeping with his politics, and though critical of elements of contemporary London, he remains an English patriot who readily slights foreigners and

*'Death shall entomb in Dust this mouldering Frame
But never reach th'eternal Part, my Fame.'*
1. Portrait of John Gay, by Jonathan Richardson (1725).

continental cities even though, or perhaps because, he does not 'wander from my native Home' (I 83).

There is little in this account of common sense and civic responsibility with which Gay's walker would have disagreed. But this is why it remains only a partial sketch. Public spirited he may be, but the walker's advice is seldom unaccompanied by examples of his self-confidence and satisfaction. Characteristically, *Trivia* is framed by two statements in which our guide sets out his exaggerated aim—'My Country's be the Profit, mine the Praise'—and then looks back on his achievement: 'And now compleat my gen'rous Labours lye, / Finish'd and ripe for Immortality' (I 22; III 407–8). In addition, comments on the benefits of pedestrianism often come with criticism of others, notably those travelling by coach, who choose or have the financial means to behave differently. Alternative lifestyles are rarely tolerated, with the effect that the walker infuses the poem with a spirit of social mistrust. Thus, while eschewing custom and superstition, he actively encourages readers to share his restless suspicion of numerous aspects of city life, from loose paving stones and recklessly driven coaches to muggers and corrupt officials. Such perceived dangers are compounded by the walker's readiness to overdramatize his role as an intrepid guide whose self-perceived courage is at odds with a fastidiousness bordering on the foppish: 'And miry Spots thy clean Cravat disgrace: / O! may I never such Misfortune meet' (I 78–9).

Such concerns also help place the walker socially. Here is a man who likes the idea of work, and praises the industrious, but who is not himself required or prepared to work, at least on the day he tours the city. Concern with the cleanliness of his dress, coupled with learning sometimes heavily worn, suggests someone who looks to impress his superiors—indicative perhaps of a man seeking patronage or work in a field which others may consider above his station or abilities. Apart from his Englishness, we know nothing of the walker's birthplace. However, his dramatic tone implies someone relatively new to London for whom the city he claims to know well is still exciting and troubling. It seems reasonable to suggest that, self-importance aside, the walker dramatizes London life to reflect better to us—his potentially greenhorn readers—his personal accomplishment in a city which, if dangerous in our narrator's telling, is not necessarily so unwelcoming when seen through Gay's eyes. Thwarted aspirations or the newcomer's sense of exclusion may also explain why the walker frequently draws attention to the idleness and corruption of his established social betters, while making it clear that he is not an associate of the court, of gentlemen's clubs, or even a theatregoer.

But equally he is ambivalent to his inferiors. Charitable to the truly destitute, the walker regards working men as superior to their privileged clients, though in personal encounters sees them as different from him and, in modern terms, relatively 'common'.

Such opinions suggest a man on the margin of urban society who uses his status to act as a seemingly dispassionate commentator on city life. What we get, of course, is a place shaped by the walker who defines, describes, and guides us through his city. The extent to which this is a personal capital becomes apparent if we compare *Trivia*'s London with a similar expedition undertaken by his predecessor, Mr Spectator, in August 1712. From his own account, readers knew this earlier narrator to be older, more mature, and better travelled than the walker; although born outside the capital, he is a long-term London resident and enjoys the friendship of a close group of trusted associates. Waking early one morning, Mr Spectator travels into the city in order to 'rove . . . till the many different Objects I must needs meet with should tire my Imagination'.[2] Like *Trivia*, the *Spectator*'s account relishes in the quotidian; however, unlike Gay's London, Mr Spectator's is characterized less by suspicion than an open-minded enthusiasm for human behaviour. In contrast to the walker's focus on pedestrianism's risks, Mr Spectator encounters chimney sweeps who pose no danger to his clothing and, far removed from the stamping and bone-crunching of *Trivia*, reports how he 'strolled' in Covent Garden. Mr Spectator goes on to discover that workmen are cheerful not crude, and the mob more humorous than menacing, while a helpful linkman is willingly overpaid for his efforts. Mr Spectator's benevolence is further demonstrated in the pleasure he derives from others' good fortune. His conclusion is that fellow Londoners should 'make every Face . . . give you the Satisfaction you now take in beholding that of a Friend'.[3]

The walker's refusal to follow this advice has gained him a generally critical response among modern commentators. For the few who consider *Trivia*'s narrator 'a sturdy man of the middling sort', others see him as a 'naïve observer' whose self-importance and rustic's poor judgement are ill-suited to the role of city descriptor, or as someone for whom the seemingly generous act of guide is an exercise in disguising 'self-interest as social concern'.[4] One of his sharpest critics, Alvin Kernan, develops this latter theme of the relationship of self to society. For Kernan, *Trivia* provides evidence of the walker's 'smug sense of his own righteousness' through conduct which 'protects him by keeping all the world outside'. Preoccupied with industriousness and scornful of recreation, the walker emerges as 'a remarkably cold man' incapable of an 'emotional response' to fellow Londoners. For Kernan, therefore, *Trivia* serves to mock a Georgic, and indeed Spectatorial, faith in social connections and the interaction of man with nature through the personality of its narrator. Petty, introverted, and with seemingly little love for life, the walker appears pedestrian indeed.[5]

*   *   *   *   *

The remainder of this essay looks more closely at Kernan's identification of the walker as unsociable—someone whose self-importance fashions an unnecessarily confrontational city in which human bonds are rejected for personal gain. More broadly it looks at what *Trivia* tells us about the chances for social interaction in the city, and the ease or difficulty of connecting with people in an urban culture that modern historians often regard as a ready source of social refinement. This theme of human connection was of interest not just to eighteenth-century pedestrians but also city commentators and to biographers who questioned the possibility of knowing another's character in an increasingly populous urban culture. In doing so, this essay suggests that we treat Gay's walker a little more leniently than some modern critics by viewing his character as, in part, conditioned by an exclusively urban environment. Certainly the London of *Trivia* is fashioned by the walker. Yet London also shapes its narrator, as well as fellow pedestrians who encounter one another only on the streets. Charges of antisocial behaviour seem harder to sustain in what is effectively a public community of strangers. Indeed, from this perspective the walker might be better identified as a reasonably accomplished citizen who takes, as he must, his chances for public sociability not when he chooses, but when the city, permits.

First, however, we should further develop the charge of unsociability. Initially such a claim may seem odd, given *Trivia*'s intensely human focus—indeed as a guide, the walker is far more concerned with identifying London by its people than its history or architecture. A trip across Covent Garden, for instance, makes only a brief reference to Inigo Jones's church of St Paul before plunging into a description of the 'Furies of the Foot-ball War' which dominates the precinct (II 348). However, for someone seemingly so interested in people, the walker pays little attention to the potential complexities of those he encounters, choosing instead to deal not with individuals but simple social types. His discussion of the prostitutes encountered around Drury Lane offers one example:

O! may thy Virtue guard thee through the Roads
Of *Drury*'s mazy Courts, and dark Abodes,
The Harlots' guileful Paths, who nightly stand,
Where *Katherine-street* descends into the *Strand.*
Say, vagrant Muse, their Wiles and subtil Arts,
To lure the Stranger's unsuspecting Hearts . . .

(III 259–64)

As befits the walker's focus with the city as a place of threat, the prostitute / client relationship is one in which stable and unsuspecting male pedestrians are unwittingly led astray by external temptation. But the walker's account scarcely tallies with those of contemporary Londoners such as the 24-year-old legal student, Dudley Ryder. His diary for 1715/16 indicates a more complex relationship in which would-be respectable men, like Ryder, actively sought out sex when emboldened by drink or by the lust to the fore in the night-time city. Ryder's journal entry for 8 August 1715 was typical of such encounters, both for its motives— 'Came from the tavern at near 12. As I came along Fleet Street had a mind to attack a whore and did so'—and, on the morning after, for its impact on a now sober author: 'Was a little uneasy . . . about what I did last night with respect to the whores. However, I have this advantage from it, that I intend never to attempt such a thing again by way of frolic as I did then.' On the evidence of his diary, Ryder's good intentions lasted until 16 November when the pattern of desire and recrimination was repeated, as it was to be on five further occasions in 1716.[6]

At their most confessional, such sources hint at the London pedestrian's 'inner voice'. Ryder's diary entry of 13 August 1716, for example, indicates the biographically interesting tension between the pedestrian's public display of equanimity and his or her concomitant questioning of an unstable inner self. At this time troubled by his love life, Ryder was given to periods of intense self-scrutiny which he contrasted with the calm displayed by fellow walkers in the Temple piazza: 'How wrongly do we judge of people's happiness by their external appearance. I was apt to envy the condition of every poor creature that passed by me whom I thought happier than I.' But Ryder was also sufficiently empathetic to appreciate that he may not have been alone in experiencing this contest of implacable public face and uneasy self-analysis. 'Perhaps', he continued, 'they were thinking how happy they should be if they could make such a gay appearance or put on such clothes as I.'[7]

Ryder's insight into the inquisitiveness of his fellow pedestrians was reiterated in a calmer observation by the Victorian biographer, Leslie

Stephen. A keen mountaineer, Stephen identified the 'true pedestrian' as one who loved walking because it proved conducive to 'tranquil and half-conscious meditation'. Walks in various locations prompted different trains of thought, but Stephen considered intimate self-reflection, 'the solitary expedition when your interlocutor must be yourself', as 'perhaps even best enjoyed, on London streets themselves.'[8] But unlike Ryder—for whom the pedestrian's self-scrutiny led to self-doubt—Stephen saw walking as a humanizing activity by which the pedestrian became 'a reflecting and individual being' who was both more interesting, and so deserving of biographical study, and more willing to socialize. The result was the formation of meaningful social groups: 'Conversation, we are told . . . is a lost art. We live too much in crowds. But if ever men can converse pleasantly, it is when they are invigorated by a good march.'[9] On what he offers in *Trivia*, it seems hard to imagine Gay's secure, yet also judgemental and complacent, walker being capable of equivalent self-scrutiny or empathy to his fellow pedestrians. Unlike Ryder or Stephen, he would undoubtedly have made a poor auto/biographer.

*   *   *   *   *

But how fair is this charge of self-absorption and unsociability? While we should be cautious of treating *Trivia* as representative of the city, Gay's London is also more than a literary construct or an exercise in decoding the bias of its narrator. As an individual's perception of a city defined by its people, the poem assumes broader historical value if we expect to see not early eighteenth-century London as it was, but how it legitimately appeared to one, and conceivably many more, of its citizens. A record of urban experience, *Trivia* highlights how the perceived city shapes the behaviour of its citizens and, though full of people, how it often worked against social contact.

The walker's experience points to four key impediments to interacting with his fellow pedestrians. First, Gay's Londoners exist not as individuals but members of a physically overwhelming and intimidating mass that appears as 'the jostling Crouds' (I 3); 'mingling Press' (II 27); 'mixt Hurry' (III 30), and 'rude Throng . . . with furious Pace', and which disrupts what little social intimacy exists by breaking 'thee from a Friend's Embrace' (III 87–8). The walker's evening tour also provides evidence of the dehumanizing effect of life among so many strangers. As a result, one person's need is viewed as another's inconvenience. The pedestrian who slips while crossing the road will 'call for Aid in vain', while a fall against a

vendor's stall prompts not help but a demand for compensation (III
125–6, 179–80). Where assistance is given, human relationships are
shaped less by professionalism than market forces, as with the constable
'Mov'd by the Rhet'rick of a Silver Fee' (III 317–18). In *Trivia*'s human
crush it appears that sympathy, when expressed, is more easily directed to
what is most distinctive, namely the city's animals that stand out from,
and suffer by, the crowd: 'O barb'rous Men, your cruel Breasts asswage, /
Why vent ye on the gen'rous Steed your Rage?' (II 233–5).

  Second, such forces work against efforts to establish personal contact
with others in the crowd. Indeed, that anyone would seek to do so
was recognized as peculiar—even by that dedicated people-watcher Mr
Spectator, who admitted his habit of 'saluting any Person whom I like'
to be 'an odd Humour I am guilty of'.[10] To look closely at pedestrians on
a main street was also a dangerous activity, since he who 'Turns oft' to
pore the Damsel's Face' will 'strike his aking Breast against the Post'
(III 102–4). Significantly, it is only the misfit and ill-at-ease peasant
who, new to the city, offers any expression in his 'enquiring Face' as he
'Bewilder'd, trudges on from Place to Place' (II 77–8). But even seasoned
Londoners discover the impracticality of socializing in a complex city
where conversation and navigation prove difficult to combine. Leaving
the Temple, the walker and his associate 'Through the long *Strand*
together let us stray', but 'With thee conversing, I forget the Way'
(II 480–1).

  Third, the walker must confront those who disguise themselves to
deceive, often by cover of darkness. During his night-time journey, the
walker identifies in quick succession the thief/beggar who, feigning
injury by day, now deploys his crutch to 'fell thee to the Ground'; then a
link-man with the power to cast the unsuspecting client into darkness,
and finally a prostitute who 'oft the Quaker's Hood prophane' to 'trudge
demure the Rounds of *Drury-Lane*' (III 135–7; 139–42; 279–80).
Other Londoners assume disguise for more innocent purposes though
with similarly restrictive effects on social interaction. Thus, 'Good
Huswives' who 'Winter's Rage despise' obscure themselves from the
weather and their fellow pedestrians, while many retreat 'underneath th'
Umbrella's oily Shed' (I 209–10) during regular downpours. Lastly, social
interaction is further inhibited by some Londoners' practice of distancing
themselves, physically and culturally, by means of the coach. If difficult to
establish among pedestrians, social contact between London's pedestrians
and its passengers proves non-existent in *Trivia*. 'Box'd within the Chair',
passengers are not only obscured from but actively contemptuous of

street culture (II 513). These, moreover, are sentiments reciprocated by the walker for whom the coach is a symbol of modern corruption, and its customers—typically an interchangeable medley of gamblers, lawyers, and fops—guilty of idleness, dishonesty, and vanity.

Though dramatized for effect, the walker's experience of social alienation corresponds with that of contemporary observers not consciously given to the mock-heroic. Dudley Ryder often found it 'difficult to get along for the crowd'[11] while an earlier commentator, Thomas Brown, described a city of such diverse cultures 'that the Inhabitants themselves don't know a quarter of them'. Common to all was Gay's theme of faceless bustle and disguise. Metropolitan pedestrians 'begin a Thousand Things before they have finished one . . . They are equally incapable both of Attention and Patience, and . . . dont allow themselves time either to Hear or See; but like Masks, work in the Dark, and Undermine one another.'[12] Foreign visitors also commented on the pace and disinterest of the crowd. Londoners, claimed Pierre Jean Grosley, 'walk very fast . . . and those who happen to be in their way, are sure to be the sufferers'. The only response was to pitch in. 'Having soon adopted the English custom', Grosley described his passage 'through crowded streets, exerting my utmost efforts to shun persons, who were equally careful to avoid me.'[13]

That the walker experiences the city on these terms helps set our narrator's character in context and, perhaps, in a better light. Eager to avoid undue contact with multiple strangers, and simultaneously impeded in his connections with would-be associates, the walker's physical and psychological withdrawal distinguishes him, as Alison Stenton shows, as an early example of the modern urban citizen. *Trivia*, however, goes further, suggesting that the walker makes an acceptable, even positive, contribution to the urban experience of others. Certainly the walker's instructions on navigating the city, although fastidious and selfish to some modern critics, are likely to have been sounder advice for eighteenth-century pedestrians. John Trusler, for example, endorsed many of Gay's instructions on the protection of person and possessions. Indeed, Trusler's later recommendation—to 'keep the wall and you will have no interruption, every one will give way'—proved less accommodating than that of the walker, whose self-preservation was tempered by concern for the old, infirm, or honest labourer to whom the wall was given up.[14] Indeed, it is arguable that Gay's walker also provides a better exponent of public sociability than pedestrians like Dudley Ryder or Leslie Stephen: Ryder because his diarist's self-analysis resulted in self-absorption; Stephen because the London walk only prompted reflection if the city's realities

could be shut out. As a result, both they and Gay's 'Proud' carriage passengers fail to act as generously as the walker for whom charity, though
somewhat smugly given, 'still moves . . . the Mind; / His lib'ral Purse
relieves the Lame and Blind' (II 451, 453–4). Interestingly, the walker's
donation is presented at the Temple, the place where a lovelorn Ryder
only has eyes for those apparently happier than he.

In his combination of social distance and impersonal charity, the
walker recalls Richard Sennett's now classic concept of the 'public man'.
This was a figure characterized by his appreciation of an inevitably anonymous urban culture defined, in its healthiest state, as 'an authentically
human but unreservedly *impersonal* amphitheatre of human interaction'
in which people participate 'without the compulsion to know them
[fellow citizens] as persons.'[15] Sennett's dating of 'public man' to the
eighteenth century is in line with early modern London's considerable
growth (from approximately 200,000 in 1600 to 900,000 in 1800),
crucially dependent on net immigration of 6,000–7,000 people per
annum in the period 1670–99.[16] Likewise his link between impersonality
and citizens' adoption of behavioural codes conforms with contemporary
essays on the impossibility of public intimacy and the value of shared
social signs, in speech, deportment or dress, for negotiating eighteenth-
century London.

Successful signs needed to be readily accessible and widely compre-
hensible to those one passed quickly in the street. Gay remarked elsewhere that dress had 'grown of universal Use in the Conduct of Life' and
now served as a point of ready reference—in the case of wigs, an 'index of
the mind'—to passers-by.[17] Of course, such signs were often not wholly
persuasive, and a minority of observers claimed to see through the codes
to detect, say, the social climber behind the would-be gentleman. But as
Richard Steele acknowledged, 'a Stranger of tolerable Sense' would always
go far if 'dress'd like a Gentleman', and undoubtedly went much further
than a more eloquent or learned peer who was 'regulated by the rigid
Notions of Frugality'. In street life it was the visual sign that gained widest
currency: 'appearance falls within the Censure of every one that sees him',
while intelligence 'very few are Judges of'.[18] Steele's observation well
captures Sennett's tension between public and personal. Thus the pavement is more a place for external, and potentially mistakable, codes than
for detailed and accurate character assessment; it is a site of negotiation
and possible deception, but cannot be the place to know individual
Londoners. Alert to the difficulties of interaction among strangers, city
commentators advised alternative locations—notably an individual's

home and neighbourhood—as the best environment to gain knowledge of someone 'as a person'. 'If we would really enquire into a man's character, we should repair to the place of his abode, and there procure information, not from his superiors on the spot, but from his neighbours of equal rank, with whom he has lived in his own natural manner.'[19]

*　*　*　*　*

Londoners' appreciation of the psychological (if not physical) distance between strangers, together with the value of the home, was likewise a theme in changing concepts of eighteenth-century biography in which 'getting to know someone' became a defining ideal. Central to this development was a growing mid-century interest in biography as the record of a person's character, rather than the study of an invariably worthy contribution to public history. In doing so, life-writing moved from an exercise in instruction through the embodiment of model human conduct to one of character formation and analysis in which a subject's exceptionalism or individualism derived less from historical greatness than our knowing them as people.

This shift in the purpose of biography—a change closely associated with Samuel Johnson's life of Richard Savage (1744), and his essays for the *Rambler* (1750) and *Idler* (1759) periodicals—had important implications for the remit and method of life-writing. First, came the potential democratization of the modern biographical subject. It was a concept epitomized by Johnson's claim that there 'rarely passes a life of which a judicious and faithful narrative would not be useful', or James Granger's decision to begin his biographical dictionary of England (1768) with 'monarchs' but to 'end with ballad-singers, chimney-sweepers, and beggars'.[20] The reasons for this approach differed between authors. For Granger the inclusion of rulers and paupers in the same volume was motivated by a rather unbiographical belief in the similarities between people: thus the anatomist would find 'little or no difference in dissecting the body of a king and that of the meanest subject'. Johnson's suggestion of usefulness, by contrast, points to the more productive, sociological effect of democratic biography from which might emerge a science of human nature.

Few readers of *Trivia* would dispute that this nature, in all its diversity, was best witnessed in the city street. But for the eighteenth-century biographer, as for Gay's walker, London's thoroughfares were not the place for the detailed knowledge required to write the life of a person. Rather, biography's full potential was achievable only by turning to the intimacy of personal relationships. Like urban commentators, biographers looked not to the street but to the home as the best location in which they could get to know their subject as a person, and therefore as a candidate for useful biography.

For Johnson this had implications for both the biographer's concept of his art and its practice. As he argued in the *Rambler*, good life-writing required an author to focus on the 'domestic privacies . . . where exterior appendages are cast aside and men excel each other by prudence and by virtue'.[21] Biographical practice in turn focused on acquiring 'personal knowledge', the source from which Johnson thought 'Lives can only be written'[22] and from which a suitably biographical 'person' might emerge. Knowledge of this kind required time and meaningful human interaction: qualities that the walker is denied in a London of busy streets, few associates, and no opportunities to stop and recuperate in coffee houses which served others as centres of human exchange. A common concern of Johnson's writings is the difficulty of getting to know another person, and of the consolidation of this knowledge in biography. What made biography challenging, but also interesting and valuable, was that character was not stable and consistent but variable and multi-layered. As Johnson and others appreciated, location shaped character. Biography was required to take account of place (and the resulting populated space), as well as personality—or, more accurately, to acknowledge the interaction between the two and its implications for how we view and what we can learn about a person.

To judge the walker harshly for his introversion is, therefore, to take him out of *Trivia's* exclusively city context. It overlooks that he is a persistently urban figure who, in his reading of signs, social distance, and giving of moderate charity, acts in ways required of public man. Streets are not the place in which the walker or fellow pedestrians should attempt intimate biography. Rather, as Gay's contemporaries understood, the true test of character in public was an individual's behaviour not with close associates—the Johnsonian route to genuine biography—but with those one encountered briefly and would not meet again. In public it was social reserve and toleration that was celebrated. 'There is', as the *Spectator* put it, 'no ordinary Part of human Life which expresseth so much a good Mind, and a right inward Man, as his Behaviour upon meeting with Strangers.'[23]

Modern readiness to criticize the walker surely also owes something to our acceptance of, indeed demand for, intimate biography in a genre profoundly shaped by the Johnsonian search for character. Moreover, if modern society is defined, as Sennett argues, by the 'fall of public man', then ours is a culture which privileges (though not necessarily protects) private life, while simultaneously challenging the perceived merit of impersonality in public conduct. To early eighteenth-century commentators, by contrast, a preoccupation with the personal, especially in the context of biography, was viewed suspiciously as corrosive of public life. Writing in the context of a sensationalist Grub Street biography market, it was Joseph Addison's belief that 'We may generally observe, that our Admiration of a famous Man lessens upon our nearer Acquaintance with him.'[24] In fact Mr Spectator and Dr Johnson, despite different attitudes to the place of personal details in biography, shared a common interest in true character, and the celebration of good character. Where they diverged was in the route to such knowledge, with route determined by place. Thus, for Johnson, genuine character was derived from the private insights of close associates at the dinner table or on the backstairs. For Mr Spectator—lone city wanderer and self-confessed outsider—estimations of 'inward Man' could not rely on intimacy but were defined by the company one kept with the pavement strangers who defined urban life.

* * * * *

It is an undeniable theme of *Trivia* that city life could often be—perhaps invariably was—difficult, tiring, and (if not always as dangerous as the walker suggests) then certainly a continual tax on one's senses and wits. In this, Gay's poem offers a useful counterbalance to the modern tendency to treat eighteenth-century participation in urban public space as a naturally refining experience. It is a reminder too that the politer and calmer Spectatorial town was as much a creation of its narrator's background, temperament, and opportunities as it was an exercise in reportage. For all his English plainness, Gay's walker is far from boorish; yet from *Trivia* it is hard to see how a day's pedestrianism is a civilizing process, simply because the realities of streets—its hazards, deceptions, and faceless crowd—give the walker little chance to socialize.

Gay's walker, of course, has no such access to privacy in a poem which offers a consistently public experience. Faced with these pressures, we may be forgiven for regarding his fortunes as bleakly unrelenting. But it is precisely because of this immersion in London life that Gay also reveals how urban culture is itself more diverse and interesting than the dichotomies of public and private, city and home, or citizen and biographical subject might initially suggest. Rather, *Trivia* reminds us that the city, and the experience of city life, is open to constant change, with subtle but largely positive implications for the character of and relationships between its pedestrians.

Change came in a number of forms. *Trivia*'s London is the capital in winter, when the cold prompted disguise and introversion through the wearing of protective clothing. However, on several occasions the walker acknowledges the year ahead and, in particular, the welcome effects of seasonal change: hence Spring brings 'Ladies gayly dress'd' and 'wanton Fawns with frisking Pleasure range' (I 151), and is followed by the agreeable strolling weather enjoyed by Mr Spectator during his travels in August 1712. As a day/night tour, *Trivia* also shows how the city's perceived character changes daily between light and darkness. As the experience of Dudley Ryder and Gay's country yeoman show, so too does the temperament of its inhabitants who by night are more prey to, but also tempted by, streetwalkers (III 285–92) — in addition to their being more hesitant as once familiar areas grow dark, or more likely to drink to incapacity.

Darkness heightens *Trivia*'s persistent theme of the city of strangers with a clear equation of the unknown with danger and risk. But, as the architectural theorist Jane Jacobs argues, perceptions of strangeness and social distance vary according to the circumstances of city life and built environment. In keeping with this, Gay shows how other events and more felicitous situations prompt levels of contact from which develop the impersonal trust networks Jacobs sees as essential for a successful city.[25] Thus, on hearing the cry 'Stop thief!', otherwise atomized and competitive pedestrians come together, albeit briefly, to chase and punish those who offend against the order of public life (III 66–70). In sunny mood, the walker also perceives himself as part of an imagined kinship network, evident when he binds himself to 'ye associate walkers, O my friends' in opposition to the coach (II 501). It may be no coincidence that the walker's happiness follows his engagement with a lone companion in the Strand—a reminder of the potential for encounters with friends or, as Susan Whyman's chapter suggests, London-based relatives to create semiprivate intimacies within a faceless crowd.

But it is perhaps in the city's topographical variations—and especially in the proximity of impersonal thoroughfares with potentially more intimate side streets—that Gay's London most influences citizens' attachment to fellow strangers. In doing so *Trivia* draws attention to a semipublic city of passageways and doorsteps that have become so rich an area for historians of gender and social identity. Such places naturally proved a mixed blessing for pedestrians and, as for the naive yeoman led down 'winding Alleys to her Cobweb Room', can become sites of confusion or entrapment (III 292). But semi-public London equally serves a positive purpose in facilitating urban sociability, either by obscuring antisocial behaviour—those seeking a quick pee, for example, should 'some Court, or secret Corner seek'—or by removing at least some of the impersonality required on the main street (II 299). As noted, the pace and volume of the 'heedless throng' made distinguishing others difficult and hazardous. Yet released from Gay's crowd or Thomas Brown's hurrying and unseeing masks, the walker is able to observe or make partial contact with those who escape to quieter 'Lanes untrod before' (I 10). Here *Trivia* offers a range of city-based relationships made possible by their relative seclusion and which, at their most passionate, include not just the fumblings of prostitute and client, but the genuine coupling of Cloacina and her watchman who 'To the dark Alley . . . move' that 'no Link-Boy interrupt their Love' (II 133–4).

Shaped by climate, time, emotion, and topography, Gay's London assumes a diversity and character which the walker sketches in an early example of what is a now popular sub-genre, the city biography. But *Trivia*'s side streets also allow the walker to make connections that are impossible or unwelcome among the crowd. Away from the thoroughfare he has, like the reflective Dudley Ryder, an opportunity to 'pensive stray' or to 'remark each Walker's diff'rent Face, / And in their look their various Bus'ness trace' (II 273–6). As a place for spectatorship the back street has something in common with London's fashionable display arena, the Mall and St James's Park, though these were locations to which people actively came to perform: 'the Rendezvous of the Gay and Gallant, who assemble to *see* and be *seen*'.[26] However, for the biographer, or indeed the plain curious, it is less the social performer with stories to tell than the lone alley figure who is of most interest. Looking in turn leads Gay to speculate on the reasons for favouring London's by-ways, and by inference, the hidden histories of individual passers-by. This is not, of course, Johnsonian biography since the walker's observations must always occur in a fleeting and semi-public urban context. Nor is it Mr Spectator's benevolent challenge to see in 'every Face . . . that of a Friend'. Based on what we know of his character, the walker has not the maturity or security to follow this advice. Nonetheless, and as Gay reminds us, glimpses of real life histories—from the secretly anxious broker to the penurious man of fashion—are possible and do occur, even in a city of strangers.

NOTES

1. Joseph Addison and Richard Steele, *The Spectator, 1711–14*, ed. Donald F. Bond, 5 vols. (Oxford, 1965; 1987), i, no. 1 (1 March 1711), 1.

2. Ibid., iv, no. 454 (11 August 1712), 98.

3. Ibid. 103.

4. Miles Ogborn, *Spaces of Modernity: London's Geographies, 1680–1780* (1998), 110; Dianne Dugaw, *'Deep Play': John Gay and the Invention of Modernity* (2001), 111; David Nokes, *John Gay: A Profession of Friendship* (Oxford, 1995), 211.

5. Alvin B. Kernan, *The Plot of Satire* (New Haven, 1965), 45–50.

6. Dudley Ryder, *The Diary of Dudley Ryder, 1715–1716*, ed. W. Matthews (1932), 71–2. For earlier and later encounters see 49, 67, 138, 274, 292, 331, 369.

7. Ibid. 294.

8. Leslie Stephen, 'In Praise of Walking', *Studies of a Biographer*, 3 vols. (1902), iii. 256, 281.

9. Ibid., iii. 259, 280.

10. *Spectator*, iv, no. 454, 98.

11. Ryder, *Diary* (18 January 1716), 167.

12. Thomas Brown, *Amusements Serious and Comical, calculated for the Meridian of London*, 2nd edn. (1702), 22, 42.

13. Pierre Jean Grosley, *A Tour to London*, 2 vols. (1772), i. 105–6.

14. John Trusler, *The London Adviser and Guide* (1786), 116.

15. Richard Sennett, *The Fall of Public Man* (1977), xix, xxi.

16. Peter Clark (ed.), *The Cambridge Urban History of Britain*, vol. ii: *1540–1840* (Cambridge, 2000), 316, 649–55.

17. *The Guardian* (1713), ed. Calhoun Winton (Lexington, Ky., 1982), no. 149 (1 September 1713), 486, 488.

18. *Spectator*, iii, no. 360 (23 April 1712), 347.

19. *The Cheats of London Exposed* (1770), 90.

20. Samuel Johnson, *The Rambler* (1750–2) in W. J. Bate and Albrecht B. Strauss (eds.), *The Yale Edition of the Works of Samuel Johnson*, 16 vols. (New Haven, 1958–90) iv, no. 60 (13 October 1750), 321; James Granger, *A Biographical History of England* (1769), 4 vols., 2nd edn. (1775), iv. 356.

21. *Rambler*, iv, no. 60, 321.

22. Samuel Johnson, 'Joseph Addison', *Lives of the English Poets*, 3 vols. (Dublin, 1780–1), ii. 39.

23. *Spectator*, ii, no. 132 (1 August 1711), 24.

24. *Spectator*, iii, no. 256 (24 December 1711), 495.

25. Jane Jacobs, *The Death and Life of Great American Cities* (2000), 66.

26. *A Trip through the Town*, 5th edn. (1735), 3.

Sharing Public Spaces

Susan E. Whyman

Readers beware! As you enjoy Gay's *Trivia* you are not just crossing the streets of London. You are crossing intellectual borders. You are entering a world where fact and fiction, history and literature, are muddied together. You will find no safe pavements dividing the fashionable West End of London from the seamy City, and no raised causeways separating walkers and riders. Gay plunges you into the heat, smells, and underbelly of an expanding commercial metropolis where people of all ranks, wealth, and ages are forced to mix together—whether they like it or not. One of *Trivia*'s many uses is to act as an entertaining mock-survival guide for sharing public space.

Gay's views of the metropolis are expressed through the words of his walking narrator, who leads the reader through London's crowded streets. You will find few signs of the polite urban culture that is praised in Joseph Addison and Richard Steele's *Spectator*.[1] Gay's London is a filthy, congested, and frightening city filled with fast moving vehicles and people. Crossing the street is dangerous, and the competition for space can degenerate into brutal warfare that has a thrilling, but dangerous frisson. 'Thy Foot will slide upon the miry Stone, / And passing Coaches crush thy tortur'd Bone' (III 175–6). The bloody confrontations that ensue are often associated with coaches, who mow down people and vehicles in their way: 'Who can recount the Coach's various Harms? / The Legs disjointed, and the broken Arms?' (II 521–2). The only way to survive in such a city is to read its signs and become a 'street-smart' walker.

This essay examines *Trivia* from the viewpoint of a cultural historian who relies on archival research and analysis of historical context. It compares the poem's evidence with that of a different type of genre—the personal letter. It also places the poem historically in the context of key changes in transport and communications. The goal of this essay is to use letters to provide a bridge from the statistical approach of the social historian to the textual world of the literary critic. This approach preserves the manuscript archive as the centre of research, but acknowledges that its texts are constructed.

As a source, personal letters are part history, part literature with literary conventions. They not only provide a private window into how individuals shared urban space, they are important to *Trivia*'s historical context. As Gay composed his verses, the way people communicated with each other was undergoing a profound change. After the civil wars of the 1640s, stable communications at last became possible and mail could be delivered without danger. By the eighteenth century, people were experiencing new patterns of mobility and separation in the face of expanding urbanization, trade, war, and empire. In contrast to the preceding centuries, there were more social transactions with those who were physically absent.[2] This led to changing views about space, time, and distance. Individuals in unfamiliar city spaces needed to develop new modes of behaviour that differed from those used in a village, where every member of society was known and endowed with rights and responsibilities.

In response, two technical innovations that reduced the effects of spatial separation reached unprecedented levels of efficiency—the provision of postal services and the use of public and private coaches. A rich, untapped postal archive demonstrates that the Restoration of 1660 was a chronological watershed for changes in mail delivery. A reorganized Post Office transported private letters several times a week on six main postal routes with links to Ireland, Scotland, and the continent.[3] In 1681, William Dockwra established a 'new Invention to convey letters and parcels . . . for a Penny', commonly called the Penny Post. He created seven central offices and 500 receiving-houses in each main street. A letter brought in at eight o'clock in the morning would be stamped by nine, and delivered at or near ten o'clock. Mails were carried six to ten times a day.[4] By Gay's time, letters had become an integral part of London life. In fact, postal revenues surged from £65,000 in 1685 to £156,000 in 1705. By 1703 the London Penny Post carried over a million items.[5]

Increased levels of wealth and commerce that created demand for postal services also stimulated use of private and public coaches. Transport to and about town was desperately needed, for at least one-sixth of the population now spent time in London.[6] At first the Crown attempted to restrict coaches to those under the rank of knight; then they tried to limit their numbers. Still, by 1636 there were over 6,000 private coaches in London.[7] By 1700, technical improvements had produced compact, more graceful coach bodies and increased comfort. 'There is an Admirable invention of springes', wrote Charles Hatton, 'wch do so prevent ye rocking of coaches yt truly I thinke coaches wth thos springes goe even in London streets full as easy as any chaires'. Hatton marvelled at the fact that 'ye springes may be easily fitted to any coach or chariot'.[8]

The use of hackney coaches also grew. By Gay's time 800 licensed London hackneys charged 5 shillings a week or 1 shilling for a mile and a half. In 1711, 200 sedan chairs were licensed.[9] Not surprisingly, the increased use of coaches and other vehicles changed the way people moved about the city. The traffic jams that Gay portrays illustrate how negotiating public streets was growing complicated. Thus the coach can be used to illustrate how people shared city spaces.

$$* \quad * \quad * \quad * \quad *$$

At first glance, personal correspondence describes a London that is similar to the city described by Gay. On closer analysis, however, we will find differences and complexities. Generally, letters complement the poem by adding a private dimension that sheds light on who came to town, why they did so, how they viewed the city, and the social conditions that they found. The poem, in turn, stimulates new ways of thinking about urban experience. There are difficulties in using Gay's poem as a source for 'real' evidence. Yet the integration of the two genres moves us closer to a more holistic understanding of Gay's London.

Gentry and middling-sort persons who journeyed between town and country wrote most of the letters used in this essay. They appear to have been experienced travellers who moved freely though urban space. In contrast, the people on *Trivia*'s streets were likely to be either permanent residents and workers or foolish newcomers from the country. For Gay's literary purposes, highlighting the differences between country bump-kins and sophisticated urbanites was useful. In personal letters, these dis-tinctions were muddied by writers who travelled back and forth between town and country. Letters thus add evidence about the fragmentation and strain placed upon nomadic families. Nothing could stem the incoming tide of people who longed for entertainment and education, consump-tion and news, politics and parliament, the social season and the marriage market, and medical, legal, and financial services.[10]

Elite and middling-sort women, who wrote many of the letters, visited London in droves. They were especially prominent on city streets, though Gay highlights working-class women in *Trivia*. Letters make clear that London was perceived as a 'women's heaven'. In 1708 when Parliament dissolved it was assumed that 'the gentlemen will be quick for leaving the town'. The ladies, however, remarked one observer, 'will not willingly go so soon'.[11] The clothes that figure prominently in *Trivia* drew women to the metropolis. Elizabeth Jervoise used buying and fitting clothes as excuses to leave Hampshire, and she begged to stay longer once in town.[12] Before Frances Cotterell attended a London wedding, she called on friends in order 'to show my cloths'.[13]

Fashion was not the only draw; nor was shopping. Women like Mrs Fauconberg and Mrs Hunlock made their visits in two hired 'chaires'. As they glided by, they liked to 'observe people that go to the chapels'.[14] They were likely to see prostitutes, as well, in all parts of town. Women strolled unchaperoned by males, despite the cautions of Gay's walker. John Verney's wife was invited to visit dangerous Spring Garden without her husband.[15]

Personal letters add life to *Trivia*'s urban panorama by fleshing out individuals in Gay's anonymous crowds. In contrast to more public texts, they also provide evidence of the emotional state of writers. Correspondence is filled with complaints of loneliness, overwork, and depression. The Mordaunts, for example, were constantly separated: some in a London townhouse, others in rented lodgings, and others in the country.[16] The North family of Covent Garden was similarly nomadic. They were also eager participants in London's cultural life. Lady Alice North owned verses by Gay's circle of friends, whilst other relations composed poetry and appended it to letters.[17] Lower down the social scale, some visitors found work and remained temporarily in town. Elizabeth Strutt came from Derbyshire and settled in London as a clergyman's housekeeper. She and her fiancé, a Derbyshire wheelwright, were thus separated for years. They too enjoyed poetry and quoted Milton and Swift in letters that helped them to remain connected.[18]

Trivia is constructed around the advice that was needed to safely share public space. Yet most country families had at least one member in town, who acted as its intermediary and guided visitors about. Although some correspondents may have been duped or molested in town, they used kinship networks to avoid such pitfalls. Most letter writers were thus amply provided with the sort of information that Gay's walker deemed important. Writers undoubtedly concealed bad experiences. Still letters generally show little of the fear for personal safety that Gay employed so effectively in his mock-heroic poem.

A Yorkshire farmer Leonard Wheatcroft, for example, sent his son to London to work for an uncle. The boy prospered so well that he eventually repurchased the Wheatcroft's former farmhouse.[19] Jedediah Strutt's brother Joseph came to London to make his fortune. He soon married, bought a draper's shop, and helped Jedediah develop Derbyshire silk factories.[20] Both *Trivia* and correspondence open windows into a time of social and economic mobility. But letters, themselves a series of narratives, tell stories about the failures and successes of unknown people. Daniel Baker came to town with nothing and was at first known as a haberdasher. Eventually he became governor of the Bridewell and Royal Africa Company. Later he thanked God 'who me from small beginings hath most wonderfully raised'.[21]

Social mobility also affected people lower down the social scale. Servants and workmen were increasingly moving to London, disrupting country patterns, and establishing urban ones.[22] In 1695, after fighting with the Verneys, their maid Betty left Buckinghamshire in a coach for London. She married a wholesale grocer and they soon had a shop.[23] In the same year, the Verneys' coachman quit service to set up a hackney coach in London. 'The truth is his wife is a proud woman', wrote a friend, and 'they think it below them to be a servant'.[24] The urban way of life was producing new mutations within the social hierarchy.

Gay himself came from Barnstaple without funds and worked as a mercer's apprentice. Though the patronage he craved was slow in coming, his talent and literary networks brought him some wealth. But mobility worked in both directions. Gay lost all of *Trivia*'s profits when his South Sea Company stock crashed.[25] In fact, London had a special attraction for people with ambitions or problems. Rebels, lovers, dissidents, and dreamers sought forbidden pleasures, escape from village restraints, and economic opportunity.[26] As letters show, the plots of literary tales like the rise of Dick Whittington (d. 1423) to mayor, often resurfaced in real life, blurring fact and fiction.[27]

Correspondence not only explains why people came to London, but also provides personal viewpoints about what inhabitants of town and country thought of the metropolis. Some writers spoke of it as the focal point of the world—a conceit also found in literary works.[28] This was often true for those who were left at home. 'Send me news' wrote Mr Hay to Sidney Evelyn in town, 'for you are at the center where every thing comes from, & what draws everything to it.'[29] As the Buckinghamshire Johnsons noted: 'London always seems to be in the road to almost every where.'[30] Once a family member left home, letters were the only way to keep in touch. Young William Hatton was ordered to write 'how I like London' and 'the fine things that are to be seen here'.[31] Letters were anxiously awaited and passed on to friends forming ongoing epistolary networks. Like *Trivia*, letters shaped images of London for readers who had never been there.

London life was the gold standard to which other places were compared negatively in emotional terms. Francis North's mother complained: 'I was afraid you had forgott yr old musty Mamma, now you have so many devertions in town.'[32] Jedediah Strutt tried futilely to lure his fiancée, Elizabeth, back to Derbyshire: 'It is not impossible that you may be happy here', he argued, 'even tho' it is true, you cannot here behold the splendor . . . of a great City'.[33] When Elizabeth finally decided to leave town and marry him, her friends wrote 'in a very taunting sort of a manner'. They 'wonder that you wou'd leave such a place', complained Jedediah, 'to come and marry a wheelwright'.[34]

Sidney Evelyn had to survive in Nottingham which boasted only '6 or 7 coaches . . . & one Hackney chair. . . . In this polite place', he noted sarcastically, 'there is no such thing as a coffee-house.' He was sure that his supper at seven 'would make you a little peevish it is so early'.[35] Representations of London in letters and literature affected how people in town and country thought about themselves. For many, it was thrilling to be at the centre and sad to be in a backwater. The dirt, filth, and danger of Gay's streets often lay submerged under more pleasant mental maps of London. *Trivia* was a reminder of the dangers of city life.

*   *   *   *   *

A first-time visitor to London may well have wondered what the city would be like. Upon arrival, letter writers often found social conditions that were similar to those described in *Trivia*. They wrote home about a city marked by diversity and congestion. In this cultural setting, there was no other alternative but to share public space. Travellers' correspondence allows us to start at the beginning of a journey to London and ride along with the visitor.

When ordinary travellers entered a cart or stagecoach, they were bumped, crushed, and thrown against bodies of people from different walks of life. As a boy, John Locke sat next to a woman 'soe grosse yt shee turnd my stomack & made me sick'. When their coach overturned, he was almost buried under her flesh.[36] On a similar journey, William Trumbull, a noted diplomat, sat squashed between 'a wrangling attorney & a scolding old woman'.[37] John Verney's coach ride was even worse. His company included 'a tanners wife on top, a cooper in the next degree, and a third person with her sucking child . . . A reeking scent', he complained, 'did frequently reach my too sensible nostrils.'[38]

Urban transportation forced physical contact with the flesh and limbs of people with whom one would never have kept company at home. The sharing of intimate space with strangers was a new phenomenon. In many villages, green fields spread out as far as the eye could see. Urban space, on the other hand, was densely packed with people, streets, and buildings. This new panorama made people stop and rethink their ideas about space and its impact on the human body. New strategies were needed, not just information, to negotiate public arenas.[39]

Alighting at a London inn, our first-time visitor might well have wished for guidance. *Trivia*'s narrator expressed fears for the visitor who entered 'the narrow Alley's doubtful Maze, / Trys ev'ry winding Court and Street in vain' (II 80–1). Even when directions were given, it was normal to get lost. If the address was known, finding it was still difficult. Buildings remained unnumbered until the 1770s, and there was no standardized format for place names.[40] Examination of addresses written on the outer sides of letters reveals that one address had many names that stood for the same location. The mail of a sea captain, Thomas Bowrey, was addressed to 'Wellclose Square', to 'Marine Square', and to 'near the Tower', to name a few of many variations.[41] Some people instructed correspondents how to write their addresses properly, but letters and walkers still went astray.

After visitors located their lodgings, they stepped onto a street where contacts were anonymous. How free were they, we wonder, to roam the streets at leisure? Although Gay focused on dangers that hampered walkers, his narrator seemed at liberty to wander across town. Historians have shown that London's streets were not as regulated as they would become later in the century.[42] Letter writers agree. They encountered obstacles as Gay predicted. Yet both men and women appear to have accommodated to urban life, strolling about in leisurely fashion and enjoying sights in neighbourhoods far from home. Merchant John Verney walked to Islington each morning to take the waters before trading at the Royal Exchange. After work he might visit his wife's in-laws in Little Chelsea, far to the west. Sometimes he walked all the way or travelled by boat to save time.[43] These distances were considerable and took people away from their usual neighbourhoods.

One of Gay's walkers might have been Robert Cotesworth, son of William Cotesworth of Newcastle. Like many younger sons of merchant families he came to London to attend school in preparation for a commercial career. Every morning he met his writing master, Mr Wright at the Hand and Pen in St Mary Axe, near Leadenhall in the City. He conversed with foreigners and learned high German and Spanish that would

'From ev'ry Penthouse streams the fleeting Snow'
2. 'Morning', plate 1 from *Four Times of Day* by William Hogarth (1738).

help him in business. After lessons, Robert might visit his sisters at their Chelsea boarding school that would hopefully 'bring them home marriageable'.⁴⁴ Travelling between eastern and western parts of the city appears to have been routine.

Of course, the degree of mobility attained was gender and class specific. Robert Shoemaker has found freedom of movement on the streets at this time, with mobility varying by rank, age, and gender. Upper and lower classes, he argues, had more liberty to roam outside home districts, especially women.[45] Our letter writers concur. Mr Atkins's wife, for example, used her urban freedoms so excessively that her husband locked her up when in town. She would only get her £120 per year if she promised to 'never be in London'.[46] Because urban life brought new opportunities for women, it had the power to undermine traditional gender roles. Correspondence often contradicts stereotypes of cloistered women found in contemporary conduct books.

If geographic mobility was a characteristic of London walkers, so was social diversity. Like Gay's narrator, letter writers encountered a city filled with 'a strange multitude . . . jumbled together'.[47] Only in London could one meet with so many different ranks of people in a range of venues. When Mary Townsend married far beneath her, London as a space of assignation was indicted. She 'would not have had a shopkeeper', complained her relatives, 'in any place but London'.[48] Urban males had their own gendered arenas, where different sorts of people were thrown together. In the City, Oliver Le Neve, a Norfolk squire, met a Frenchman at Garraway's Coffeehouse where he transacted business.[49] Clubs and taverns were other mixed social venues. Gay wrote letters from his publisher's where book buyers congregated. Shortly after *Trivia* was printed he remarked: 'I write this from Mr Lintot's Shop where pray direct to me for the future, being just come to Town. . . .'[50]

Both genders and all classes attended London theatres, where they observed each other from differently priced sections. The Cotterell family sat in 18*d.* seats at the playhouse, 'whilst ye vulgar' sat nearby on those that cost 'twelve penny'.[51] The 'vulgar' were important to Gay as theatre-goers. When his play *The What D'ye Call It* opened, Gay remarked in a letter: 'The common people of the pit and gallery received it at first with great gravity and sedateness, some few with tears; but after the third day they also took the hint, and have ever since been very loud in their clapps.'[52] Sitting in an audience was a cultural experience shared by a mix of social groups. Members of the audience looked across at people whom they would never encounter socially, and the objects of their view stared back. Both laughed and clapped during the performance and shared streets on the way home.

Later Gay's play, *Polly*, though a commercial success, was criticized by the government. 'Most of the Courtiers, though otherways my friends', wrote Gay, 'refuse to contribute to my undertaking, but the City and the people of England take my part very warmly, and I am told the . . . Citizens will give me proofs of it by their contributions.' Apparently they did so, for in its published form *Polly* realized £1,200.[53] Both Gay and letter writers described a city where people of diverse ranks shared public space. As urban theorists have maintained, early modern cities often bred alienation and isolation. Sharing spaces with different groups, however, might also produce awareness that new types of urban sociability were possible.[54]

After a day out in London, letter writers returned to mixed neighbourhoods that cut across social and cultural divisions. Indeed the city developed as an amalgam of villages where people of all classes clustered together. Heterogeneous communities emerged in every part of town with gradations of status spreading out laterally from broad streets to cramped alleys, and vertically within individual houses: shopkeepers below; servants at the top; household and lodgers in between. By 1716, the shopkeeping middle class had spread throughout every neighbourhood. Until the mid-eighteenth century, artisans, and retailers continued to reside next to their clients.[55]

Lawrence Stone believed that 'the landed classes lived among their own kind in what was known . . . as "the polite end of town"'. *Trivia* and letters demonstrate that this model overlooked the in-filling and intermingling that took place in neighbourhoods.[56] St Martin-in-the-Fields, Westminster was a good example. Within a few hundred yards of the most fashionable residences, manual labourers and paupers lived in desperate poverty. As Jeremy Boulton and Tim Hitchcock have demonstrated, the poor were more visible than their habitations in side streets and back alleys might suggest.[57]

Moreover, lodgers who rented rooms dominated the mixture of people who lived in one building. Unlike Paris with its grand town houses, there were few large freestanding houses in London. Gentry families poured their money into country estates. In the season they leased a fashionable house and then let rooms to lodgers—both rich and poor. A floating mass of tenants thus occupied rooms in larger buildings and spent much time in coffee houses, where they received mail.[58] St Martin-in-the-Fields parish poll books show 'about one-third of the population were lodgers in other people's homes'.[59]

Gay does not treat this topic, but personal letters confirm statistical studies. A country friend of the Le Neves, for example, lodged at an apothecary's house in Coleman Street near business colleagues.[60] In 1694, John Evelyn's daughter Susan reported that a friend 'is to lye in Dover St at her sister's . . . who has lent her her house, she being out of town'.[61] In 1708 Evelyn's grandson John tried to obtain use of part of a house from

Sir Thomas Frankland. They bickered as to which side and rooms in the house were the most desirable and fretted over how much to pay. It was hoped, John Evelyn was told, that Frankland would agree to 'change his side'.[62]

Many epistolary remarks confirm the congestion found in *Trivia* and demonstrate a severe housing shortage. In April 1702 it was reported the 'town fills . . . and all the best lodgings will be quickly taken'.[63] In 1710, London was 'thought to be fuller this winter than the last 40 years'.[64] Public spaces were also crowded. In 1714, the Evelyns complained that they were unable to get into Henry VII's chapel to 'hear the musick' at Queen Anne's funeral. Even people who paid a guinea for a seat in the Abbey had the same problem.[65] After one London wedding, the crowd was so dense, that the Norths had to 'fight our way thro' to the coaches'. [66]

Some thought that street congestion was driven by greed. In Cheapside, Jedediah Strutt observed that the cause of the 'vast concourse of people, of the Hurry & bustle they were in, & the eagerness that appear'd in their countenances, was getting of Money, & whatever some Divines would teach to the contrary, this is . . . the main business of the life of Man'.[67] 'Walking in London', summed up John Verney, 'differs from doing so in the country. The roughness of the treading, the rubbing by people and the bustle of 'em wearies the body and giddies . . . the head.'[68] As Gay maintained, crossing the street could be dangerous (III 169–74). During the Glorious Revolution, even a high official was not safe from 'ye Rabble'. An observer reported that 'a seaman, a common fellow took the wall of him and thrust him into the kennel with his mace and sword before him'.[69]

In normal times, however, correspondence shows people successfully adapting to the mobility, diversity, and congestion of urban space. Knowing the city was the strategy that Gay's narrator recommended, and with the help of kinship networks, visitors became informed walkers. Yet the growing number of pedestrians and vehicles eventually called for new strategies. Under these circumstances, a family coach became more important. We can observe a new private way of sharing public space by using coaches as a case study.

*   *   *   *   *

The symbol of the congested city was the newly popular coach that wreaked havoc on London's streets. That is why references to it were so prevalent in literature and correspondence. That private coaches were highly dangerous was obvious to letter writers. Letters were rife with reports of accidents. In 1726 Gay wrote to Swift about Lord Bolingbroke, 'who was thrown into the river with the glasses of the coach up, & was up to the knots of his perriwig in water'.[70] As Sir William Trumbull was leaving London, the perch of his coach cracked and broke. Fortunately, he was able to hire a hackney coach, but his servants had to walk home.[71] One traveller declared that 'he encounter'd more difficulties in his journey from London . . . than he had met with in crossing the Alps'.[72] There was nothing more fearful than a drunken coachman, who held your life in his hands. It was best to lodge him with his employer in London, where his sobriety might be monitored.[73]

Not only were coaches dangerous, they soaked up space, even when they were unoccupied. On arriving in town, coach owners had to make provision for their vehicles, as they would for a person. If there were no coach house, space would be rented. House hunters often assessed a street's status by noting how many coaches were kept.[74] Once families were established in town, their coaches became divisive markers in the game of conspicuous consumption. In 1697, Susan Draper took pains to recount the elegant retinue of a bride attended by six coaches. The latter, she maintained, made 'no small noyse'.[75]

As Gay observed, coaches not only caused traffic jams, they created divisions between walkers and riders: 'In sawcy State the griping Broker sits, / And laughs at Honesty, and trudging Wits' (I 117–18). Like the enclosure of land, the coach provided a private place for its owner, who was now enclosed in leather. Riding in a coach became a new private strategy for negotiating public space. It lifted its owner above the crowd and separated its riders from the populace. Instead of just knowing city streets as *Trivia* suggested, coach riders adopted the strategy of separating themselves from the masses. The social gulf that resulted was confirmed with every journey.

As a status symbol, ownership of a coach immediately proclaimed that a family possessed wealth. Accounts show that they were the most expensive items in urban budgets. In 1708 Sir John Evelyn paid 53 guineas for a pair of coach horses,[76] and accoutrements and trimmings could mount to as much as £100.[77] Even the well-off Evelyns made a formal plan to save money by using hackneys and horses.[78] Coaches were therefore a visible divisive marker that set off riders from walkers.

But if coaches drove wedges between rich and poor, they united members of the coach-owning classes. When John Grimston, a squire in Beverley, inherited money, he was told to 'get a coach and six genteel horses. . . . 'Tis expected a young heir so rich should launch a little out of the humdrum style.'[79] It was therefore aggravating when Simeon Weld, a well-esteemed landowner, had trouble gaining an inside place on the coach to London.[80] The Welds' neighbour did not have this problem. He sold his estate and was reported 'gone to London in great equipage'.[81] Riding in one's private coach was simultaneously a withdrawal from public space and a union with others of the same status.

Coaches united their London owners in many ways. When they were used to make visits, for example, they created social networks and cemented patronage. As I have shown elsewhere, the daily routine of urban visiting was a highly developed ritual based on enforced reciprocity.[82] People often found it irksome, but to forgo it might cause loss of prestige. When Lady Wentworth 'began to keep her visiting day', her relations grew unhappy. 'I am to be a constant piece of furniture for her drawing room', noted one kinswoman, who had to return the hated visit by riding in a coach.[83] After a difficult journey from the country, the Weld family arrived in London, tired and ill. Yet visitors arrived 'within a quarter of an hour after we came to town . . . and stay'd with us an hour, which was very troublesome'.[84] Members of the Langton family of flax merchants had a different problem. When they left London for Cumbria, they were forced to take leave of each friend that had come to see them.[85]

Whether visiting was done by foot or by coach affected power and status. Fortunately, the urban social structure was increasingly open to upwardly mobile families at this time. If a coach owner possessed other attributes including manners, a good marriage, and political connections, he might rise in status. Gay himself had longings to own a coach, though he had come to London from Devon as a lowly apprentice, a fact noted by Samuel Johnson.[86] Gay certainly had coaches on his mind when he wrote *Trivia*. In his personal letters before the poem's publication, he included only one long quotation from *Trivia*. Significantly, it described the evil effects of London coaches (I 83–104).[87] These same verses duly appeared in *Trivia* along with other pejorative passages about them.

In his private comments, however, Gay admitted the powerful attraction of coaches, and there were even jokes about his buying one. 'Gay has gott so much money by his art of walking the streets', wrote a friend, 'that he is ready to sett up his equipage.'[88] Gay wittily admitted to this paradox in a letter to Thomas Parnell: 'What I got by walking the streets', he remarked, 'I am now spending in riding in Coaches.'[89] Later in life he repeatedly mentioned the high cost of coaches. When Swift accused him of laziness in 1731, he insisted defensively: 'I spend no shillings in coaches or chairs to levees or great visits.'[90] Gay, it seems, had ambivalent feelings about coaches and their riders.

This period is known for its unclear, often porous boundaries that separated those with gentility from the lower orders. One way to claim gentle status in an anonymous urban environment was to make visits in a coach. Barriers on the road to elite status might be evaded by driving a coach assuredly through London's streets. This act was part of a strategy to cope with public arenas by creating private pathways through urban space.

*   *   *   *   *

As Georg Simmel noted, 'Cities demand a lot of mental work from those who wish to make sense of them.'[91] Gay surely anticipated issues of urban sociology such as metropolitan anxiety and the development of compensatory street codes. Early modern cities naturally caused some people to feel alienation and isolation. Yet sharing spaces with different social groups also produced new strategies for moving about town.[92] Intimate body contact in crowded spaces led to competition, conflict, and accentuation of class divisions. The coach increasingly enclosed elite riders and protected them from walkers. The boundaries between walkers and riders, however, remained unclear. Walkers like Gay hired or shared a wide range of vehicles on a regular basis throughout their lives. One could buy and lose a coach many times over as financial conditions changed. The ownership of a coach, moreover, enabled some people to cross over the line that demarcated gentle status.

The boundaries between city and country, or the east and west ends of town, were equally porous. I also want to extend the idea of permeable borders to the genres of poetry and letters. It is useful to think of them as overlapping texts that shared areas of adjacent grey between them. The opening statement of this essay cautioned: 'Readers beware . . . you are crossing intellectual borders'. Though distinct vocabularies and methods divide writers, current scholarly practice is blurring disciplinary boundaries across the humanities.

Both *Trivia* and letters shed light on a fluid historical moment marked by increased urbanization. Both genres tell a series of little stories using literary conventions. Yet despite similarities, there are important differences. Gay's text is an imaginative representation of urban culture that plays with and entertains us through language. It offers multi-layered allusive references to classical and literary sources that are often missed by historians. The aesthetic values of the period come alive in *Trivia* in a way that ordinary correspondents cannot capture.

Letter writers, on the other hand, add a private dimension to our understanding of the urban landscape. Their narratives put flesh on anonymous crowds and the social context that form the backdrop to Gay's poem. Letters have been thought of as conveying actual experience, at least before literary theory questioned the constructed nature of archival evidence. Even given this fact, correspondence has some unique attributes that help to mitigate the problem. When both outgoing and incoming letters exist, readers can listen to conversations that employ contemporary language. There has been healthy debate as to whether first-person voices can be heard by later generations. But we do not have to abruptly choose either one or the other side of the argument. We can enrich our research by integrating a wide range of sources that speak to questions that we want to answer from different cultural perspectives.

Historians must continue to study parish registers and personal accounts. They must also read Gay's *Trivia* for a more capacious understanding of early eighteenth-century London. In doing so, they will be emulating the poet's interdisciplinary outlook. *Trivia* is itself a mix of genres. Moreover, it deals with issues raised by our modern-day categories of sociology, economics, geography, urban planning, classics, and art history. The resulting sum is greater than its parts. If John Gay were alive today, he might boast that he knew all about 'interdisciplinarity'. One of the many ways that we can read *Trivia* is to celebrate its own mix of cultural spaces.

NOTES

1. Joseph Addison and Richard Steele, *The Spectator (1711–1714)*, ed. Donald F. Bond, 5 vols. (Oxford, 1965).
2. Anthony Giddens, *A Contemporary Critique of Historical Materialism: Power, Property, and the State* (1981) i. 5.
3. The Post Office Archive (POA) in London describes all aspects of postal service.
4. William Dockwra, *The Practical Method of the Penny Post* (1681).
5. POA, Treasury Letter Books; Howard Robinson, *The British Post Office* (Princeton, 1948), 80–1, 86.
6. Edward A. Wrigley, 'A Simple Model of London's Importance in Changing English Society and Economy, 1650–1750', *Past and Present*, 37 (1967), 44–70.

7. John Crofts, *Packhorse, Waggon and Post* (1967), 113; Ralph Straus, *Carriages and Coaches* (1912), 58–60, 90.

8. British Library Additional (BL Add.) MS. 29576, fo. 31, Charles Hatton to Christopher Hatton, 21 March 1700.

9. John Ashton, *Social Life in the Reign of Queen Anne* (New York, 1929), 376, 381.

10. Susan Whyman, *Sociability and Power in Late-Stuart England: The Cultural Worlds of the Verneys 1660–1720* (Oxford, 1999), 58.

11. Verney Letters, Princeton University Library microfilm edition, Reel (R) 53-571, John Verney to Thomas Cave, 17 April 1708; R54-112, Thomas Cave to John Verney, 19 July 1709.

12. Hampshire Record Office, Jervoise Papers MS 44M69/F6, Elizabeth Jervoise to Thomas Jervoise III, 13 October 1709.

13. BL Add. 72518, fo. 4, Frances Cotterell to Sir William Trumbull, 28 March [1708?].

14. Bodleian Library (Bodl), D. D. Weld MS *c*.13/5/7, Margaret Weld to Sir James Simeon, 7 October 1707.

15. Verney Letters, R37-60, Elizabeth Palmer to John Verney, 25 June 1683.

16. Elizabeth Hamilton, *The Mordaunts: An Eighteenth-Century Family* (1965), 5.

17. Bodl North MS b.14, fos. 100–3, List of Lady Alice North's books; d.23, fo. 116, Brownlow North to Francis North, 27 May 1760. Peter Lewis and Nigel Wood (eds.), *John Gay and the Scriblerians* (1988).

18. Derbyshire Record Office (DRO) Strutt MS D5303/3/4/1, Jedediah Strutt to Elizabeth Woollat, 3 February 1755; D5303/1/2, Elizabeth Woollat to Jedediah Strutt, n.d., fragments.

19. DRO MS D5433/1; Leonard Wheatcroft, 'The Autobiography of Leonard Wheatcroft of Ashover, 1627–1706', in Dorothy Riden (ed.), *A Seventeenth-Cenutry Scarsdale Miscellany*, Derbyshire Record Society xx (1993), 78.

20. DRO D2943M/F9/2, Frederick Strutt, *The Strutts of Derbyshire*, ed. R. Harold Paget (1898), preface.

21. Whyman, *Sociability and Power*, 121; Phillips Auctioneers Catalogue, Sheffield Park MSS, Sussex., item 250, 2 July 1981, 41.

22. Verney Letters, R53-519, Charles Chaloner to John Verney, 2 November 1707.

23. Verney Letters, R48-619, Elizabeth Lillie to Ralph Verney, 15 December 1695.

24. Verney Letters, R53-519, Charles Chaloner to John Verney, 2 November 1707.

25. Samuel Johnson, *The Lives of the English Poets*, 2 vols. (Oxford, 1905), ii. 274.

26. Whyman, *Sociability and Power*, 60.

27. Gwynedd Sudworth, *Richard Whittington, London's Mayor* (1975); Lennard Davis, *Factual Fictions: The Origins of the English Novel* (New York, 1983), 153.

28. [Richard Burridge], *A New Review of London* (1722).

29. BL Add. MS 78476, J. Hay to Sidney Evelyn, 23 December 1733.

30. Bodl MS Don. *c*.191, fo. 43, Robert Johnson to Barbara Johnson, 24 July 1785.

31. BL Add. MS 29576, fo. 100, William Hatton to Christopher Hatton, n.d. [1702?].

32. Bodl North MS d.23, fo. 35, Alice Guilford to Francis North, 19 January, n.y.

33. DRO Strutt MS D5303/3/4/1, Jedediah Strutt to Elizabeth Woollat, 3 February 1755.

34. DRO Strutt MS D5303/5/2 A. Dethickes to Elizabeth Woollat, 5 November 1755.

35. BL Add. MS 78476, Sidney Evelyn to Mary Evelyn, 7 August 1738.

36. Bodl Locke MS *c*.24, fo. 170 John Locke to John Locke senior, 25 October 1656.

37. Berkshire Record Office, Trumbull MS D/ED C.3 Sir William Trumbull to Elizabeth Trumbull, Tuesday night, n.d.

38. Verney Letters, R46-140, John Verney to Mary Verney, 11 October 1682.

39. Henri Lefebvre, *The Production of Space*, trans. Donald Nicolson-Smith (Oxford,1991); Miles Ogborn, *Spaces of Modernity: London's Geographies, 1680–1780* (New York, 1998).

40. For examples of early house numbering see Guildhall (GH) Baker MS 16,927, fo. 8ᵛ. In 1779, Edward Baker is told to direct his mail to 'No. 10'; Bodl MS Don. *c*.191, fo. 43, Robert Johnson to Barbara Johnson, 24 July 1785, addressed to Miss Johnson at No. 1 Kensington Square.

41. For example, GH Bowrey MS 3041/4, fo. 79. A letter of 30 December 1760 is addressed 'To Mr. Thomas Bowrey/Marchant living in Marine Squair'.

42. Robert Shoemaker, 'Public Spaces, Private Disputes? Fights and Insults on London's Streets 1660–1800', in Tim Hitchcock and Heather Shore (eds.), *The Streets of London: From the Great Fire to the Great Stink* (2003), 54–68.

43. Whyman, *Sociability and Power*, 61, 73.

44. Edward Hughes, *North Country Life in the Eighteenth Century: The North-East 1700–1750* (1952), 360–4.

45. Robert Shoemaker, 'Gendered Spaces: Patterns of Mobility and Perceptions of London's Geography, 1660–1750', in Julia Merritt (ed.), *Imagining Early Modern London: Perceptions and Portrayals of the City from Stow to Strype, 1598–1720* (New York, 2001), 144–65.

46. Whyman, *Sociability and Power*, 60.

47. *The Country Gentleman's Vade Mecum or His Companion for the Town* (1699), 7.

48. Verney Letters, R16-26, Elizabeth Adams to Ralph Verney, 11 November 1659.

49. BL Add. MS. 71573, fo. 37^v, Oliver Le Neve to Peter Le Neve, 1 September 1686.

50. John Gay, *Letters of John Gay*, ed. C. F. Burgess (Oxford, 1966), 28–9, no. 20, John Gay to Thomas Parnell, [26 March 1716].

51. Cotterell MS Papers, Jane Cotterell to Miss Fanny Cotterell, 24 August, n.y.

52. Gay, *Letters*, 19, no. 15, Alexander Pope and Gay to John Caryll, 3 March [1714/15].

53. Gay, *Letters*, 79–80, and note 3, no. 55, Gay to Jonathan Swift, 18 March 1728/9.

54. John J. Macionis and Vincent N. Parrillo, *Cities and Urban Life* (Upper Saddle River, NJ, 1998), 110; Richard Sennett (ed.), *Classic Essays on the Culture of Cities* (Englewood Cliffs, NJ, 1969).

55. Whyman, *Sociability and Power*, 63.

56. Lawrence Stone, 'The Residential Development of the West End of London in the Seventeenth Century', in B. Malament (ed.), *After the Reformation: Essays in Honor of J. H. Hexter* (Philadelphia, 1980), 167–212 (188).

57. Jeremy Boulton 'The Poor among the Rich: Paupers and the Parish in the West End 1600–1724', in Mark Jenner and Paul Griffiths (eds.), *Londinopolis* (Manchester, 2000), 197–227; Tim Hitchcock, *Down and Out in Eighteenth-Century London* (2004).

58. Whyman, *Sociability and Power*, 63, 72; M. Dorothy George, *London Life in the Eighteenth Century* (1965), 94–6.

59. Boulton, 'The Poor among the Rich', 206 and *Neighbourhood and Society* (Cambridge, 1987).

60. BL Add. MS 71573, fo. 32, Oliver Le Neve to Peter Le Neve, 28 April 1686.

61. BL Add. MS 78433, Susan Draper to Mary Evelyn, 2 August 1694.

62. BL Add. MS 78442, Sir John Evelyn to Martha Evelyn, 7 August 1708.

63. Verney Letters R51-705, Elizabeth Adams to John Verney, 9 April 1702.

64. Verney Letters R54-326, Elizabeth Adams to John Verney, 26 October 1710.

65. BL Add. MS 78442, Sir John Evelyn to Martha Evelyn, 17 August 1714.

66. Bodl North MS d.23, fo. 44, Louisa North to Francis North, 13 January 1755.

67. Richard S. Fitton, *The Strutts and the Arkwrights, 1758–1830: A Study of the Early Factory System* (Manchester, 1958), 109, Jedediah Strutt to Elizabeth Strutt, 1765.

68. Verney Letters, R40-27, John Verney to Ralph Verney, 22 May 1685.

69. BL Add. MS 71573, fo. 51, Oliver Le Neve to Peter Le Neve, 11 July 1688.

70. Gay, *Letters*, 54–5, no. 40, John Gay to Jonathan Swift, 16 September 1726.

71. Berkshire Record Office, Trumbull MS D/ED C.3, fo. 45, Sir William Trumbull to Elizabeth Trumbull, Tuesday Night, Gerard St., n.d.

72. Bodl MS Don. *c*.191, fo. 14, Robert Johnson to Barbara Johnson, n.d.

73. Verney Letters, R34-165, Ralph Verney to John Verney, 11 November 1680.

74. Whyman, *Sociability and Power*, 104.

75. Bl Add. MS 78433, Susan Draper to Mary Evelyn, 26 July 1694.

76. BL Add. MS 78442, fos. 5–6, Sir John Evelyn to Martha Evelyn, 2 October 1708.

77. Whyman, *Sociability and Power*, 103; Harold Nockolds (ed.), *The Coachmakers* (1977).

78. BL Add. MS 78442, fos. 27–8, Anne Evelyn to Sir John Evelyn, 23 September [1709?].

79. East Riding of Yorkshire Archives Service, Grimston of Garth MS 42/2/49, T. Robinson Esq. to John Grimston, 26 March 1752.

80. Bodl D. D. Weld MS *c*.13/5/11, Margaret Weld to Sir James Simeon, 4 April 1704.

81. Bodl D. D. Weld MS *c*.13/5/16, Margaret Weld to Sir James Simeon, 24 November 1704.

82. Whyman, *Sociability and Power*, 87–109.

83. Add. Ms. 22226, fo. 37ᵛ, Anne Wentworth, Countess of Strafford to Thomas Wentworth, Earl of Strafford, 30 November 1711.

84. Bodl D. D. Weld MS *c*.13/5/9, Margaret Weld to Sir James Simeon, 9 August 1701.

85. Joan Wilkinson (ed.), *The Letters of Thomas Langton, Flax Merchant of Kirkham 1771–88*, Manchester, Chetham Society, 38 (1994), 145, Thomas Langton to William Langton, 26 March 1773.

86. Johnson, *Lives of the English Poets*, ii. 267.

87. Gay, *Letters*, 15–16, no. 13, Gay to Charles Ford, 30 December 1714.

88. Gay, *Letters*, 27, no. 19, Gay, Charles Jervas, John Arbuthnot, and Alexander Pope to Thomas Parnell, [February 1715–16].

89. Gay, *Letters*, 29, no. 20, Gay to Thomas Parnell, [26 March 1716].

90. Gay, *Letters*, 116, no. 74, Gay and Alexander Pope to Jonathan Swift, 1 December 1731; 122, no. 77, Gay to Jonathan Swift, 16 May 1732.

91. John Macionis and Vincent Parrillo, *Cities in Urban Life* (Upper Saddle River, NJ, 1998), 159.

92. Ibid. 121, 139–41, 159; Georg Simmel, *On Individuality and Social Forms: Selected Writings*, ed. Donald Levine (Chicago, 1971); Sennett, *Classic Essays*.

Spatial Stories: Movement in the City and Cultural Geography

Alison Stenton

What is the place of geography in literature, or literature in geography? For many years, literary critics have analysed the ways in which places are described in literary texts; more recently geographers have become interested in not only the same literary descriptions, but also how geography itself might be read as a text. In John Gay's poem *Trivia: or, the Art of Walking the Streets of London* (1716), with its descriptions of London street life at the turn of the eighteenth century, the place of geography is of interest to both disciplines. Since London is a subject of the poem, a geographic approach to the text might focus on how this urban space is represented by one contemporary writer; alternatively, the literary critic might be interested in how London is represented in a poetic mode. Where the two disciplines overlap, however, is perhaps less clear: because the London represented by *Trivia* is not just historical fact but also an imaginative fiction, what does a geographer do with descriptions of imagined space?

To look at *Trivia* through the lens of cultural geography, however, is not simply to fillet the text for detail of particular places; rather it is to take a more critical approach to representation, and in doing so, to refocus attention from specific places to *spaces*. Moving from geography to cultural geography destabilizes a binary relationship between fact and fiction to make room for something new—a geography that is neither fact nor fiction, but both: a representation of space that is always, in part, imaginative. Cultural geography is the result of what is often described from within the discipline as a 'turn', as some geographers have adopted both a historical and culturally relative approach to their work and, at the same time, have become aware of the reassertion of the subject of 'space' within the field of cultural studies.[1] Within cultural geography, then, 'space' is not synonymous with 'place', and the geographic approach is more critical than a fact-finding survey of a particular place, or a tabulation of data about any chosen area. This new geography is interdisciplinary: it recognizes that geography is cultural, that 'culture is spatial', and that this is a reciprocal relationship. As Derek Gregory explains:

> Geography . . . is not confined to any one discipline. We routinely make sense of places, spaces and landscapes in our every day lives—in different ways and for different purposes—and these 'popular geographies' are as important to the conduct of social life as are our understanding of (say) biography and history.[2]

As geographers like Gregory apply postmodern critical theory from a host of related disciplines, they argue that any inquiry that takes space as its subject must accept that all representations of peoples and places are interpretative, and, moreover, that all of these spaces are constructed. As Mike Crang points out, not only do 'geographers deploy imaginative techniques' in what might traditionally have been assumed to be factual representation, but that which they choose to represent is also critical because space is not simply *there* (as a place—a city, country, or continent), but is *produced* by the forces that control and define it.[3] What this means in practice is that geographical inquiry and representation is always one story, however fact based or thorough. Spaces are constructed, and because those who choose to represent them are implicit in that construction, there can never be a full and complete view or a final word, only multiple representations drawn as a result of a multitude of different agendas.

Appropriating the metaphor 'space' for geographical inquiry, then, pluralizes the subject of scrutiny and casts a critical eye on the ways in which one might survey and represent peoples, places, and cultures. In early modern and eighteenth-century descriptions of space, imaginative geographies are found in maps and descriptions as well as poetry. As Bernhard Klein has argued, early modern geographic discourse was 'neither fixed nor static, but a highly flexible means of organising cultural knowledge' which 'enabled geographers to construct a range of different, even contradictory, graphic models for the political and social space of the nation'.[4] Reading detailed descriptions of British regions—also called chorographies—Klein finds that these texts are imaginative because they describe a lived-in, changing space which appears differently from observer to observer and from one day to the next. In other words, the detail on which they rely paints a vivid picture of one moment, and as seen by one pair of eyes. The human agency involved in describing space disrupts any claim to fact making chorography, like *Trivia*, an imaginative geography.

Alongside considerations about the role of imagination in geographic inquiry, cultural geographers working with literary texts have also wondered how we might focus not only on the geography *in* the text (the place, say, London), but also on 'the geography *of* the text'.[5] For James Kneale, a geographer working with fantasy literature, this approach requires the reader to see beyond specific places, into the spaces represented in the text; how, for example, characters in a novel, or the narrator of a poem, use, occupy, move through, and change the spaces that are described.[6] For Kneale, this is to look for the 'kinetic geography' of the text; to recognize how spaces work within the writing itself (its pace and progression, for example), and to accept that any one space—an urban space, perhaps, like London—is not merely the sum of its constituent parts—its population, trade, town planning, transport—but is also represented and constructed by the way its people move about it, the connections they make with others, and the routes they create as a result.

With this line of inquiry, it is not difficult to understand *Trivia* in terms of its 'kinetic geography': as the narrator of the poem is a walking poet, the London he describes is a travelled-through space. What is more difficult, however, is to consider the ways in which London is represented as a travelled-through space, and how these representations or stories of the city work within the poetic mode. Walking some of the spaces of *Trivia* as they exist in actual topography is a useful way of identifying a fiction: whilst a reader might be given the impression of progression, the text in fact skips and jumps between locations and so reflects no walkable route. Moreover, walking some of the spaces described in *Trivia* raises many interesting questions about the ways in which spaces are represented in the poem. Does the city aid or obstruct the walker? It is clear that the walker's purpose is to find the path of least resistance, even though he isn't really going anywhere. In light of this, how does the individual occupy travelled-through spaces, when these spaces are, by definition, occupied by many others at different times? The advice offered by *Trivia* is for an individual intent on finding his or her way through a public, often crowded, space: 'For Ease and for Dispatch, the Morning's best: / No Tides of Passengers the Street molest' (II 7–8). At times, the urge to get through without incident is expressed either as a kind of smug discourse of practical travelling, or even a sort of militant pedestrianism: 'Let Beaus their Canes with Amber tipt produce, / Be theirs for empty Show, but thine for Use' (I 67–8); 'Let not the Chairman, with assuming Stride, / Press near the Wall, and rudely thrust thy Side' (III 153–4). In *Trivia*, the sense of needing to protect your own course in the city, a course that is forever impeded by everyone else, is a constant theme.

For cultural geographers, a need to make one's way through the city is intimately connected with the idea of the city itself; the city is a 'riot of meanings, of significance' which 'cannot be read . . . unaided', but must be learned, imagined and recognized; only once it is possible to read the space, it is then also possible to get through it.[7] In *Trivia*, being London-literate is important, from being able to read shop signs swinging above walkers' heads—'Be sure observe the Signs, for Signs remain, / Like faithful Land-marks to the walking Train' (II 67–8)—to a more instinctive sense of understanding how London works:[8]

> Does not each Walker know the warning Sign,
> When Wisps of Straw depend upon the Twine
> Cross the close Street; that then the Paver's Art
> Renews the Ways, deny'd to Coach and Cart?
>
> (II 307–10)

Knowing how to read the signs keeps you moving; not being able to read literal and figurative signs leaves you stranded, just as the (illiterate) peasant at the junction of the Seven Dials 'dwells on ev'ry Sign, with stupid Gaze' (II 79), and finds himself brought to a standstill at the crossroads. Part of being able to 'read' the city is to understand how it works. As the peasant's hopeless journey around St Giles' illustrates, even if actual street signs do not signify, the ebb and flow of London's inhabitants do, if you can recognize the city's timetable.[9] In *Trivia*, London is a city which runs by routine, and those who live and work in it read space temporally; they 'Need not the *Calendar* to count their Days' when '*Mondays* and *Thursdays* are the days of Game' (II 406 and 412). As days of the week are signified by changing trades, so the months of the year are also marked by the buying and selling of seasonal wares: flowers in the summer; walnuts in the autumn; rosemary and bay in winter. Things appearing in the streets, in other words, signify time. In *Trivia*, the coming and going of these things are more than visible signs, they are audible and noticeable by smell, too, announced by the cries of the city's various traders, and carried on the wind—'Successive Crys the Seasons Change declare, / And mark the Monthly Progress of the Year' (II 425–6).[10] In this city space, then, all the senses are employed in 'reading' and the space itself is a constantly moving, changing scene like a drama that is improvised around its changing scenery.

As *Trivia*'s city space is forever in motion, the walker's own movements join forces with the swarming people and changing scenes, and, at the same time, plot a single course through the crowds. For urban theorists, the role of the individual in relation to everyone else is significant, as Lewis Mumford suggests: 'If the individual would participate at all in the social, political and economic life of the city, he [*sic*] must subordinate some of his individuality to the demands of the larger community and in that measure immerse himself in mass movements.'[11] Mumford goes on to describe this process of immersion as 'a common life and . . . significant collective drama', which, though often a cause of irritation and friction, is a necessary part of city life.[12] Adopting a similar performative metaphor for life on the street, Jane Jacobs argues that:

Order is all composed of movement and change, and although it is life, not art, we may fancifully call it the art form of the city and liken it to the dance . . . to an intricate ballet in which the individual dancers and ensembles all have distinctive parts which miraculously reinforce each other and compose an orderly whole.[13]

Whether a drama or a ballet, for these urban theorists movement in the city is vital to its life and its order. Jacobs implies that people occupying busy pavements operate a kind of mutual surveillance, where the vast majority of individuals observe and move around each other in order to ensure safety. For the narrator of *Trivia*, safety in the street is hoped for, but never guaranteed, and the moving crowd more often signifies danger, especially at night. As the poet embarks upon his night-time journey, he prepares himself as if going into battle: 'Summon at once thy Courage, rouze thy Care, / Stand firm, look back, be resolute, beware' (III 23–4). As the day ends, the streets fill with a moving mass of people: 'Team follows Team, Crouds heap'd on Crouds appear' (III 27), and the walker's advice is all about avoidance: 'Where the Mob gathers, swiftly shoot along, / Nor idly mingle in the noisy Throng' (III 51–2). Fear of the crowd is fear of robbery and injury; of mixing with all and sundry, and being literally swept away or ripped apart by the mob. In *Trivia*, it is not just the innocent individual who is at risk; mob rule also ensures that the wily pickpocket who hides amidst the crowd is dealt rough justice when caught: 'dragg'd amid the Rout, / . . . plung'd in miry Ponds, he gasping Lies, / Mud chokes his Mouth, and plaisters o'er his Eyes' (III 73–6). For any individual, then, the force (and pull) of the crowd is formidable and dangerous.[14]

As Gay's walker in *Trivia* strives to avoid the throng, one contemporary city walker, *The London Spy* (1698–1700), is rather less resistant to its

'Thick-rising tents a canvas City build'

3. View of a frost fair on the River Thames looking towards London Bridge (c.1715).

pull. In this text, 'the Spy'—a countryman new to town—explores the city with a street-savvy school friend, and the pair weave their way through London's streets with a chorographic thoroughness that leaves no well-known path unwalked.[15] As in *Trivia*, the crowd features heavily as a threat, but unlike the poet, who regularly stands to one side to allow the tides of people to pass, the Spy and his friend give themselves over to the flow. At the New Exchange, for example, the pair wade into the chaos of a space famed for its many, and various, trades: 'We . . . jostled in amongst a parcel of swarthy buggerantoes' and 'squeez'd amongst coasters and English traders'.[16] In even the thickest and most famous of crowds—such as that at Bartholomew Fair—the pair push their way through 'with a great deal of elbow-labour, and much sweating'.[17] Getting involved in the thick of things like this is physical; for the Spy and his friend, throwing themselves into the *body* of Bartholomew Fair brings them into close contact with people in the crowd:

> In Compassion to one of the female gender, who was labouring in the crowd like a fly in a cobweb, I laid my hands upon my friend's shoulders, and by keeping her between my arms, defended her from the rude squeezes and jostles of the careless multitude.[18]

For *Trivia*'s walker, maintaining order by avoiding physical contact is one way of occupying urban space by placing the individual's course over and above the movements of everyone else. Here, the walker may not get involved quite as intimately as the Spy, but all the same he takes to the streets (keeping to the wall) and is fiercely opposed to riding in a coach; in other words, he determines to walk and finds a way to get through whilst also keeping contact to a bare minimum. This, then, is something like Jacob's urban ballet: a choreographed approach to city space that, as Miles Ogborn points out, retains 'the privacy of the individual whilst responding to the public context'; it is a 'feeling of being in, if not wholly part of, the crowd', as everyone dances around one another without risking any close contact.[19] For Richard Sennett, the eighteenth century was a time when physical contact in the city still signified *order*. He cites Hogarth's famous engraving of Gin Lane as evidence of the corrosive effect of gin on society, and its ability to break down social order; it is 'a social scene in which . . . the people have no corporeal sensation of one another, nor of the stairs, benches, and buildings in the street'; physical contact is absent from the scene.[20] In this reading, *Trivia* represents a stage somewhere between an expectation of regular physical contact (like *The Spy*), and the beginnings of a desire for sensory withdrawal, perhaps best signified in the modern age by the personal-stereo-wearing commuter of today. *Trivia*'s walker is between these poles: a resolute pedestrian, yes, but not a carefree wanderer.

If *Trivia* is evidence of an early modern need to be an individual in the city, what does this mean for the movements of the walker, and the stories the poem tells about his journey through the city's spaces? As a man taking his own course through the town, his path, according to Michel de Certeau, traces an invisible, individual 'poem' on the urban space, one that is 'other' to the one he composes as the 'song'.[21] This invisible 'poem' is itself a story about the use of space; it is unnoticed by the walker, even as the 'song' he writes turns his own experience of getting about London into good advice. As the walker explains his reasons for the journey— 'How to walk clean by Day, and safe by Night' (I 2)—he also exposes his path through life as a leisured, though not idle (in 'well-hammer'd Soles'), comfortable, but not wealthy (no cane with an amber tip for him) man of the middling sort. In this position, his own path is one of continual movement because he has no reason to stop and get involved in trades, fairs, or games; his role is didactic and aimed at others of the same class, who are likely to want to occupy space in the same way.[22] Resisting involvement and keeping moving, the walker is able to disconnect from the city he describes and take what is sometimes described by literary critics as a gently ironic stance on the chaos and filth of the city space.[23] Hence, his movements, like his text, keep him removed from the city itself in favour of observing things with a more critical, mocking eye. By keeping moving, the narrator is a walker *through*, and not a worker *in* the city, which means that he is able to withdraw physically and socially from its spaces. In Sennett's reading, constant movement in the city acts as a social anaesthetic that 'dulls the body'; it is for this reason that modern cities are designed to be moved through, so that each person is able to retain a sense of autonomy, even in the densest of crowds: 'movement articulates, specifies, individualizes experience'.[24] In the London of 1716, the chaos of the city prompts the narrator of the *Trivia* to find a way to keep himself to himself as an act of resistance to the collective chaos of urban space.

Yet despite the poet's expressed intention to keep apart from the city he describes in his poem, the kinetic geography of *Trivia* suggests that there are other stories at work besides a warning against what to avoid, and what to steer your way past. In recent years, literary critics have noted that *Trivia* does not maintain a consistently satiric tone throughout the poem; where one might imagine there to be disgust—as in the descriptions of the Fleet River, for example—in fact there is conflict: a sense of aversion to the city's filth, but admiration for the ways in which those who live in this space make the most of it.[25] In the same way that the narrator is unable to maintain a consistently ironic stance, so he is similarly unable to *not* get involved in the city's public realm. In the first place, the walker's movements about the town, though his own, have a public purpose: he embarks upon the journey not unlike a geographer in the field—'for the publick Safety, risque thy own' (II 6)—with the right equipment (solid shoes, a good coat and cane), and the stated intention of writing about the city (composing a song) in such a way as will benefit others. Here, Gay's tongue is firmly in his cheek as to how far one really needs a guide to getting by in this city, but nevertheless it is a guide to the town all the same, and one the narrator thinks the space itself would recognize and find useful: 'The busy City asks instructive Song' (II 220). Hence, Sennett's suggestion that keeping moving is antithetical to the life of—and to being alive *to*—the city is not entirely borne out by the representations of space in the poem. The poet is, in fact, no different from the space he describes; like himself, the city itself keeps moving to stay alive—the Fleet River (in the shape of its Goddess, Cloacina) rises and falls, carrying away the city's waste; street traders everyday set up and take down their stalls; rivers freeze then thaw—the movement he represents as an individual picking his way through the crowd echoes throughout the city space to indicate that movement is not merely for the benefit one the individual, but is an essential part of city life and necessary for all.

Perhaps crucial to understanding how movement through the city space is represented in *Trivia* is in the 'song' that the poet himself produces, and what he does with it. As a representation of London, some literary critics have noted that, at best, *Trivia* is impressionistic; certainly there is no clear picture of the city in the text, only glimpses of places, people, sights and sounds.[26] In my own attempt to walk some of the spaces represented in *Trivia*, it was abundantly clear that using the poem like a map was impossible because places are not represented in an orderly or logical way—the journey is more like sticking a pin in a map, than following a linear route; space is not mapped with the same chorographic thoroughness as *The London Spy*. Standing back from Gay's representation of space, therefore, is revealing; in *Trivia*, the poet represents the city as he moves through it, bringing to life the spaces he walks into, with detail of others who live, work and play there—it is a 'spatializing action', not a stable picture.[27] At Covent Garden, for example,

Where *Covent-garden's* famous Temple stands,
That boasts the Work of *Jones*' immortal Hands;
Columns, with plain Magnificence, appear,
And graceful Porches lead along the Square:
Here oft' my Course I bend, when lo! from far,
I spy the Furies of the Foot-ball War . . .

(II 343–8)

Here, a double focus of kinetic geography is at work: the walker represents how Londoners appropriate space for their own purposes (what de Certeau would consider to be an act of resistance to planned urban space), and, in addition, he identifies his working methods—'Here oft' my Course I bend', signifying that walking to, and passing through, the space is the best way to view it and write about it.[28] The walker, then, sees his text as something composed on the hoof and *of* the hoof: it is a geographer's notebook or a journalist's story, the result of investigations and fieldwork, written up and laid open for others to see.[29] At no time does the text suggest it offers a complete view, only representations of spaces that change by the hour, as witnessed by the walker himself. The temporal gauging of the space reflects its movement and changeability, just as the footsteps of the walker sound out a rhythm for his song that marks the passing of time like a ticking clock.

As the geography of the text is revealed to be kinetic, the story of a city space that *Trivia* paints is best placed 'High-rais'd on *Fleetstreet* Posts' (III 415) so that all who pass by are able to read it as they go. The poem's final resting place in 'Grub Street' may be ironic, a hint, perhaps, that this is an inferior piece by a *pedestrian* author, but nevertheless it is the right place for the poet to leave it. Pinned to a lamp-post, it is just another thing thrown up by the city itself, like a broadside ballad dropped by a hawker into the street.[30] Moreover, left to be read in the street famous for hack writing, it also marks the end of the walker's path like a point on a map, and exposes the city to be a space which will be forever viewed in different ways by a multitude of other walkers and writers.

NOTES

1. For useful discussions of the development of the new cultural geography and its relationship with postmodernism and cultural studies see Don Mitchell, *Cultural Geography: A Critical Introduction* (Oxford, 2000), Mike Crang, *Cultural Geography* (2004), and Edward Soja, *Postmodern Geographies: The Reassertion of Space in Critical Social Theory* (1989).

2. Derek Gregory, *Geographical Imaginations* (Cambridge, Mass., 1994), 11.

3. Crang, *Cultural Geography*, 44. For a full discussion see Henri Lefebvre, *The Production of Space*, trans. Donald Nicholson-Smith (Oxford, 2000). Scholars working within the field of ethnography have also challenged the idea that space is *there*, by arguing that cultures are not static, but rather move about to form connections and lay down routes that link them with a multitude of other peoples and places. See James Clifford, 'Traveling Cultures', in Lawrence Grossberg, Cary Nelson, and Paula A. Treichler (eds.), *Cultural Studies* (1992), 96–116, and his *Touring Cultures: Transformations of Travel and Theory* (1997); Chris Rojek and John Urry (eds.), *Routes: Travel and Translation in the Late Twentieth Century* (Cambridge, Mass., 1997).

4. Bernhard Klein, *Maps and the Writing of Space in Early Modern England and Ireland* (Basingstoke, 2001), 8.

5. Marc Brosseau, 'The City in Textual Form: *Manhattan Transfer's* New York', *Ecumene*, 2 (1995), 89–114 (90).

6. James Kneale, 'Secondary Worlds: Reading Novels as Geographical Research', in Alison Blunt et al. (eds.), *Cultural Geography In Practice* (2003), 39–51.

7. Crang, *Cultural Geography*, 51.

8. See also Addison on street signs in Angus Ross (ed.), *Joseph Addison and Richard Steele, Selections from the* Tatler *and the* Spectator (1988); *The Spectator*, no. 28 (2 April 1711), 283–6.

9. See also Penelope Corfield, 'Walking the City Streets: The Urban Odyssey in Eighteenth-Century England', *Journal of Urban History*, 16 (1990), 132–74 (142).

10. See Sean Shesgreen, *Images of the Outcast: The Urban Poor in the Cries of London* (Manchester, 2002).

11. Lewis Mumford, 'What is a City?' (1937) in Richard T. Le Gates and Frederic Stout (eds.), *The City Reader*, 2nd edn. (2000), 102.

12. Ibid. 94.

13. Jane Jacobs, 'The Use of Sidewalks: Safety' (1961) in Le Gates, *The City Reader*, 107–11 (110).

14. Fear of pickpockets amidst the London crowds is a theme of many London travel guides throughout the eighteenth century. See for example John Fielding, *A Description of the Cities of London and Westminster* (1776), xxxii in which readers are advised 'to avoid crowds, leave your watch at home, and to carry no more money in your pocket, than will barely serve for the purpose of the day'.

15. 'Their journey is mapped onto the topography of the city in a way that both emphasizes its subtle differentiations and draws high and low together'. Miles Ogborn, *Spaces of Modernity: London's Geographies 1680–1780* (1998), 107.

16. Ned Ward, *The London Spy*, ed. Paul Hyland (East Lansing, Mich., 1993), Part III, 45–62 (58, 61).
17. Ibid., Part X, 171–88 (187).
18. Ibid., Part XI, 189–207 (189).
19. Ogborn, *Spaces of Modernity*, 113.
20. Richard Sennett, *Flesh and Stone: The Body and the City in Western Civilization* (2002), 21.
21. Michel de Certeau, *The Practice of Everyday Life*, trans. Steven Randall (Berkeley, 1988), 93.
22. In this description, the walker cannot really be described as a flâneur because although he is an observer who 'walks at will', he does not do so without purpose, nor does he 'absorb the activities of the collective—often formulated as "the crowd" '. See Chris Jenks, 'Watching your Step: The History and Practice of the Flâneur', in Chris Jenks (ed.), *Visual Culture* (2002), 142–60 (146).
23. See for example Eugene Kirk, 'Gay's "Roving Muse": Problems of Genre and Intention in *Trivia*', *English Studies*, 62 (1981), 259–70.
24. Sennett, *Flesh and Stone*, 309.
25. Stephen Copley and Ian Haywood, 'Luxury, Refuse and Poetry: John Gay's *Trivia*', in Peter Lewis and Nigel Wood (eds.), *John Gay and the Scriblerians* (1988), 62–82.
26. William Bowman Piper, *Reconcilable Differences in Eighteenth-Century English Literature* (1999), 90–112.
27. De Certeau, *The Practice of Everyday Life*, 119.
28. Ibid. 91–110.
29. Sven Armens's description of *Trivia* as a 'Hogarthian newsreel' makes sense here. See Sven M. Armens, *John Gay: Social Critic* (New York, 1954), 79.
30. Leslie Shepherd, *The History of Street Literature* (Newton Abbot, 1973).

'All besides the Rail, rang'd Beggars lie': *Trivia* and the Public Poverty of Early Eighteenth-Century London

Tim Hitchcock

John Gay's London is replete with beggars and the beggarly self-employed. His streets are alive with shoeblacks and beggars, ballad singers and pickpockets. Much more than the narrator of *Trivia*, or London itself, it is the people of the street who form the primary object of Gay's attention. They wait to assault the unwary passer-by.

> Where *Lincoln's-Inn's*, wide Space, is rail'd around
> Cross not with vent'rous Step; there oft' is found
> The lurking Thief, who while the Day-light shone,
> Made the Walls eccho with his begging Tone:
> That Crutch which late Compassion mov'd, shall wound
> Thy bleeding Head, and fell thee to the Ground.
>
> (III 133–8)

They positioned themselves in the roadway, offering services every urbanite needed and entertainments found nowhere else. Gay warns: 'Though thou art tempted by the Link-man's Call, / Yet trust him not along the lonely Wall' (III 139–40).
And

> Let not the Ballad-Singer's shrilling Strain
> Amid the Swarm thy list'ning Ear detain:
> Guard well thy Pocket; for these *Syrens* stand,
> To aid the Labours of the diving Hand . . .
>
> (III 77–80)

The 'laborious beggar sweeps the Road', and a full cast of beggarly street workers is introduced. The chimney sweeps, oyster sellers, link boys, purveyors of hand bills, chairmen and errand boys fill the public spaces of the capital (II 453–6; II 33, III 190–4, III 139, II 335). And perhaps most emblematically, Gay dedicates over sixty lines to that newly invented eighteenth-century street figure, the shoeblack. He depicts the shoeblack's creation from the earthy, open-air coupling of the goddess Cloacina and a shit bespat scavenger. Created from the very stuff of Fleet Ditch, Gay's shoeblack goes on to grow into his profession:

> At first a Beggar's Brat, Compassion mov'd;
> His Infant Tongue soon learnt the canting Art,
> Knew all the Pray'rs and Whines to touch the Heart.
>
> (II 142–4)

By his mother's intervention, he is then trained in the arts of the oily rag. Shoeblacking as a named occupation was only a couple of decades old when Gay wrote *Trivia*, and the poem represents the first extended treatment of shoeblacking as an occupation in any genre.[1]

∗   ∗   ∗   ∗   ∗

By focusing the reader's attention on the poor and marginal in early eighteenth-century London, Gay contributes to the creation of an increasingly important set of stereotypes that in turn had a profound impact on the evolution of social policy. This chapter explores the origins and content of Gay's stereotypes and suggests that they were at odds with the experience of the living poor on the streets of London as reflected in the records of crime and social policy. This chapter also suggests that the yawning gap between Gay's stereotypes and the experience of the urban poor helped to determine the shape of workhouses, hospitals, and prisons.

Sixteenth- and seventeenth-century pauper stereotypes were made up of either the settled, deserving poor—the elderly cottager and overburdened family that formed the objects of the Old Poor Laws (1598–1601)—or else, the rogue and the vagrant. The wandering and unsettled poor, in particular, were objects of a well-established 'rogue literature', which from the early sixteenth century depicted them as dangerously subversive, using 'canting' language, and creating what amounted to an organized underworld of vagrants and beggars bent on cheating honest citizens and even threatening the state. In part, this early stereotype was a response to the religious, economic, and social disruptions of the sixteenth century, and in particular of the crisis-ridden

1590s.[2] But whatever its origin, this image was made traditional in the works of John Awdeley, Thomas Harman, Robert Greene, Thomas Dekker, and Samuel Rid, and retained a power and authority in British thinking throughout the next three centuries.[3] Bowdlerized dictionaries of canting slang, and thinly revised editions of sixteenth-century texts were published in most decades of the eighteenth and nineteenth centuries, and their impact can be seen in even the most apparently authoritative life-writings.[4]

From approximately the late 1680s, however, a new series of images began to inflect and overlay both literary and visual depictions of the poor. In Marcellus Laroon's *Cries of London*, first published in 1687, for instance, beggars and the beggarly poor were invested with a new individuality and a newly important place on the streets of London. 'Drawn after life', Laroon's *Cries* took a rather unpromising European tradition and made it central to our image of eighteenth- and nineteenth-century London. He included beggars in a continuum of street traders that bridged the gap between the most marginal denizens of London streets and more financially secure traders. Samuel Pepys believed he could name eighteen people who had served as the models for Laroon's *Cries*.[5] Gay's own careful peopling of London's streets with traders and beggars, and his account of their activities in *Trivia*, reflects the growing importance of this group of men and women. But even the poor themselves came to see 'crying' as a distinct and distinctly metropolitan activity. Although the term has an older etymology, it was only in the 1710s that 'crying' goods 'about the streets' became a common expression in the mouths of witnesses at the Old Bailey. Between 1674 and 1720, for instance, this expression is used five times: once in 1684, three years before Laroon's publication, and then four times between 1713 and 1719.[6] In the decades after 1720 it became ever more common. A couple of generations after the publication of *Trivia*, at the end of 1770s, Israel R. Potter entered London a ragged pauper, who went on to cry 'Old Chairs to Mend' on the streets for over thirty years. His first impression of the city was dominated by its street merchants: 'my curiosity was not a little excited by what is termed the "cries of London"'.[7] What Laroon helped to create, and Gay helped to popularize, was a new and distinctly urban vision of the labouring urban poor.

Most sixteenth- and seventeenth-century accounts of working people assumed them to be essentially rural workers. The concept of poverty itself was structured around the realities of a predominantly rural economy. The Old Poor Law, for instance, despite its many connections to the essentially urban phenomenon of European civic humanism, was predicated on the belief that most paupers lived in closed rural parishes.[8] In Laroon's work the urban street became the natural environment for the working poor for the first time. He helped to create a new urban stereotype that included beggars and thieves among a broad working class.

Literary stereotypes were evolving at precisely the same moment as this visual tradition. Thomas D'Urfey, Tom Brown, Ned Ward, Joseph Addison and Richard Steele, Jonathan Swift, Jane Barker, Daniel Defoe, and John Gay himself all helped to create a series of much more clearly articulated stereotypes than can be found in the works of earlier writers.[9] This new image was derived from a conjunction of the still plundered and reprinted body of sixteenth-century rogue literature and from the Spanish picaresque tradition, and in particular Miguel de Cervantes's *Don Quixote*.[10] But what these authors created was a peculiarly non-threatening stereotype that emphasized a series of new characteristics. In common with earlier rogue literature, eighteenth-century stereotypes were almost exclusively male and preyed on the naivety of their contemporaries, but unlike earlier formulations, they were not essentially vicious or dangerous, and nor were they culturally divided from other working people. Where sixteenth-century rogues had been imagined as the 'foreign' poor, unknown to the communities upon which they preyed, eighteenth-century rogues were perhaps lonely, but still acknowledged members of a single community. They were also distinctly urban in character. For many writers they were figures of fascination and almost admiration, located in an exciting and new urban landscape, threatening only to the inexperienced country bumpkin.

The starting point in this literary evolution was Thomas D'Urfey's *Collin's Walk through London and Westminster* published in 1691, just four years after Laroon's *Cries*. But where D'Urfey first set out, many others followed. Ned Ward sits comfortably between the older rogue literature tradition and these new literary developments, and in his *The History of London Clubs* (1709) he creates an image of the beggarly poor that can stand in for many others. He includes a beggars' club among the many others he details:

This society of old bearded hypocrites, wooden legg'd implorers of charity, strolling clapperdugeons, limping dissembers, sham-disabled seamen, blind gun powder blasted mummers and old broken limb'd labourers, hold their weekly meeting at a famous boozing ken in the midst of old street . . . they sing this song, which is call'd the beggars new ballad . . .

> What tho' we make the world believe
> That we are sick and lame,
> Tis now a virtue to deceive,
> The Righteous do the same.
> In trade dissembling is no crime
> And we shall live to see
> That begging in a little time,
> A common trade will be.[11]

In the process, Ward locates beggars among the whole panoply of working Londoners, eliding a division that earlier writers would have sought to emphasize.

Twelve years after the publication of *Trivia*, John Gay himself created perhaps the most famous eighteenth-century literary beggar of them all in the form of his narrator in *The Beggar's Opera*. The beggar may not figure in the story, but he does represent beggars in general, and his life and attributes exemplify Gay's begging characters and their relationship to the broader economy. He lives in the crowded back alleys of St Giles', and makes money by writing ballads—the sort of street profession which would seem to belie his occupation as a 'beggar'. With the rogues of an earlier epoch, and with Ned Ward's characters, he also attends 'weekly festivals' of beggars in the 'great room' of an alehouse.

For both Ward and Gay, beggars were healthy (even when disabled) and smart. They also held a powerful place on the street. In several encounters with beggars depicted by Joseph Addison and Richard Steele in *The Spectator* (1711–14) it is clear that the beggar in this period could frequently gain the upper hand. In one incident Steele recounts how:

at the corner of Warwick-Street, as I was listning to a new ballad, a ragged rascal, a beggar who knew me, came up to me, and began to turn the eyes of the good company upon me, by telling me he was extreme poor, and should die in the streets for want of drink, except I immediately would have the charity to give him six pence to go in the next alehouse and save his life. He urged, with a melancholy face, that all his family had died of thirst. All the mob have humour, and two or three began to take the jest; by which Mr Sturdy carried his point . . .[12]

For later writers, beggars and street traders become even more significant. One important aspect of the eighteenth-century picaresque novel was its frequent inclusion of 'low' characters. Heavily influenced by Cervantes and the Spanish picaresque tradition, novelists such as Francis Coventry, Henry Fielding, and Tobias Smollett included street beggars and paupers among the cast of characters encountered by their flawed heroes. The

'Beneath the Lamp her tawdry Ribbons glare,
The new scour'd Manteau, and the slattern Air'

'You'll see a draggled Damsel, here and there,
From Billingsgate her fishy Traffick bear'

'The little Chimney-sweeper skulks along,
And marks with sooty Stains the heedless Throng'

'Proud Coaches pass, regardless of the Moan,
Of Infant Orphans, and the Widow's Groan'

4. Four figures from *The Cryes of the City of London Drawne after the Life* by
Marcellus Laroon (1711), first published 1687

eponymous hero of *Pompey the Little*, a particularly irritating lapdog, was looked after by a blind beggar for several months; while Smollett's Humphry Clinker started his expedition as a workhouse child and idle vagrant, dressed in rags so tattered they failed to preserve his modesty.[13]

Early eighteenth-century literature brought to the fore a new and newly- engaging literary character—an adult man, full of cunning, whose experience formed a distinct and important component of the lives of the labouring poor in general. By creating a series of characters that could stand in for a broader working class, these authors effectively erased and redrew the older sixteenth- and seventeenth-century distinction between the pauper and the vagabond. In a world without surveys and question-naires, in which records were constructed in a linear format that denied the opportunity to apply many analytical strategies, where every figure was the crudest estimate, the heightened verisimilitude of eighteenth-century imaginative literature exercised a uniquely powerful authority over the beliefs and actions of its readers. Without pie charts and surveys, the source of knowledge about the poor and about social problems was more likely to derive from novels, poetry, and ephemera, than would ever be the case again.[14] What Ned Ward, Gay, Addison and Steele, and the later picaresque novelists did was to create an image of beggarly poverty that was significantly at odds with the experience of Londoners, but which could be applied to the poor in general.

*   *   *   *   *

The moment one steps beyond the shimmering image of the literary beggar and red-cheeked street seller, they disappear in a storm of dust and lies. The historical evidence for eighteenth-century London beggary and street employment suggests a very different experience. Court and administrative records suggest that London poverty was dominated by women, and characterized by illness, old age, and pregnancy. It is exem-plified by people like the unfortunately named Jane Austin. By the third week in February 1762, for instance, Jane Austin found herself in a des-perate situation. She lost her lodging in White Hart Yard, after being beaten and thrown onto the streets by the man she was living with, John Duggin. Homeless and friendless, both the beating and a long-standing chest complaint undermined her ability to keep body and soul together. The weather that week was cold and stormy, and temperatures ranged between 29 and 43 degrees Fahrenheit.[15] First, she applied to the overseer of the poor of the parish of St Martin-in-the-Fields for admission to their workhouse. Her settlement was investigated, and the parish decided she had no claim upon it. As a result Jane was turned back onto the street.[16] For the next three days she begged about the parish, in the Strand and Covent Garden, sleeping in doorways at night. By the third day she was desperate. Starving and still suffering from the wound in her side, she knocked at the door of Elizabeth Stewart's apartment in a low lodging house belonging to Ann James in New Bedford Court, a narrow alley just off the Strand. Inside Jane found several women working in the room, and begged to be given a seat by the fire. She was allowed in, and spent the rest of the afternoon warming herself, while more fortunate women— poor but employed—worked around her. In the evening she shared a pint of purl—hot beer and gin mixed together—and at ten, when Elizabeth Stewart returned from an errand, Jane asked to be allowed to sleep in front of the fire for the night.

The next morning, after a long night disturbed by Jane's groans, Elizabeth Stewart had had enough of charity. She asked the lodger upstairs, a black man named Michael Reading, to accompany Jane out of the house. Reading took her arm and directed her to the door and down the stairs. Jane fell, and Reading grabbed her around the waist, and together they ended up in a tangled heap on the street. A couple of minutes later Jane was dead. The coroner later brought in a verdict of 'natural death'.[17]

Like Jane Austin, many of the people working on London's streets throughout the eighteenth century were simply desperate. In 1763 a prospective buyer was shown over a vacant house in Stonecutters Street, which runs between Fleet Market and Shoe Lane, just north of Fleet Street. Squatting was commonplace, and there were plenty of abandoned and half-finished houses which could be used for shelter in an emergency.[18] In this instance, the buyer discovered the bodies of two almost naked women in the front room, and in the garret found two women and a girl, alive, but on the verge of starvation. The bodies were of two women, both of whom were called 'Bet', who had worked as casual porters in Fleet Market. They were typical of the large number who made a casual living on the streets, either as porters, or prostitutes (if they could), or beggars or shoeblacks, or as casual domestics. The boundary between begging and working was always a very subtle one. Frequently women would go from door to door, asking for broken food, or a bit of household work. They might buy a single mackerel from Billingsgate and attempt to hawk it through the streets, with the insurance that if they could not sell the fish, at least they would eat that night. Prostitution was famously characterized as 'amphibious' by Daniel Defoe;[19] but there is a larger sense in which every poor person was forced to dive into and out of whatever opportunity arose.

In Stonecutters Street, the other three women in the house were again largely typical of a wider group of the beggarly poor. In the garret, a woman named Pattent lived for several months. She was an out-of-place servant, who had gone to the Fleet Market to look for casual labour, and had been told by one of the 'Bets' about the house on Stonecutters Street. Pattent lived in the garret as best she could taking what employment she could—sleeping in the house at night, and working in a cook-shop in exchange for food, during the day. Elizabeth Sturridge, one of the other women in the garret, was only 16. An orphan, she had been employed by a washerwoman for six years in Fleet Market until she fell ill. Discharged and with nowhere to go, having been refused relief by her parish of settlement, and unusually ignorant of her rights under the Poor Law, she slept on the streets for weeks, before finding a bit of shelter in the house.[20] When she was strong enough she went out begging, coming back to Stonecutters Street at night. A couple of days before they were discovered, Pattent pawned her apron for 6 pence, which they spent on food.[21]

If we look for a moment at the records of the criminal justice system, the actual characteristics of the population who filled the streets become clearer. Of a sample of 153 individuals apprehended for begging and loitering in the City of London between 1738 and 1742 over half were adult women. For a very brief period in the autumn of 1705 the Governors of the Poor for London recorded the place of settlement of everyone apprehended for vagrancy, and whether or not they were in receipt of a parish pension. The results again confirm a distinctly non-literary pattern.[22] Of twenty-nine individuals apprehended in October of 1705, fifteen of them were adult women, seven were men, and seven were children.[23] The lives of the people represented by these statistics is at odds with the literary stereotype. There was violence, and desperation, theft, drink and charity, hard work and hard hearts. There was conflict with parish officers, justices, constables, and watchmen, and limited, if casual, support from those around you. It was also a world made up substantially of women and young people, and one in which everyone was forced to negotiate a complex set of systems and resources, individual relations, and public attitudes, in order to survive.[24]

*   *   *   *   *

It is, of course, a rather banal observation that fiction is indeed fiction, or that poetry requires a certain licence and contrivance. But this particular discontinuity had the effect of creating an important disjuncture in thinking about social policy that radically impinged on the lives of Londoners.

If any single development is typical of the social policy of the period it is the move to an institutional response to the poor, the ill, and the simply inconvenient. Workhouses, hospitals, foundling hospitals, and madhouses are all characteristics of the institutions of the eighteenth-century metropolis. Where seventeenth-century poor relief had been largely given in the form of cash doles and relief in kind, eighteenth-century relief took the form of bed and board in an institution. The Corporation of the Poor re-established in 1698, the Westminster Hospital in 1716, and the foundling hospital in 1741 are well-known highlights in this development.[25] But the meat and gristle of the system can be found in the parochial workhouses of the capital. The first London example was established in 1719, and this was followed by dozens more in the 1720s and 1730s.[26] By 1776, there were 86 parochial workhouses within the bounds of London, Westminster, and Middlesex, housing 15,180 individuals—perhaps 2 per cent of the population of the capital. Nicholas Hawksmoor designed them, the entrepreneur Matthew Marriott ran them, and the Society for the Promotion of Christian Knowledge provided the rules and the intellectual underpinnings that determined how they were meant to work.[27] And what is clear in the very bricks and mortar of these developments is that the pauper that glistened in the minds' eye of every workhouse projector and administrator was a literary beggar rather than a real one. This is not to argue that workhouse designers based their ideas on literature, but rather that literary representations incorporated and publicized broader assumptions about the poor, and in doing so helped to reinforce a series of unreliable stereotypes. Works like *Trivia* shared and publicized, selected and reinforced specific preexisting prejudices, prejudgements, and assumptions.

When the parish of St George Hanover Square built its workhouse in 1725–6—a design which was published and widely copied—the house was evenly divided down the middle, with half being given over to adult men.[28] Indeed, the assumption of a gendered symmetry is a common aspect of almost all eighteenth-century workhouse and hospital designs. Without research or inquiry, the founders of these institutions simply assumed that the population they were catering for was equally divided between men and women, with children added on as an extra. This despite the fact that at least two-thirds of parish pensioners were in fact women; something every overseer should have known, simply as a result of handing out the money.[29]

More than this, while workhouses and healthy male beggars are perhaps at the core of this relationship between social policy and literary invention, we should not forget the equally important literary origins of a range of other social policy initiatives. The Magdalene Hospital established at mid-century has frequently been associated with the rise of a more sentimental version of womanhood by historians of prostitution and the working class. And the Foundling Hospital and to a lesser extent the Marine Society have been implicated with an essentially literary sentimentalization of childhood. These charities pedalled an odd combination of an increasingly romantic notion of the child, and a hard-headed notion of the uses to which child flesh might be put—all tied together with high adventure and glory.[30]

In other words, what one is faced with when examining London's institutional infrastructure is a set of assumptions about who was poor and why that bore only a very tenuous relationship to the actualities of poverty. Each type of institution was informed by its own version of literary poverty. Indeed, many of the voluntary and specialized institutions of mid-century could only flourish while middling-sort and elite patrons maintained a sentimental interest in the supposed objects of their charity.[31] Literature and print culture played a central role in maintaining such an interest. From the last decade of the seventeenth century there developed a growing specialization of institutional provision that mapped easily onto a gradually changing literary landscape, but which apparently responded to the letters page of new journals, rather than the demands of the poor. At the same time, however, the realities of poverty, the needs of the poor, their gender and their circumstances remained largely unchanged, although increasingly at odds with the language used to describe them as a class.

The poor could not afford to ignore the resources available through this institutional infrastructure. They needed to access them in order to support a complex economy of makeshift. As a result, what was created was a constant battle—to and fro—between the designers of institutions, the drafters of by-laws, and the administrators of workhouses and hospitals, on the one hand, and the ill and poor on the other. Surprisingly, it was a battle that, despite the odds, the poor frequently won. From the passage of the Act of Settlement in 1661 every English and Welsh pauper had a parish of settlement, a parish from which they could claim poor relief. In the generations that followed the Act this legal construction gradually came to take on the character of a 'right to relief'. By the early eighteenth century, paupers increasingly knew how to demand relief from their parish, and what to do if they were refused. In London the Lord Mayor sat in judgement on appeals from paupers and as frequently as not issued orders demanding beleaguered parish overseers and work-house masters provide pensions and a workhouse place.[32]

When Mary Brown, a 17-year-old prostitute and orphan went into labour, she asked the advice of her landlady and bawd, Mrs Davies. A long discussion ensued in the house in Jackson's Alley, off Bow Street, where Mary had entertained men for several years. The question on everyone's lips was 'which is the casualty parish?', or in other words, where is the best casualty department in town? One young woman suggested St Martin-in-the-Fields, but was answered, 'No, no, St Clement is the best casualty parish—send her there!' Mary was hustled into a coach, and presented herself at the door of the workhouse. And while the workhouse mistress vainly attempted to restrict her access by insisting that the overseer be summoned before she would be admitted, the demands of nature ensured that Mary soon found herself in the well-appointed lying-in ward, giving birth to a healthy boy. When she was later examined as to her settlement, she gave perhaps the one story that would allow her to stay. She claimed to have been born on shipboard between Ireland and England, and hence completely outside the system of settlement.[33]

In hundreds of thousands of similar encounters the poor confronted the workhouses and charities of the capital, frequently citing their legal settlement in support of their claims for relief, and gradually forced changes in the policies of these apparently carceral institutions. What began as a series of institutions designed for a mythical figure (a male beggar) evolved into a group of institutions that by the end of the century more clearly reflected the shape of London beggary. To take just a single example, the workhouse at St George Hanover Square designed with the help of Nicholas Hawksmoor and opened in 1725–6, was forced to re-allocate its internal space within a single year. By 1727–8 much of the men's ward had been turned over to female paupers and a separate infirmary for the sick poor had been built.[34] In institution after institution a similar accommodation was made.

*   *   *   *   *

To return to *Trivia*, what Gay achieves is a distillation of a new image of the poor. Gone are the rogues and vagabonds who filled the nightmares of sixteenth-century commentators. Gone also are the settled poor huddled in back streets, dependent on the parish for their meagre livelihoods. Instead, one finds a vibrant and unified world of economics and poverty that elides the most prominent forms of male begging (cap-in-hand street-corner mendicity) with the desperate economics of men, women, and children who struggled to make a living as ballad sellers and prostitutes, shoeblacks and errand boys. In common with Laroon and Defoe, Addison and Steele, Barker, Coventry, and Smollet, John Gay solidified and popularized an image of the labourious poor that, in turn, filled the imaginations of eighteenth-century poor law administrators and projectors. In the process, these authors helped to fuel the creation of a malformed system of relief that was ill-suited to the actual needs of poor Londoners. It was only the demands of the poor themselves, backed up with the dubious authority of the Act of Settlement, which could begin to set the system to rights.

NOTES

1. There is no substantive account of the history of shoeblacking and shoeblacks before the nineteenth century. For a brief discussion see Tim Hitchcock, *Down and Out in Eighteenth-Century London* (2004), 52–61.
2. For two recent authoritative accounts of the evolution of social policy in the sixteenth and seventeenth centuries see Steve Hindle, *On the Parish? The Micro-politics of Poor Relief in Rural England c.1550–1750* (Oxford, 2004) and Paul Slack, *From Reformation to Improvement: Public Welfare in Early Modern England* (Oxford, 1998).
3. For discussions of the history of rogue literature and in particular its veracity and generic qualities see Jodi Mikalachki, 'Women's Networks and the Female Vagrant: A Hard Case', in Susan Frye and Karen Robertson (eds.), *Maids and Mistresses, Cousins, and Queens: Women's Alliances in Early Modern England* (Oxford, 1999); A. L. Beier, *The Problem of the Poor in Tudor and Early Stuart England* (1983); Gámini Salgado, *The Elizabethan Underworld* (Stroud, 1992); Alfred F. Kinney (ed.), *Rogues, Vagabonds, and Sturdy Beggars: A New Gallery of Tudor and Early Stuart Rogue Literature* (Amherst, Mass., 1990); Linda Woodbridge, *Vagrancy, Homelessness, and English Renaissance Literature* (Urbana, Illi., 2001); William S. Carol, *Fat King, Lean Beggar: Representations of Poverty in the Age of Shakespeare* (Ithaca, NY, 1996).
4. Even W. H. Davies, in his *Autobiography of a Super Tramp* (1908) uses many of the tropes and conventions of rogue literature in his avowedly realistic depictions of his own wandering life.

5. Sean Shesgreen, *Images of the Outcast: The Urban Poor in the Cries of London* (Manchester, 2002), 88. For a full and authoritative account of Laroon's *Cries* see Sean Shesgreen (ed.), *The Criers and Hawkers of London: Engravings and Drawings by Marcellus Laroon* (Palo Alto, Calif., 1990).

6. See *Old Bailey Proceedings Online* (**www.oldbaileyonline.org**, 17 July 2005), July 1684, trial of Ann Jones, Elizabeth Jones (t16840702-5); February 1713, trial of Susan Perry (t17130225-27); February 1715, trial of William Clark (t17150223-21); May 1716, trial of John Corny (t17160517-15); July 1719, trial of Susannah Cook (t17190708-55).

7. Israel R. Potter, *The Life and Remarkable Adventures of Israel R. Potter* (1824; New York, 1962), 68–9.

8. Paul Slack, *From Reformation to Improvement* (Oxford, 1998), 5–52.

9. For eighteenth-century literary visions of the poor see Judith Frank, *Common Ground: Eighteenth-Century English Satiric Fiction and the Poor* (Palo Alto, Calif., 1997).

10. For the impact of Cervantes's work on English literature see Ronald Paulson, *Don Quixote in England: The Aesthetics of Laughter* (Baltimore, 1998).

11. Ned Ward, *The History of London Clubs: or The Citizens Pastime, Particularly The Lying Club, The Beggars Club* (1709), 7.

12. Joseph Addison and Richard Steele, *The Spectator, 1711–14*, ed. Donald F. Bond (Oxford, 1965), no. 454 (11 August 1712), iv. 101.

13. Francis Coventry, *The History of Pompey the Little; or The Life and Adventures of a Lap-Dog*, ed. Robert Adams Day (1751; Oxford, 1974), 82–105; Tobias Smollett, *The Expedition of Humphrey Clinker*, ed. Angus Ross (1771; 1967), 112–13. It is worth noting that *Pompey the Little* shares many generic qualities with Miguel de Cervantes, *A Dialogue between Scipio and Berganza* (1613).

14. For a recent account of the interrelationship between the rise of quantitative social investigation and the evolution of social policy see Sandra Sherman, *Imagining Poverty: Quantification and the Decline of Paternalism* (Columbus, Oh., 2001).

15. The barometer at Greenwich was low throughout the week and fell sharply towards its end. Astronomical observations could only be made on 20, 24, and 26 February, the other nights being too cloudy. The Astronomer Royal described 20 February as 'very hazy'. On 15 February the recorded temperature at Greenwich was 29 degrees; on 24 February it was 42 degrees, and on 26 February, 43 degrees. See James Bradley, *Astronomical Observations Made at the Royal Observatory at Greenwich from the Year MDCCL to the Year MDCCLXII* (1805), ii. 215, 303, 391, 412.

16. For recent work on the history of the laws of settlement and their impact see James Stephen Taylor, 'The Impact of Pauper Settlement, 1691–1834', *Past and Present*, 73 (1976), 42–74; K. D. M. Snell, 'Pauper Settlement and the Right to Poor Relief in England and Wales', *Continuity and Change*, 6 (1991), 375–415; Nicholas Rogers, 'Policing the Poor in Eighteenth-Century

London: The Vagrancy Laws and their Administration', *Histoire sociale/ Social History*, 24 (1991), 127–47; Nicholas Rogers, 'Vagrancy, Impressment and the Regulation of Labour in Eighteenth-Century Britain', *Slavery and Abolition*, 15 (1994), 102–13; Tim Hitchcock and John Black (eds.), *Chelsea Settlement and Bastardy Examinations, 1733–1766*, London Record Society 33 (1999). For a more pessimistic analysis of the role of the settlement see David Feldman, 'Migrants, Immigrants, and Welfare from the Old Poor Law to the Welfare State', *Transactions of the Royal Historical Society*, 6th series, 13 (2003), 79–104. For a recent general account of the Old Poor Law see Lynn Hollen Lees, *The Solidarities of Strangers: The English Poor Laws and the People, 1700–1948* (Cambridge, 1998).

17. Westminster Abbey Muniment Room, Westminster Coroner's Inquest, 28 February 1765, 'Jane Austin'. For the best recent account of the black community of eighteenth-century London see Gretchen Gerzina, *Black London: Life before Emancipation* (1995).

18. For a recent account of pauper strategies for securing accommodation in eighteenth-century London, see Tim Hitchcock, *Down and Out in Eighteenth-Century London*, 49–74.

19. Andrew Morton (pseud. for Daniel Defoe), *Every-Body's Business is No-Body's Business; or Private Abuses, Public Grievances: Exemplified in the Pride, Insolence, and Exorbitant Wages of our Women Servants, Footmen, etc.* (1725), 7.

20. Elizabeth Surridge could have appealed to either a Justice of the Peace or the Lord Mayor for an order commanding her parish of settlement to provide relief. The fact that she does not appear to have done so reflects either timidity or lack of experience.

21. For a detailed account of the events on Stonecutters Street see M. Dorothy George, *London Life in the Eighteenth Century*, 2nd edn. (1965), 173–4.

22. London Metropolitan Archives (LMA, formerly CLRO), 'Vagrant Books (4), together with five loose pages and a bill of mortality, 1738–42', Misc. MS 322.5. This same broad gender pattern can also be found among vagrants removed from Middlesex. See Rogers, 'Policing the Poor', 127–47.

23. LMA, 'Courts of the President and Governors of the Poor of London, 1702–5', MS New 377c/1/22, fos. 246–7.

24. For an excellent recent analysis of the lives of a subset of eighteenth-century street traders see Paula McDowell, *The Women of Grub Street: Press, Politics, and Gender in the London Literary Marketplace, 1678–1730* (Oxford, 1998).

25. For these institutions see Stephen MacFarlane, 'Social Policy and the Poor in the Later Seventeenth Century', in A. L. Beier and Roger Finlay (eds.), *London 1500–1700: The Making of the Metropolis* (1986), 252–77; J. G. Humble and Peter Hansell, *Westminster Hospital, 1716–1974*, 2nd edn. (1974); Ruth McClure, *Coram's Children: The London Foundling Hospital in the Eighteenth Century* (New Haven, 1981). For a recent account of the

evolution of private madhouses see Elaine Murphy, 'The Metropolitan Pauper Farms, 1722–1834', *London Journal,* 27 (2002), 1–18.

26. For a comprehensive gazetteer of early eighteenth-century foundations see Tim Hitchcock, 'The English Workhouse: A Study of Institutional Poor Relief in Selected Counties, 1696 to 1750', Ph.D. thesis (Oxford, 1985), 258–81.

27. Tim Hitchcock, 'Paupers and Preachers: The SPCK and the Parochial Work-House Movement', in Lee Davison et al. (eds.), *Stilling the Grumbling Hive: The Response to Social and Economic Problems in England, 1689–1750* (Stroud, 1992), 145–66; for the architectural history of early workhouses see Kathryn Morrison, *The Workhouse: A Study of Poor Law Buildings in England* (Swindon, 1999), 3–20.

28. For this design see Morrison, *The Workhouse*, 15–16.

29. For the gendered patterns of poor relief see Steven King, *Poverty and Welfare in England 1700–1850: A Regional Perspective* (Manchester, 2000), 164–70.

30. For these institutions see Donna Andrew, *Philanthropy and Police: London Charity in the Eighteenth Century* (Princeton, 1989).

31. For a specific discussion of this relationship see Sarah Lloyd, 'Pleasing Spectacles and Elegant Dinners: Conviviality, Benevolence, and Charity Anniversaries in Eighteenth-Century London', *Journal of British Studies,* 41 (2002), 23–57.

32. Hitchcock, *Down and Out in Eighteenth-Century London,* 49–74.

33. Westminster Archives Centre, 'St Clement's Settlement and Bastardy Examinations Book', MS B1187, fos. 147–50. I am grateful to Dr John Black for this reference.

34. Kevin Siena, *Venereal Disease, Hospitals, and the Urban Poor: London's 'Foul Wards', 1600–1800* (Rochester, NY, 2004), 139–40.

'Nauceious and Abominable'? Pollution, Plague, and Poetics in John Gay's *Trivia*

Mark Jenner

Critics have often noted how *Trivia* repeatedly draws attention to the multifarious hazards of urban pollution. The reader is told how in rain 'the Kennels . . . rush in muddy Torrents to the Thames' (I 159–60), how grease, paint, and soot can ruin the clothes of the unwary pedestrian, and how horses, carts, and coaches cast mud, mire, and beer-froth onto those walking along or standing by the street.

For many nineteenth- and early twentieth-century commentators, the muckiness of these passages lent the poem a 'real' quality; its topographical references and its preoccupation with grime and with manners led them to suggest that *Trivia* was an outstanding source for the social history of the 'habits and customs of the time'.[1] Gay's poem was said, in particular, to exemplify and reveal the sanitary mores of early modern London. In the 1920s, for instance, William Henry Irving declared that 'With a realism . . . unparalleled in his time except by Swift, [Gay] . . . describes the wretched condition of the pavements' and itemizes 'with sufficient particularity all the steams' and stinks of the metropolis. 'No wonder the plague visited every generation!', Irving concluded.[2]

Since the Second World War, academic commentary on the poem has generally reacted against this kind of approach. The new social history of the 1960s and 1970s often constructed its disciplinary identity by contrasting its archival and quantitative approach with earlier more impressionistic surveys based upon print culture. Whereas scholars like Irving or G. M. Trevelyan regarded works of literature as revealing traces of the past, the new generation of social historians was often dismissive of self-consciously 'literary' texts.[3] Their taste in documents expressed an anti-poetic aesthetic: if sources were not statistical or quantifiable, they should at least be in prose. Highly crafted verse like *Trivia* with its epigraph from Virgil was seen as a dangerously unreliable source for English social history.

Literary scholars, too, generally rejected the idea that *Trivia* was a real-istic account of London life. Some contrasted Gay's treatment of foulness and the Fleet River with Jonathan Swift's harder edged *A Description of a City Shower* (1710) or Ned Ward's more demotic *The London Spy* (1698–1702).[4] Many other critics concentrated on the poem's formal and generic properties, debating and delineating its relation to Virgil, Horace, and Juvenal.[5] More recent publications have analysed the work with reference to Augustan notions of authorship,[6] and to the eighteenth-century preoccupations with luxury and politeness.[7] All these readings stress how the poem's imagery is a set of representations, not an exact sanitary survey of the capital.

Nevertheless, even the most detailed demonstration of *Trivia*'s inter-textual character rarely disputes that the poem responds to, and even springs from, the actual mire of the city. At the beginning of their subtle discussion of *Trivia*'s ambiguous engagement with the sordid world of commerce, Stephen Copley and Ian Haywood show how the poem deployed an 'accumulation of local detail', which exemplified 'the general squalor of the London environment . . . and [its] inadequate . . . sanita-tion'.[8] For instance, the River Fleet, so crucial to the Cloacina episode that Gay inserted in 1720, was, they determined, 'a "nauseous and abom-inable sink of public nastiness"'.[9]

This phrase has echoed through the critical commentary on *Trivia* from Pat Rogers's 1972 cultural geography of dullness to Laura Brown's 2001 discussion of Augustan poems about showers and sewers.[10] Significantly, it appears in M. Dorothy George's 1925 study, *London Life in the Eighteenth Century*.[11] This work deservedly remains a classic. Grounded in the meth-ods of economic and social analysis developed at the London School of Economics in the early twentieth century, based on a wide range of crim-inal and administrative records as well as on the reports of social reformers, and sometimes presenting its findings in a statistical fashion, *London Life* is much closer to our conception of history than is Irving's account of the capital.[12] Small wonder, then, that literary scholars regularly turn to it for a sense of historical 'reality' and the social-historical context of Augustan verse about the metropolis. Unusually, Copley and Haywood followed up George's footnotes and quoted other passages from the text that she had cited, in order to give readers further 'empirical historical knowledge' about the lamentably insanitary condition of the capital at the time Gay was writing.[13] But what is this apparently transparent empirical source? What can a comparison of it and *Trivia* tell us about the nature of Gay's poem or about representations of London's dirty environment?

It was Daniel Defoe who described the Fleet as a 'Nauceious and abominable Sink of publick Nastiness'; the phrase is found in his *Due Preparations for the Plague* of 1722.[14] This fact reveals a significant tension within the critical commentary around *Trivia*. Copley and Haywood rightly emphasized that Gay's poem 'cannot be seen simply as a piece of "realistic" loco-descriptive poetry', not least because there was 'no available poetic mode in which such a possibility is conceivable'. They quoted Defoe in an introductory section which summarized and supplemented what 'numerous historians have pointed out' about the state of the London environment. In their study, as in those of both Rogers and Brown, passages from a work of one member of the eighteenth-century literary canon—Defoe—were taken as an indication of historical actuality, while the work of another—Gay—was said to demand 'to be read primarily as a literary construction'.[15] At one level they were, of course, absolutely right. Like so much of Defoe's writing, *Due Preparations* is much concerned with matters of fact.[16] It quotes statistics and documents about the plague epidemic then raging in Marseille, and about the 1665 outbreak in London.[17] It is not a frothily poetic confection like *Trivia*, but neither is it straightforwardly loco-descriptive.

M. Dorothy George, however, employed it as if it was. The phrase appears in her vivid survey of the housing of eighteenth-century London, revealing the 'bad character' of the 'unfortunate places' in which the city's workers lived.[18] One problem with *London Life* is that George often built up a picture of the poor state of London's local government, streets and scavenging by quoting from the proposals of private projectors or from pamphlets advocating administrative reform, as if they were 'straight' descriptions of the capital. Characteristically, when George quoted Defoe, she discussed neither his polemical purpose nor the circumstances in which he wrote the pamphlet, nor did she pause to consider whether these might have affected the image of metropolitan life that he presented.

Yet Defoe's pamphlet was designed to stir people into action. The passage from which George quoted concludes a section urging London's magistrates not to be satisfied with having merely issued orders for street cleaning, and further urging them to cleanse the evil-smelling tide-ditches and watercourses around the city. The intensity of the language which he used to describe such sewers—'unsufferably Nauceous', 'notorious Fountains of Stench'—was anything but neutral.[19] It sought to stir his contemporaries into more extensive and expensive reforms of the urban environment, ones which would have hurt the livelihoods of the capital's pig-keepers, butchers, and dyers.[20] Furthermore, this section marks a turning point in his argument. For after mentioning Fleet Ditch, Defoe emphasized that it was even more important for his readers to cleanse their own bodies.

> It is true that the nauceious Places . . . I have mention'd, are of dangerous Consequence . . . But I must say, that People ought to turn their Thoughts to Cleansing a worse Jakes than that of the Tide-Ditches . . . or Fleet-Ditch . . . and that is, that the People . . . should Universally cleanse themselves, cleanse their Bodies of all Scorbutick Distempers, ill Habits, and especially bad Digestures, gross Distempers, and the like . . .[21]

Defoe's account of the Fleet was not, therefore, simply a revealing description of one particularly unpleasant part of London. It was part of a rhetorical strategy which advocated new priorities in public cleansing and the cleansing of the public.

Furthermore, his representation of the city fostered the mood of a moment, not some perennial anxiety about the metropolitan environment. In the early 1720s, England experienced a wave of fear about the possible reappearance of plague.[22] The disease had struck the French port of Marseille and there was every expectation that it would reach London.[23] Readers thrilled and quaked over newspaper reports of the sufferings of southern France;[24] the press was full of remedies which claimed to cure or ward off the infection.[25] In these circumstances, people saw London's social and physical environment in a new light and sniffed its air with perturbation. Pamphleteers warned of the insanitary condition of the capital's graveyards;[26] doctors denounced the city's fetor and the carelessness with which it was cleaned.[27] Such expressions of concern were not confined to the anxiety-makers of Grub Street and Warwick Lane.[28] Residents of one ward petitioned the London court of aldermen complaining of the health hazard presented by the 'Stench and Nastiness' of the slaughter houses pouring their waste into the Fleet.[29] For the first time in more than a decade, the City of London Grand Jury and the Middlesex Sessions focused upon the need to clean up the metropolis.[30] Walpole's government drew up legislation for thoroughgoing control of social relations. The Quarantine Act of 1721 not only greatly strengthened controls over shipping but also included a proposal to use the army to enforce the isolation of infected communities. Other figures contemplated even more drastic measures. Sir Richard Mead argued that it was necessary to ensure effective 'police' of the population;[31] Sir Richard Bradley, another physician member of the Royal Society, proposed the relocation of the poor from the East End to Hounslow and Blackheath.[32] In *Due Preparations*, Defoe, who reckoned that it was 'not so much the Poor living close and not cleanly that Infects them . . . but . . . their going abroad among one another' not only told the elaborate and fantastical story of a householder who barricaded himself in his house and thus, Crusoe-like, survived the 1665 plague by severing social ties, but also recommended the wholesale removal of children from London so that the city would better withstand the plague.[33]

Rather than being an anthology of helpful documentary snapshots of the streets and sewers figured in Gay's verse, the pamphlet to which a generation of critics have turned for the 'real historical background' to *Trivia* is in fact a highly rhetorical text produced at a time when thresholds of tolerance had been lowered. Defoe's representations of the Fleet and other areas of the metropolis expressed and contributed to a heightened and atypical sense of risk. Indeed if one accepts Mary Douglas's argument that dirt is a perceptual category,[34] then one could argue that *Due Preparations*, like other medical writing of the early 1720s, created a pollution problem: at this moment dirt became dangerous and thus culturally visible in a new way.

In saying this, I am not proposing that in 1716 it would have been perfectly sensible to raise a blue flag on the banks of the Fleet. Nor am I suggesting that because Defoe's pamphlet can be shown to have fictive qualities, we should then conclude that it and *Trivia* are equivalent and identical products of discourse. On the contrary. Comparing Gay's poem with pamphlets of the early 1720s (and it was, after all, reissued in a somewhat revised form in 1720), highlights how little anxiety *Trivia* displays about epidemic disease. Death in London is certainly acknowledged: Doll, the fruit-seller, is decapitated (II 381–98);[35] the poem notes the ritual marking of the door of the house in which someone has died (II 467–74). John Chalker maintained that in *Trivia* not only is 'there . . . dirt everywhere', but also that 'ill-health is common'.[36] Yet Gay's description of how before the onset of rain 'Ungrateful Odours Common-shores diffuse, / and dropping Vaults distil unwholesome Dews' (I 171–2) evokes a distasteful rather than pestilential, or even disgusting environment. These are not Defoe's 'fountains of stench'. Similarly, when Gay wrote of the 'mix'd Fumes' of Thames Street compounded from the 'Steams' of tallow chandlers' shops and cauldrons, from stale fish and from barrels of whale oil, he did not, as Sven Armens claimed, suggest that townspeople were 'in imminent danger from unhealthy smells and diseases',[37] only that such vapours 'the wrinkled Nose offend' (II 247–53).

These scenes may have led Irving to think of former plagues, but Gay did not steer the reader in that direction.

If anything, *Trivia* dwells more on the health hazards of fashionable living than on the mephitic exhalations of the London poor or the infectious potential of the capital's bad sanitation. It is the 'Beaus' that loll at ease in gilded Chariots who are said to 'lazily insure a Life's Disease' (I 69–70). The only reference to physicians is an ironic one to the asses that were led through the streets so that their keepers could sell their milk, an accepted (if expensive) remedy recommended for recuperation from gout, coughs, consumption, and other diseases of the dwindling beau and love-sick maid (II 13–16).[38] Gay presents commercial sex as far more hazardous than the mire of metropolitan thoroughfares, urging the walker/reader to beware of the dark but less muddy alleys in which harlot-like Cloacina had consorted with the scavenger (II 129–34, III 127–32), and telling the moral fable of the Devon yeoman who lost money, credit, and nose to the poxed and 'fraudful' urban prostitute (III 285–306).

Trivia does refer in passing to the 'sickly Head' of Want (II 444) and warns of the 'Rheums and Coughs' which plagued households suffering from 'the Dearth of Coals' (I 123, 138) in cold, wet weather, but these passages are in tension with the linguistic verve and vitality with which the labour of the city is described. The poem notes the handbills puffing the supernatural therapeutic power of quackish practitioners which are proferred to the walker if he looks sickly or pale, but implies that such figures are no more efficacious than the tailors touting for business alongside them (II 539–42). Above all Gay echoes commonplaces about the salubrity of the simple life and about how prevention is better than cure. He announces that walking will maintain youthfulness and 'Rosiecomplexion'd Health' (I 73–4). The physician, George Cheyne, declared walking 'the most Natural and effectual *Exercise*';[39] Gay claims that it wards off gout, the stone, rheumatism, jaundice, coughs, and asthma (II 505–10). All these were chronic and non-infectious conditions often ascribed in the early eighteenth century to fashionably high living;[40] the epidemic fevers and plagues which contemporaries associated with stench, miasma, and urban pollution are not mentioned here.[41]

Genre springs to mind as a possible explanation for Gay's silence on the latter themes: nowadays pestilence does not strike us as the stuff of verse. However, there was a well-established poetic tradition of grand historical accounts of such plagues; these included works which translated or imitated Lucretius, such as Thomas Sprat's *The Plague of Athens*, and religious epics like George Wither's account of the plague of 1625.[42] This form had not expired in early Hanoverian England. In 1721, for instance, Christopher Pitt published a thirty-page poem on the plague of Marseille.[43] Furthermore, to develop a section with scenes of death, disease, and suffering would have been in keeping with *Trivia's* Virgilian form. Book III of *The Georgics* concludes with a long section that describes the devastating ravages of plague on cattle and other creatures. (I quote from Dryden's 1697 translation.)

> Here from the vicious Air, and sickly Skies,
> A Plague did on the dumb Creation rise: . . .
> Sheep, Oxen, Horses fall; and, heap'd on high,
> The diff'ring Species in Confusion lie: . . .

It was a disease which could spread to humans, for if they wore clothes made from infected creatures,

> Red Blisters rising on their Paps appear,
> And flaming Carbuncles; and noisom Sweat,
> And clammy Dews, that loathsom Lice beget:
> 'Till the slow creeping Evil eats his way,
> Consumes the parching Limbs; and makes the Life his prey.[44]

In 1714, when Gay was working on *Trivia*, these lines would have been extremely resonant.[45] During that year Middlesex was ravaged by a cattle plague so severe that the government called a national day of fasting.[46] Yet Gay did not develop this dimension. Halfway through the third book of *Trivia*, however, he did gesture towards such themes. Warning against picking a fight rather than giving the wall, he reminds his reader of what happened after Oedipus had killed his father in what was, after all, an altercation between two pedestrians: 'Hence sprung the fatal Plague that thinn'd thy Reign' (III 221). The poem then pauses to describe the ostrich-plumed pomp of an aristocrat's funeral and to mouth conventional sentiments about the transience of life (III 225–36), before swiftly moving on to advise '*Of avoiding Paint*' (III 237–46). It does not plunge into the plague pit or the 'poor's holes' where the indigent were buried in mass graves.[47]

It is characteristic of the poem that plague is figured as the consequence of classical parricide rather than of cloacal pollution. Challenged by his friend and fellow poet, Thomas Parnell, 'to make fine Pictures' out of the disorder of urban life, and seeking to create more than burlesque out of the interplay of high and low, in *Trivia* Gay transmuted the dirty and demotic into a polite literariy and demonstrated his own command of this mode by daringly testing its boundaries in passages of virtuosic poetic alchemy which made mini-epics from the invention of the patten and the genealogy of the shoeblack.[48] In the process, the hazards of urban life are rendered not as dangers which can lead to general social catastrophe, but as inconveniencies which spatter the walker's clothes or delay his progress through the streets.

Such attention to the possible inconveniencies of urban living picks up more general preoccupations in Restoration and Augustan London. From the 1660s and 1670s onwards the regulation of the metropolitan environment came to focus more and more upon the 'conveniency of passage' through the streets of the capital. This concern had, of course, always been present—no commercial centre can function in a state of perpetual gridlock; the maintenance of roads and streets was a priority of medieval city government. However, whereas early seventeenth-century City orders for street cleaning harped upon the dangers to the general health posed by the noxious and pestiferous smells which would result from accumulations of filth and stagnant water, late seventeenth- and early eighteenth-century precepts for cleaning and maintaining public space concentrated on the removal of things and people that blocked the thoroughfares.[49] In November 1671, for instance, Sir George Waterman proclaimed against the 'great quantities of Ashes soile and filth' thrown into the streets and the general negligence of the inhabitants in cleaning the streets, because it was to the 'great annoyance of . . . passengers & hindrance of ye Trade of this Citty'; in October 1686 the Lord Mayor ordered the constables of the City to keep the streets 'free & cleare from stopps'; in February 1692 an order went out for the streets to be cleansed as they were blocked in a way that was 'to ye great hindrance & annoyance of passengers'.[50] Furthermore, the concerns of metropolitan magistrates and grand jurymen increasingly focused on offenders who impeded trade, traffic, and polite passengers.[51] In January 1716, for instance, the year *Trivia* was published, the City of London Grand Jury presented the Hackney Coachmen standing in narrow streets as 'a Great Stoppage to Passengers' and 'as a Comon & Great Annoyance & Publick Damage of Passengers Going to & fro'. The following year they complained that their behaviour on stands near the Bank of England was 'to the Detriment and hazard of the Lives of Passing[e]rs Passing and repassing' there.[52] Such precepts and presentments implicitly imagined the metropolis as a set of thoroughfares in which people and traffic circulated with ease and elegance.

Such an ideal can be glimpsed in the engraving included in the first two editions of *Trivia*, an image which has received astonishingly little critical attention (Fig. 5).[53] It presents a pleasantly salubrious scene—the pavements along which four figures (two men, two women) are perambulating are flat, white, and even. The walks are separated from the cobbled street by the posts introduced in the City after the Great Fire (1666) which had become standard in wider and more fashionable metropolitan thoroughfares by the 1710s. The illustrator has included none of the vignettes of the discomforture of the polite which were common in early eighteenth-century engravings of street life.[54] The woman carrying an umbrella in the centre of the scene is treading gingerly, but is in no apparent danger of tripping. The trades portrayed on the margins of the image present no threat to pedestrians. In the right-hand corner there is a shoe-black boy at work, with his customer's foot resting on a stool; silhouetted in a doorway in the right-hand background is a figure carrying a sack or parcel.[55] If the women in the doorway and window of the house on the left are servants, then their labour is unobtrusive and does not impinge upon the pedestrian passing before them. They are certainly not whirling or twirling 'the sprinkling mop' or 'stunted Beesom' (II 422, 91) in a way that might spray the clothes of passers-by, the kind of behaviour that was evoked by Gay, described by Swift,[56] and painted by Edward Penny in a genre scene of the 1760s, which was made into an engraving in the 1770s and then adapted to serve as the frontispiece of the 1807 joint edition of *Trivia* and Samuel Johnson's *London.*[57]

Augustan editions of *Trivia* were, therefore, illustrated with a vision of polite urban space, not with some Hogarthian scene of shattered wheels and sprawling limbs like the 1738 engraving, *Night.*[58] But it is also clear that this space does not function efficiently. The roadway at the centre of the picture is impassable. The coach that is approaching the viewer will not be able to proceed. Ironically, two of the 'sturdy Pavior[s]', whose 'thumps', Gay says, 'smooth the broken Ways' and serve both the goddess Trivia and the walker, are causing the obstruction (I 11–13).[59] The street is being relaid. In the foreground is a pile of cobblestones waiting to be rammed down and made into its surface. The labour and the labourers that sustain, and, indeed make possible, the circulation of the city's traffic, here block the way. We do not see the inevitable confrontation. Unlike Hogarth's depictions of them in Beer Street and in his painting of a signboard, the paviours in this illustration neither interact with nor acknowledge the people around them.[60] They cannot be said to threaten the better-dressed pedestrians. Nor is there any suggestion that the heap of

The Second Edition.

LONDON:

'Now all the Pavement sounds with trampling Feet,
And the mixt Hurry barricades the Street.'

5. Street scene, title page vignette in *Trivia*, second edition (1716).

rubbish with which they are working will snap the axle of the approaching coach or tumble its passengers and horses into a sewer. The vehicle is in no danger of being overturned (compare III 335–44).

We have no idea whether Gay had any hand in the composition or the content of this engraving; nor do we know if he appreciated the witty inclusion of umbrellas, canes, coat sleeve, and the other symbols of fashionable pedestrianism which were placed around Bernard Lintot's imprint of the Crossed Keys on the title page of *Trivia*'s first edition (Fig. 9). However, the way it depicts both the incommodious and the convenient aspects of urban life, delicately suggesting that you might not be able to have the one without the other, catches something of the poem's nature. For not only did these verses about walking allow Gay to join the coach-riding classes,[61] they also demonstrated that he could indeed produce 'fine Pictures' while 'in populous City pent, Where Houses thick and Sewers annoy the Aire'.[62]

NOTES

In writing this piece I benefited from conversations with Mike Cordner, Natasha Glaisyer, Mark Hallett, Tim Hitchcock (who suggested the connection to the 1714 cattle plague), Frank Romany, and Patrick Wallis. I wish that I had been able to discuss it with my late and much missed colleague, Stephen Copley, who wrote so well about *Trivia*. My thanks, above all, to Patricia Greene for her encouragement, assistance, and support.

1. John Ashton, *Social Life in the Reign of Queen Anne*, 2 vols. (1882), i. v; John Gay, *Trivia*, ed. W. H. Williams (1922), xvii–xix. This tendency may derive in part from the repeated characterization of Gay's work as second-rate. Diane Dugaw, *'Deep Play': John Gay and the Invention of Modernity* (2001), 59–74.

2. W. H. Irving, *John Gay's London* (1928; 1968), 153, 164. Written in the early years of the emergence of English as an academic subject, Irving's treatment of *Trivia* has a hybrid quality. One chapter uses verse to illustrate the 'amusements' of eighteenth-century London. Others look forward to formal 'literary' analysis, discussing the conventions of, and models for, verse accounts of early modern London.

3. For an extreme example of this, see Peter Laslett, 'The Wrong Way through the Telescope: A Note on Literary Evidence in Sociology and Historical Sociology', *British Journal of Sociology*, 27 (1976), 319–42. For a corrective, see Keith Thomas, *History and Literature* (Swansea, 1988).

4. e.g., John Sutherland, 'John Gay', in James Clifford and Louis Landa (eds.), *Pope and His Contemporaries: Essays Presented to George Sherburn* (Oxford, 1949), 205; John Chalker, *The English Georgic: A Study in the Development of a Form* (1969), 167–9.

5. e.g., Diane S. Ames, 'Gay's *Trivia* and the Art of Allusion', *Studies in Philology*, 75 (1978), 199–222; Eugene Kirk, 'Gay's "Roving Muse": Problems of Genre and Intention in *Trivia*', *English Studies*, 62 (1981), 259–70; Anne McWhir, 'The Wolf in the Fold: John Gay in *The Shepherd's Week* and *Trivia*', *Studies in English Literature 1500–1900*, 23 (1983), 413–23.

6. Peter Stallybrass and Allan White, *The Politics and Poetics of Transgression* (1986), 102–18; Brean S. Hammond, '"A Poet, and a Patron, and Ten Pound": John Gay and Patronage', in Peter Lewis and Nigel Wood (eds.), *John Gay and the Scriblerians* (1988), 23–43.

7. Stephen Copley and Ian Haywood, 'Luxury, Refuse and Poetry: John Gay's *Trivia*', in Lewis and Wood (eds.), *Gay and the Scriblerians*, 62–82; Thomas Woodman, *Politeness and Poetry in the Age of Pope* (1989).

8. Copley and Haywood, 'Luxury, Refuse and Poetry', 67, 63.

9. Ibid. 63.

10. Pat Rogers, *Grub Street: Studies in a Subculture* (1972), 146; Laura Brown, *Fables of Modernity: Literature and Culture in the English Eighteenth Century*

(Ithaca, NY, 2001), 26. See also, David Nokes, *John Gay: A Profession of Friendship* (Oxford, 1995), 215.

11. M. Dorothy George, *London Life in the Eighteenth Century* (Harmondsworth, 1965), 94.

12. On George's work and methods see Adrian Wilson, 'The Politics of Medical Improvement in Early Hanoverian London', in Andrew Cunningham and Roger French (eds.), *The Medical Enlightenment of the Eighteenth Century* (Cambridge, 1990), 5–9. Irving's *John Gay's London* was reviewed in literature and history journals, indicating the permeability of disciplinary boundaries in the 1920s. See *American Historical Review*, 35 (1930), 342–4 and *Review of English Studies*, 6 (1930), 228–30.

13. Copley and Haywood, 'Luxury, Refuse, and Poetry', 64.

14. Daniel Defoe, *Due Preparations for the Plague, As well for Soul as Body* (1722), in W. R. Owens and P. N. Furbank (eds.), *Writings on Travel, Discovery and History by Daniel Defoe*, 8 vols. (2002), v. 48.

15. Copley and Haywood, 'Luxury, Refuse, and Poetry', 63–5.

16. On Defoe and ideas of fact and fiction, history and the novel, see Lennard Davis, *Factual Fictions: The Origins of the English Novel* (New York, 1983); Robert Mayer, *History and the Early English Novel: Matters of Fact from Bacon to Defoe* (Cambridge, 1997); Simon Schaffer, 'Defoe's Natural Philosophy and the Worlds of Credit', in John Christie and Sally Shuttleworth (eds.), *Nature Transfigured* (Manchester, 1989), 13–44.

17. Defoe, *Due Preparations*, 35–7, 46–7, 54, 73, 145–6.

18. George, *London Life*, 94.

19. Defoe, *Due Preparations*, 45.

20. There was already a furious debate about the damage which quarantine could do to English trade. Paul Slack, *The Impact of Plague in Tudor and Stuart England* (1985), 326–37.

21. Defoe, *Due Preparations*, 48.

22. George did note this in passing. *London Life*, 97, 344 n. 117.

23. C. F. Mullett, 'The English Plague Scare of 1720–23', *Osiris*, 2 (1936), 484–516; Slack, *Impact of Plague*, 326–37; Larry Stewart, 'The Edge of Utility: Slaves and Smallpox in the Early Eighteenth Century', *Medical History*, 29 (1985), 54–7.

24. For examples of this reportage, see Daniel Defoe, *A Journal of the Plague Year*, ed. Paula Backscheider (New York, 1992), 218–25.

25. e.g., M. Jenner, 'Quackery and Enthusiasm, or Why Drinking Water Cured the Plague', in Ole Grell and Andrew Cunningham (eds.), *Religio Medici: Medicine and Religion in Seventeenth-Century England* (Aldershot, 1996), 313–39.

26. M. S. R. Jenner, 'Death, Decomposition, and Dechristianisation? Public Health and Church Burial in Eighteenth-Century England', *English Historical Review*, 120 (2005), 615–32.

27. e.g., [Robert Samber], *A Treatise of the Plague* (1721), 6–10; G. Pye, *A Discourse of the Plague* (1721), part II, 23–7; S. M., *A Treatise of the Plague* (1721), 12–17.

28. The College of Physicians was based in Warwick Lane.

29. London Metropolitan Archive (LMA, formerly CLRO), Court of Aldermen Papers, January–April 1721, Petition marked as entered 10 January 1721.

30. LMA, City of London Sessions Papers, October 1721, Grand Jury Presentment, 7 October 1721; LMA MJ/OC/1 fos. 126–8, esp. fo. 127; MSP, December 1720 (48 61); MJ/SBB/78 (Sessions Book 794 pp. 61–2); WJ/O/C/1 fos. 5ᵛ–6, 7, 17, 20; E. G. Dowdell, *A Hundred Years of Quarter Sessions: The Government of Middlesex from 1660 to 1760* (Cambridge, 1932), 193–4.

31. Richard Mead, *A Short Discourse concerning Pestilential Contagion*, 6th edn. (1720), 44. This is a very early usage in an English medical context. For 'police' and 'medical police' see J. M. Beattie, *Policing and Punishment in London 1660–1750* (Oxford, 2001), 77–9; George Rosen, *From Medical Police to Social Medicine* (New York, 1974); Ludmilla Jordanova, 'Policing Public Health in France 1780–1815', in *Nature Displayed: Gender, Science, and Medicine 1760–1820* (London, 1999), 143–59; Patrick E. Carroll, 'Medical Police and the History of Public Health', *Medical History*, 46 (2002), 466–80.

32. Richard Bradley, *Precautions against Infection* (1722?), 13–16.

33. Defoe, *Due Preparations*, 41–4, 58–80 (80).

34. M. Douglas, *Purity and Danger* (1966).

35. Chalker, *English Georgic*, 176–7; Regina Janes, 'Ariosto and Gay: Bouncing Heads', *English Literary History*, 70 (2003), 447–63.

36. Chalker, *English Georgic*, 178.

37. Sven M. Armens, *John Gay: Social Critic* (New York, 1954), 83.

38. George Cheyne, *An Essay on the Gout*, 3rd edn. (1721), 27; Richard Blackmore, *A Treatise of Consumptions and other Distempers Belonging to the Breast and Lungs* (1724), 111–22; P. Dubé, *The Poor Man's Physician and Surgeon* (1704), 103.

39. George Cheyne, *An Essay of Health and Long Life* (1724), 106.

40. Roy Porter and George S. Rousseau, *Gout: The Patrician Malady* (New Haven, 1998); Roy Porter, 'Consumption: Disease of the Consumer Society?', in John Brewer and Roy Porter (eds.), *Consumption and the World of Goods* (1993), 58–81; John Gabbay, 'Asthma Attacked? Tactics for the Reconstruction of a Disease Concept', in Peter Wright and Andrew Treacher (eds.), *The Problem of Medical Knowledge: Examining the Social Construction of Knowledge* (Edinburgh, 1982), 31.

41. This is an enormous oversimplification. Eighteenth-century theories of contagion were extremely complicated and did not preclude an environmental understanding of the origins of disease. See e.g., Arnold Zuckerman, 'Plague and Contagionism in Eighteenth-Century England: The Role

of Richard Mead', *Bulletin of the History of Medicine*, 78 (2004), 273–308; D. C. Brunton, 'Pox Britannica: Smallpox Inoculation in Britain, 1721–1830', Ph.D. thesis (University of Pennsylvania, 1990), chapter 2; J. V. Pickstone, 'Dearth, Dirt, and Fever Epidemics: Rewriting the History of British "Public Health", 1780–1850', in Terence Ranger and Paul Slack (eds.), *Epidemics and Ideas: Essays on the Historical Perception of Pestilence* (Cambridge, 1992), 128–35.

42. Thomas Sprat, *The Plague of Athens* (1659); George Wither, *Britain's Remembrancer* (1628), Spenser Society, nos. 28–9 (Manchester, 1880); Raymond Anselment, *The Realms of Apollo: Literature and Healing in Seventeenth-Century England* (Newark, NJ, 1995), 91–130.

43. C. Pitt, *The Plague of Marseilles: A Poem* (1721).

44. John Dryden, *Virgil's Georgics*, iii. 721–22, 829–30, 840–44 in W. Frost and V. A. Dearing (eds.), *The Works of John Dryden* (Berkeley and Los Angeles, 1987), v. 233, 236–7.

45. In May 1714, Gay was working on a poem dealing with urban smoke, crowds, and noise. Alexander Pope, *The Correspondence of Alexander Pope*, ed. George Sherburn, 5 vols. (Oxford, 1956), i. 222–3. By 30 December 1714, he had completed 300 lines of *Trivia*. John Gay, *The Letters of John Gay*, ed. C. S. Burgess (Oxford, 1966), 15–16.

46. John Bates, *A Fast Sermon Preach'd at Hackney, Novemb. the 3d 1714. Upon Account of the Present Mortality of the Cattle* (1714); Thomas Simmons, *A Lesson from the Beasts* (1714). See also Thomas Bates, 'A Brief Account of the Contagious Disease which Raged among the Milch Cowes near London, in . . . 1714', *Philosophical Transactions*, 30 (1717–19), 872–85; Bradley, *Precautions against Infection*, 33–5; John Broad, 'Cattle Plague in Eighteenth-Century England', *Agricultural History*, 31 (1983), 104–6.

47. *Some Customs Consider'd Whether Prejudicial to the Health of this City* (1721), 8.

48. In this letter of 4 May 1714, Parnell wrote that Gay was 'content' to write of 'smoak . . . crouds, and . . . noise', and Pope condemns the idea of publishing a 'ludicrous trifling Burlesque'. It is unclear whether this burlesque was an early version of verses that became *Trivia* or another composition altogether. Even if it was the latter, Pope's injunction surely contributed to the literary ambition of Gay's verses. Pope, *Correspondence*, i. 222–3.

49. See M. S. R. Jenner, *A Cleanly City?*, forthcoming, for a full account of this.

50. LMA, Journal of the Common Council [Jnl.] 47, fo. 150^v; Jnl. 50, fo. 188^v; Jnl. 51, fo. 115^v.

51. Robert Shoemaker, *The London Mob: Violence and Disorder in Eighteenth-Century London* (2004), 1–26.

52. LMA, City of London Sessions Papers 1716/1, Grand Jury Presentment January 1715/16; City of London Sessions Papers 1717/3, Grand Jury Presentment, 1 May 1717. See also M. S. R. Jenner, 'Circulation and Disorder: London Streets and Hackney Coaches, *c*.1640–*c*.1740', in Tim

Hitchcock and Heather Shore (eds.), *The Streets of London from the Great Fire to the Great Stink* (2003), 40–53.

53. In the first edition this scene appears at the top of the first page; in the second edition it is included on the title-page.

54. Mark Hallett, *The Spectacle of Difference: Graphic Satire in the Age of Hogarth* (New Haven, 1999), 169–95.

55. Although the figure is too indistinct to permit confident identification, its outline resembles images of a chimney sweep carrying a sack of soot.

56. Jonathan Swift, 'A Description of a City Shower' in Roger Lonsdale (ed.), *The New Oxford Book of Eighteenth-Century Verse* (Oxford, 1987), 16–17, lines 19–22.

57. Giles Waterfield and Anne French, *Below Stairs: 400 Years of Servants' Portraits* (2003), 126–8; John Gay, *Trivia: or The Art of Walking the Streets of London: A Descriptive Poem, by Gay. To which is added. Dr. Johnson's London, A Satirical Poem* (1807).

58. William Hogarth, *Hogarth's Graphic Works*, comp. Ronald Paulson, 2 vols. (New Haven, 1965), ii. 167.

59. They are often incorrectly termed 'scavengers' or 'streetsweepers'. Irving, *Gay's London*, 419; Christopher Hibbert, *London: The Biography of a City* (1969), 145.

60. For a reproduction and discussion of Hogarth's painting of a paviour's sign (part of which we know only from a later engraving), see Lawrence Gowing, *Hogarth* (1971), 14. The engraving is in Samuel Ireland, *Graphic Illustrations of Hogarth*, 2 vols. (1794–99), ii. 46–8. For the paviours in Beer Street, see Paulson, *Hogarth's Graphic Works*, i. 207–9, ii. plates 197–8; on its iconographic exchanges with images of urban (re)construction see Hallett, *Spectacle of Difference*, 201–6.

61. Gay, *Letters of John Gay*, 27, 29; Nokes, *John Gay*, 209.

62. John Gay, *The Shepherd's Week* (1714), 'The Proeme' in John Gay, *Poetry and Prose*, eds. Vinton A. Dearing and Charles E. Beckwith (Oxford, 1974) i. 91. Gay here is quoting from Milton's *Paradise Lost*, Book IX, 1. 445.

Artless and Artful: John Gay's *Trivia*

Clare Brant

To represent 'literary criticism' is to condense a discipline diverse within itself to a falsely single approach. Literary critics don't all do the same thing. All critical methodologies have proponents and opponents, and sometimes they quarrel madly. However, there are, I think, some literary critical approaches to texts that are relatively uncontentious—we might agree it is necessary to read a text closely, and to supply it with some sort of context. Even those basics have had arguments attached: formalist readings, which would focus on verse form, narrative structure, and poetic effects, have given way to more historically minded readings of poetry, which explain its significance in terms of literary history and culture. The two can overlap—who writes, who reads, and how?—but also diffuse into the question of what a poem does which is comparable to other productions of its time. Such comparisons might not all be literary. An older generation of critics were attuned to the parallels between Augustan verse and Palladian architecture, through their common aesthetic of order and proportion. More recently, critics have explored manifestations of gender, class, and race in discourses to which literature is one contributor but not the only one. Readings start with an assumed position on the question are we reading to learn about the poem, or about what the poem is about, or both? So, with *Trivia*, are we reading to form an understanding of Gay as a writer, the poem as a poem, or the text as a representation of London?

In the hope of touching on all these considerations, I propose to start by discussing aspects of genre that literary critics interested in Gay's *Trivia* have tended to go to first and dwell on longest; then suggest some other paradigms for reading the poem, and end by looking briefly at some work on theorizing the city in later periods, and how useful it is—or not—for reading Gay's poem on London.

Genre is an obvious place to start from. What kind of poem is it? Most eighteenth-century texts indicate a relation to genre in their titles or subtitles. *Trivia* does this. A contemporary reader might guess from seeing 'the Art of Walking' that this would be a longish poem, with some sort of narrative or progression, and a humorous imitation of classical poems, principally Virgil's *Georgics*, which taught the art of agriculture. Such comic reinventions—thus William King's poem, *The Art of Cookery* (1708)—went down well in the early eighteenth century, not least because they satisfied a commonly made injunction (adopted from Horace) that literary works should be useful and entertaining. *Trivia* identifies itself as belonging to a mock genre through the pun of its title, meaning tri-via, three roads, and trivia in the sense of trifles.[1] The 'mock' in mock genres indicates imitation—like mock-turtle soup—and burlesque, or imitation for comic purposes. Gay and his friends Pope, Swift, Arbuthnot, and Parnell who made up the Scriblerian Club favoured the term 'heroic-comical'. Like postmodern irony, it's not always clear how heroic-comic homage relates to pastiche; what is clear is that an element of play is involved. Many of Gay's works play games with genre—most famously *The Beggar's Opera*, known as a Newgate pastoral, in which thieves and whores replace shepherds and shepherdesses. *Trivia's* title evokes 'Art' ostensibly with reference to pedestrianism, but it too plays with conventions. The art of walking ought to be a non-sequitur—walking is something we can all do, to the point of banality. But then walking is also something we all have to learn, and Gay's class-conscious society made a distinction between doing things functionally and doing them as an art—hence the art of conversation, as distinguished from mere talking, separated the polite from the hoi polloi. Pleasantly self-deprecating, *Trivia* nonetheless claims significance for the tri-via, the crossroads, the classical trope for a meeting—or parting—of ways. Coleridge described mock-heroic as 'making the great little and the little great'; Gay's title anticipates crossing points between high and low which are not simply two-way streets but busy junctions.

To decide upon genre, some critics try to sort out Gay's classical borrowings. Dianne Ames ranks *Trivia* 'among the most sophisticated and most accomplished exemplars of neoclassical allusiveness'.[2] Each allusion is meant to be recognized, she argues; though Gay imitates ancient poets, he does so on a principle of 'inept decorum': 'Much of the humor of *Trivia* proceeds from carefully bungled or splendidly mangled imitations of the English Augustan canon of Latin poets: Vergil, Horace, Ovid, and Juvenal.' Virgil's high purity coexists with Horace's annoyance, Juvenal's virulence, and Ovid's fancifulness; moralizing, amusement, satire, and fantasy mingle in a concordia discors.[3] Displacement of allusions thus looks like learned wit: by putting 'high' text into 'low' context, you create a joke. But allusion can be more slippery than simple, if ingenious, comic misplacings. Ames takes the epigraph to be a joke, with Gay 'in the guise of a kind of Martin Scriblerus whose enthusiasm is greater than his taste'.[4] The epigraph, a non-ironic quotation from Virgil's third Eclogue, asks what customs and path we follow en route across the city. Readers who knew this might also know what happens next. The dunce accused of murdering a sorry tune on pipes at the crossroads goes on to split the honours in a serious poetry contest. Does allusion stop with words directly quoted, or can it supply meanings from a quotation's setting? Can it do both? Bruce Redford argues it can, and that in what he calls 'two-tiered allusion', one meaning (the quotation) can complicate another (the quotation plus its setting).[5] If that complication is allowed, the epigraph is not a label of dunce for Gay, or an ironic label of dunce for Gay, but an ironic observation about literary judgements including those that mistake Gay for a dunce—a point Gay then makes in plain English!

Yet something remains elusive, puzzling. The poem has a complex, even contradictory mixture of genres, everyone agrees, but resolving these into the otherwise helpful term 'urban georgic' doesn't help sort out what ironies matter.[6] We are no wiser: 'The range of interpretive possibilities, shaped by generic judgments, offers us John Gays who are practical instructors upon, deplorers of, realists about, and delighted participants in "The Art of Walking the Streets of London" '.[7] One should beware identifying Gay's own views with those of the poem: the many denunciations of coaches in the poem, for instance, contradict the corpulent, indolent Gay's own fondness for riding rather than walking.[8] One should also beware of identifying Gay with the walker, or even, as one critic puts it, 'approximately Gay'.[9] The pronouns used for the protagonist slip about between I, thou, and he; identifications are evasive. Indeed assumptions of a walker need care: Gay's Index refers to an Author, and to Walkers, but only once not to any Walker, who in the poem is mostly evoked through second person pronouns.

Like its genre and persona, the poem's narrative has puzzles. Gay's urban walk is notable for its lack of purposeful topography.[10] Unlike other satirical accounts of London in the late seventeenth and early eighteenth centuries, it is not a walk to anywhere. It does not take in the standard sights, like the Guildhall, the Exchange, or St Paul's; nor does it offer a circuit of London low-life through taverns or brothels or a sexual tour of parks.[11] Other writers before and after Gay deployed a narrator who repairs to the edge of London in order to reflect upon it from a figurative distance. Gay takes up the epic position of *in media res*, being in the thick of things, using a division of three books to structure discussion of preparation for walking, walking by day, and walking by night. The walker's purpose is curiously vague: is he on business? Pleasure? The indeterminacy allows him to represent a more generalized class of readers—ostensibly, 'honest' men who are neither aristocrats nor artisans, yet sufficiently part of that class aspiring to politeness to understand both the aspiration of improving themselves (the art of . . .) and the joke of 'art' to describe something as literally pedestrian as walking. For all that critics now assume the idea as ludicrous, some readers did appreciate the practical advice. Thus one praised Gay light-heartedly for having written a sort of *Rough Guide* to London: 'Whilst I walk Streets, thy Precepts I'll imbibe / *Trivia* shall be my Convoy and my Guide.'[12] The section in Book I about giving way selectively on the wall side of the street assumes a readership attuned to the significance of social position mapped onto street movement. This was not new or ironic: Tom Brown wrote in 1700, 'Here a sooty chimney-sweep takes the wall of a grave alderman, and a broom-man jostles the parson of the parish.'[13] It has been argued that Gay uses stylistic inflation to satirize the dullness of the walker.[14] The walker may well be an ironic hero,[15] but the social sensitivity of jostling limits the degree to which the walker is a consistently ironic figure.

So there's more to the poem than classical jokes, though some critics would have you believe the classical jokes are the only ones. Although classical allusions and genres are to the fore, they may distract us from considering what part earlier English literature is playing in *Trivia* (Gay was interested in Chaucer, Spenser, and Milton, who has a significant presence in the poem). For instance, Gay uses a discourse about danger in the urban environment against which his poem supposedly provides useful warnings. The art of walking in *Trivia* is significantly an art of avoiding threat.[16] Gay proposes a solution, circumspection, which can be compared to, even if it doesn't 'borrow' from, a religious trope of safe walking. At least some early eighteenth-century readers would have known books like Thomas Taylor's *Circumspect Walking* (1631 and much reprinted) described as 'so many several steps in the art of walking'.[17] Religious differences, like political differences, were foregrounded by writers before Gay, like Thomas D'Urfey. His burlesque *Collin's Walk through London and Westminster* (1690) follows a bigoted peasant round the city, with a delight in arguments leading to fights that looks back to Samuel Butler's *Hudibras* (published in parts, 1663–78). Gay's classicism seems to absorb anything really contentious into the unifying pleasure of learned wit, but it's important to remember this choice is ideological, and presented humorously—also an ideological choice.

Nonetheless, *Trivia* is anxious. A mock-heroic motif of danger unites the three books: dangers such as inclement weather; falling roof tiles; uneven terrain; roadworks; dangerously driven carts and carriages; getting lost; falling prey to pickpockets and prostitutes. Seen from the middle-class pedestrian's point of view, danger connects physical stumbles, *faux pas*, and social pitfalls. One of the most repeated words in the poem is *miry*. Mire is an Anglo-Norman word; along with mud, it's used again and again to describe the streets, a motif that classical allusion doesn't wholly account for. Literary critics have taken up Swift's anxiety about dirt, filth, and the excremental, and noted how other Scriblerians combined politeness and lavatorial humour: Pope's *Dunciad* is full of it. *The Dunciad* also expresses an interest in mire: like Gay, Pope rhymes mud with flood.[18] In the Thames, the Fleet Ditch, and other rivers, he locates a stagnant, fetid element that breeds creatures which buzz and shine like insects around muck. One can read this as a literal comment on London's waterways, but it's also metaphorical: the insects are as irritating as dunces, bad writers who buzz about annoying true writers. Their element is a modern ooze that contrasts with the pure springs of Helicon to which the Augustan poet laid claim.[19]

Gay sees the waterways and streets as unclearly divided. Though one critic has described him as 'a swain of the streets',[20] his discourse of mire is not simply anti-pastoral. Mud collapses a binary of earth and water. Here Gay's choice of a winter setting is important: 'Winter my Theme confines; whose nitry Wind / Shall crust the slabby Mire, and Kennels bind' (II 319–20), and the Index entry for Summer declares '*Summer* [is] *foreign to the Author's Design*'. The comically inflated dangers of walking are most in evidence in winter, true, but though winter produces more abject substance—more mud—it also provides a means of controlling it, through the crisping operations of frost and ice. Gay includes an account of the frozen Thames and a frost fair, but interestingly makes little use of the purificatory power of snow. Snow is simply 'fleeting' (II 404). One could contrast Ambrose Philip's *A Winter-Piece* published in 1709 in which frost transforms the natural world into a glittering scene of beauty and art. In Philip's poem, winter shows

> The face of nature in a rich disguise,
> And brightn'd every object to my eyes.
> For ev'ry shrub, and ev'ry blade of grass,
> And ev'ry pointed thorn, seemed wrought in glass;
> In pearls and rubies rich the hawthorns show,
> While through the ice the crimson berries glow. . .
>
> $(31–40)$[21]

Frost becomes a metaphor for culture, especially the poet's ability to transform and fix nature into art. If frost acts as an emblem of poetry, mud is its opposite. Thus Philip's poem ends with a thaw, returning his traveller to 'a miry country' (line 51). One could read Gay's preoccupation with mire in terms of a jocular inversion of a popular conceit: other writers playing with conventions of *rus in urbis* focused on the dust of summer as an anti-pastoral phenomenon. But I think mire is worth further investigation. Mud falls into the category of thick, greasy life, according to a historian of disgust. Like decaying matter, mud 'redefines everything downwards'; like impure substances, it disgusts because it sticks.[22] Mire clogs poetic feet, yes, but if the joke was only a mock-heroic one, the word wouldn't recur so frequently.

Mire is dirt, and perfectly exemplifies Mary Douglas's succinct definition of dirt as matter out of place. Another early eighteenth-century writer who addressed social anxiety about matter out of place was Bernard Mandeville. His *Fable of the Bees* (1714–29) used rational paradox rather than Swiftian irony to propose that dirty matter on the streets was a precipitate of economic vitality. Where there's muck there's brass. Just as now traffic fumes are an index of economic activity,[23] so the piles of horse dung, rubbish, and mud churned up by the wheels of carts on early eighteenth-century London streets were to Mandeville evidence, however distasteful, of London's valuable status as a world-class centre of trade, with all its concomitant advantages of culture and consumption. David Nokes has observed that Gay's walker is neither a gentleman of leisure nor a man on business;[24] his unspecified occasion for walking gives him an indeterminate relation to economic activity. He covers distance more purposively than the rakes who featured in many Restoration poems about rambling;[25] he also pauses, to savour a quiet alley, to browse at bookstalls, or to study people (II 271–84). The poem recognizes many forms of work—some sixty occupations are cited[26]—yet concerns itself with the perceptions of the walking class rather than the working class. Although the working class has to walk (and here one might remember that prostitutes are called streetwalkers), the poem separates walkers from workers with some awkwardness, in which metaphors of dirt play a part. An urban underclass is present in the poem in stylized ways, notably a stress on how the dirt-poor are figures of dirt.

In turning up this street, the literary critic leaves behind the classics and heads for psychoanalysis, by way of cultural materialism. Labour underpins two episodes normally read in terms of Ovidian supernatural machinery, or stories of interventions by gods that explain phenomena fancifully through myth. One concerns the invention of the patten, an overshoe whose wooden sole with an iron ring lifted the wearer a little out of the mire (Fig. 6). Patty, a Lincolnshire milkmaid, struggles with mud until Vulcan devises the patten to protect her. The second episode also comically mixes classical and modern life: the son of Cloacina, goddess of the sewers, thinking himself an orphan, laments his lack of a trade; his mother furnishes him with brushes and oil, donated by various gods, so transforming him into a useful shoe-cleaning boy. Gay's addition of the Cloacina sequence to the poem's 1720 edition suggests muck was a theme he wanted to pick up again. Humorous and fanciful, these episodes pastiche aetia, or myths of origins. Dianne Ames acclaims them as 'rococo spoofs of baroque treatment of myths'.[27] Yet for all their 'heroic-comical' significance, both these episodes deal with mire. The patten is a prophylactic, preventing mire from getting onto walkers' shoes. The shoe-boy is an agent of mire's removal:

> . . . useful to the walking Croud,
> To cleanse the miry Feet, and o'er the Shoe
> With nimble Skill the glossy Black renew.
>
> (II 154–6)

The great unwashed service middle-class cleanliness: 'What though the gath'ring Mire thy feet besmear, / The Voice of Industry is always near' (II 99–100). Yet one of the dangers faced by the walker is of being spattered with mud by the brooms of streetsweepers (see Fig. 7).

'Safe thro' the Wet on clinking Pattens tread.'
6. Pattens (1710–20).

> When waggish Boys the stunted Beesom ply,
> To rid the slabby Pavement; pass not by
> E'er thou hast held their Hands; some heedless Flirt
> Will over-spread thy Calves with spatt'ring Dirt.

(II 91–4)

Mud still features in advertisements for floor-cleaners as a signifier of outside coming in; here, mud violates the surface of the person.

Why does mud matter? Clean shoes get the poem's serious attention: 'The Foot grows black that was with Dirt embrown'd' (II 155). The poet jokes that when he drops into Lord Burlington's place, he has to do so with cleaner shoes. Clean stockings matter too. Straying into gender, in an age when a woman's reputation was ideally unspotted, a literal spattering of mud on a man's leg had a trace of sexual meaning. Calves were a masculine body part much more on display than now. Some men even wore calf-stuffers in search of a firming and uplifting effect—like a Wonderbra. Mire on stockings or cravats was the cultural forebear of egg on tie but it involves less agency. Gay's portentous advice to the walker to anticipate and avoid 'the muddy Dangers of the Street' (I 194) and to 'Mind only Safety, and contemn the Mire' (III 130) comically proposes that care might prevent contamination, but the poem's incidents are described in a poetic present tense that makes all the dangers happen, imaginatively. For example, in Book I by day the walker must watch out for people who carry walking canes under their arms: 'The dirty Point oft checks the careless Pace, / And miry Spots thy clean Cravat disgrace' (I 77–8).

In Book III, by night the walker must sniff out the dangers of fresh paint:

> Where the nail'd Hoop defends the painted Stall,
> Brush not thy sweeping Skirt too near the Wall;
> Thy heedless Sleeve will drink the colour'd Oil,
> And Spot indelible thy Pocket soil.

(III 237–40)

Clothes conspire with the outside to let muck in. The poem's anxiety about fear of dirt is a heroic-comical joke about modernity as not heroic, as timorous in comparison to the ancients; it's also a psychosexual dramatization of abjection in a specific cultural location.

Cloacina's lover, the bootboy's father, pushes the soil cart. Mud's affinity with excrement—indeed in 1716 half the muck probably was excrement—points to psychoanalytic frameworks: in true mock-heroic form, the unconscious rises to the surface, as mire. Hence its repression in the gravel walks of the well-heeled, walks whose geometric straightness contrasted with twisty city streets, and whose crunch contrasted with squelchy mud. One way of reading Gay's fascination with mire would be to suggest that, like Pope's with ooze, it is infantile. It's been suggested that literature's representation of urban space offers readers the pleasure of exploring, of practising a relation to space otherwise confined to child-hood.[28] Against this, other commentators define the urban condition as unpleasant because it imposes involuntary touch. Elias Canetti argues in *Crowds and Power*: 'The repugnance of being touched remains with us when we go about among people; the way we move in a busy street . . . is governed by it.'[29] Urban touch is unpredictable and random, disturbing because it returns us to polymorphous perversity. Touch threatens in a city and sight is no defence; as de Certeau puts it, urban experience is 'prey to contradictory movements that counterbalance and combine them-selves outside the reach of panoptic power'.[30] Sight is a limited sense in the city; 'lower' senses—smell, touch, hearing—express the city just as well if not better. How does that work in a genre that mixes high and low? Does the body get rewritten as a joke like everything else, or despite the vulnerability in which it is clothed, is it still a reliable source of sense impressions? I think the latter.[31] But one can see in eighteenth-century texts like *Trivia* that sight has to work for its position as the most privi-leged of the senses, in Freud's words.

For the rest of this essay I want to explore *Trivia* in relation to work on the city in later periods, with special attention to the way cities prob-lematize vision. Much thought has been given to the nineteenth-century Parisian flâneur who has become a figure widely and loosely taken to represent urban spectating. The origins of the word flâneur are obscure and its definition disputed; I'll take Walter Benjamin's view of the flâneur as a melancholy fantasist, economically insecure and sexually fragile, a figure who represents the spirit of modern angst, produced by an urban condition of excitement, boredom, and horror.[32] To some feminists, the flâneur embodies the male gaze, which in Lacanian psychoanalysis repre-sents desire, mastery, and unconscious fear of women. Others, worried by excessive regard for the visual, argue the flâneur's gaze is a creation of modernism as much as masculinity, and note the flâneur was an urban eavesdropper, tuned into sound as much as sight.[33] Gay's walker is obviously not a flâneur in Benjamin's sense, but like a flâneur, he listens as well as sees. Gay and other writers stressed the heteroglossia of urban experience. London is wondrous because of the variety of talk one can hear.[34] Gay's walker hears women and children as well as men—ballad singers, apple-sellers, prostitutes, apprentices, orphans.[35] Sound filters in people out of view, explaining perhaps the curious popularity of the 'Cries of London' as a subject of engravings.[36]

For the flâneur, the panoptic power broken up by the city is restored by being always on the watch. *Trivia* restores it through imagery, especially burlesque of classical similes. The picture of Doll's head bouncing along the ice like Orpheus's is one such moment; another is Gay's description of a wig bedraggled by the rain:

> Thy Wig alas! uncurl'd, admits the Show'r.
> So fierce *Alecto's* snaky Tresses fell,
> When *Orpheus* charmed the rig'rous Pow'rs of Hell.
> Or thus hung *Glaucus'* Beard, with briny Dew
> Clotted and strait . . .
>
> (I 202–6)

Not all Gay's imagery is visual, but allusion is a kind of remembered picture brought alongside. My point is that Gay is doing something else besides imitating the ancients: he is using that imitation to stabilize a visual field called into question by the eighteenth-century city. Perhaps surprisingly, a number of the images get Index entries. Imagery offers a double field of vision. It's the literary alternative to panoptic power.[37] Other eighteenth-century writers besides Gay experimented with imagery to describe urban landscape: thus Lady Mary Wortley Montagu wrote to Lady Bristol in 1718 that Constantinople showed

an agreeable mixture of Gardens, Pine and Cypress trees, Palaces, Mosques and public Buildings, rais'd one above another with as much Beauty and appearance of Symetry as your Ladyship ever saw in a Cabinet adorned by the most skillful hands, Jars shewing themselves above Jars, mix'd with Canisters, babys and Candlesticks. This is a very odd Comparison, but it gives me an exact Image of the thing.[38]

De Certeau argues the city manifests what he calls a forest of gestures (think of graffiti).[39] To compensate for the city's bewilderment of vision, *Trivia* uses mock-heroic as a wood whose grotesqueries are known.

There's another way in which *Trivia* engages with vision: by invoking signs as an emblem of the city's potential readability. Side-headings act like signposts in the poem, as does the Index, a prosaic aid to finding your way back around the poem. The weather is described as a series of signs, and street signs mean the literate don't get lost. At the Seven Dials in Covent Garden

Here oft the Peasant, with enquiring Face,
Bewilder'd, trudges on from Place to Place;
He dwells on ev'ry Sign, with stupid Gaze,
Enters the narrow Alley's doubtful Maze,
Trys ev'ry winding Court and Street in vain,
And doubles o'er his weary Steps again.

(II 77–82)[40]

City people were having to learn to live with new signs and in newly regulated ways. In 1716, the same year that *Trivia* was published, an Act was passed to regulate wheeled traffic in London.[41] Section IV of this Act tackled a growing abuse of 'borrowing' gentlemen's coaches without their permission to attend at funerals; this was to be prevented by requiring mourning coaches to display a number. If you get into a cab now you probably don't think much of reading the number on top, the company name on the side, the driver number, but you distinguish a cab from a car by that signage. It's an urban hermeneutics that has taken a while to build up, and *Trivia* shows how.

To return, unlike Gay's walkers, to where we started out: London is a subject of *Trivia*, but not the only subject, and in any case, London is treated imaginatively, its contours as much literary as literal. The poem's subject matter includes 'Art', ostensibly in relation to walking but also through its own demonstration of the art of writing. In 1716 a dozen other works besides *Trivia* used 'art' in their titles or subtitles, works on arithmetic, punning, surveying land, gardening, letter-writing, husbandry, printing, angling, and navigation. Creative labour and practical skills are linked. The art of poetry encompassed skills that defined writers as poets rather than versifiers or hacks. The walker has mastered the art of walking better than more artless walkers who get jostled, spattered, and lost. With anchor-points in other literary texts as well as the streets of London, the poem points up a gap between the poet and walker which is comparable to the gap between artful and artless. *Trivia* plays with a persona more artless than the poet in order to make the art of walking into a dynamic topographical joke about the artfulness of literature.

NOTES

1. Early to mid-eighteenth-century writers preferred the adjective trivial to the noun trivia; thus in Samuel Johnson's *Dictionary* (1755). 'Trivia' was used to refer to a commonplace or trifle; it also retained a sense of the trivium, the three subjects of grammar, rhetoric, and logic in the medieval division of knowledge.

2. Dianne S. Ames, 'Gay's *Trivia* and the Art of Allusion', *Studies in Philology*, 75 (1978), 199.

3. Ibid. 200.

4. Ibid. Martin Scriblerus was a character invented by the Scriblerian Club as a figure for pedantic wrong-headedness and false scholarship. *Memoirs* in his name, written by Arbuthnot, were published in the second volume of Pope's prose works in 1741.

5. Bruce Redford, *The Converse of the Pen: Acts of Intimacy in the Eighteenth-Century Familiar Letter* (1986), 97–118 on allusion in the letters of Thomas Gray.

6. On generic complexity and urban georgic, see Anne McWhir, 'The Wolf in the Fold: John Gay in *The Shepherd's Week* and *Trivia*', *Studies in English Literature, 1500–1900*, 23 (1983), 414, 422. Eugene Kirk, 'Gay's "Roving Muse": Problems of Genre and Intention in *Trivia*', *English Studies*, 62 (1981) 270, argues for *Trivia*'s 'generic multifariousness'. In *John Gay: A Profession of Friendship* (Oxford, 1995), 206, David Nokes declares the poem is a town georgic which 'defiantly resists generic classification' because though its sources are clear, its tone is not. Stephen Copley and Ian Haywood argue that the poem is driven by contradictions including ones of genre: 'Luxury, Refuse, and Poetry: John Gay's *Trivia*' in Peter Lewis and Nigel Wood (eds.), *John Gay and the Scriblerians* (1988), 67.

7. Kirk, 'Gay's "Roving Muse" ', 259.

8. He was ever on the cadge for a lift; friends joked he would spend the profits of *Trivia* on a coach. Gay confessed to Parnell, 'what I got by walking the streets I am now spending in riding in Coaches'. John Gay, *The Letters of John Gay*, ed. C. F. Burgess (Oxford, 1966), 29, no. 20 (26 March 1716).

9. Calhoun Winton, *John Gay and the London Theatre* (Lexington, Ky., 1993), 51.

10. Gay wrote the poem while he was in Hanover but I don't think that makes any difference.

11. For example, Ned Ward, *A Frolick to Horn-Fair* (1700); *A Walk to Islington* (1701); *The Field Spy, or the Walking Observator* (1714); anon, *The Holiday Ramble, or A Walk to Pancridge* (1703). Broadly speaking, early eighteenth-century literature of the city was either rambling, as if the city was so disorderly the appropriate literary form for it could only be a loosely structured one, or that disorder was overcome through the polished couplet. The compromise quadrameters of *Hudibras*-roughly energetic, loosely composed—disappeared from the literary scene.

12. James Heywood, 'To Mr. Gay, on his Poem entitled *Trivia, or, the Art of Walking the Streets of London*' (1724). Quoted by W. H. Irving, *John Gay: Favorite of the Wits* (New York, 1962), 135–6. On imitations of *Trivia*, see Irving, *Favorite of the Wits*, 124.

13. Thomas Brown, *Amusements Serious and Comical*, ed. Arthur L. Hayward (1700; 1927), Amusement III: London, 12.

14. Alvin B. Kernan, 'The Magnifying Tendency: Gay's *Trivia, or the Art of Walking the Streets of London*', *The Plot of Satire* (New Haven, 1965), 36–50.

15. Nokes, *Profession of Friendship*, 211.

16. Compare [John Bancks], *A Description of London* (1751): 'Tipsey barrow-women tumbling, / Dukes and chimney-sweepers jumbling' (lines 23–4).

17. Or Henry Osland's *The Christian's Daily Walk, or Profitable Instructions* (*c.*1660). A topographical poem by William Draper, *The Morning Walk, or City Encompass'd* (1751) assumes this discourse, alternating rhapsodic addresses to the deity with descriptions of the lamentable godlessness of London.

18. For example, *Dunciad*, II 270–1 on the Fleet Ditch: 'The King of Dykes! Than whom no sluice of mud / With deeper sable blots the silver flood'.

19. The city river becomes a trope for the generation of writers from Grub Street whom Pope writes off as dirty irritants. W. H. Irving, *John Gay's London* (Cambridge, Mass., 1928; 1968), 163, notes the Fleet Ditch, not covered until 1768, 'became a stock figure for Grub Street verse'.

20. Anne McWhir, 'The Wolf in the Fold', 421.

21. Text taken from Roger Lonsdale (ed.), *The New Oxford Book of Eighteenth-Century Verse* (Oxford, 1983), 85.

22. William Ian Miller, *The Anatomy of Disgust* (Cambridge, Mass., 1997), 38–42, 63. Thus the mud on Elizabeth Bennett's skirts in Jane Austen's *Pride and Prejudice* disgusts Miss Bingley.

23. Compare Iain Sinclair's account of the postmodern walker: 'Walking, moving across a retreating townscape, stitches it all together: the illicit cocktail of bodily exhaustion and a raging carbon monoxide high.' Quoted in Iain Borden et al. (eds.), *The Unknown City* (Cambridge, Mass., 2001), 163.

24. Nokes, *Profession of Friendship*, 210. He quotes Tom Woodman, '"Vulgar Circumstance" and "Due Civilities": Gay's Art of Polite Living in Town', in Lewis and Wood (eds.), *John Gay and the Scriblerians*, 88: 'Walking thus has a fairly precise class orientation as a golden mean between *nouveau riche* selfishness and idleness and the vulgar labours of the lower classes.'

25. For example, John Wilmot, Earl of Rochester's *A Ramble in St. James's Park* (1680).

26. As counted by Irving, *John Gay: Favorite of the Wits*, 127.

27. Ames, 'Gay's *Trivia*', 214.

28. 'Travel (like walking) is a substitute for the legends that used to open up space to something different'. Michel de Certeau, *The Practice of Everyday Life*, trans. Steven Rendall (Berkeley, 1984), 106–7.

29. Elias Canetti, *Crowds and Power*, trans. Carol Stewart (1984), 15.

30. *The Practice of Everyday Life*, 95. De Certeau argues that the *here-there* of walking evokes that phatic function which is the first verbal function

acquired by children (99). One might also note how this echoes the *fort-da* game explained by Freud as a child's taking control over his mother's comings and goings. The perambulations open to adults are closed to the less mobile child—though again one should note that the term for an infant carriage, a pram, is a contraction of the word perambulation. Pushed about in a pram, small children can participate in the art of walking. Compare the late twentieth-century 'stroller' for children too young to walk far. Though discussions of walking as an urban experience now consider gender—thus Elizabeth Wilson, 'The Invisible Flaneur' (1992) in *The Contradictions of Culture: Cities, Culture, Women* (2001), 72–9—few (any?) consider it from other than an adult, able-bodied perspective.

31. Compare how cinema reorders the senses through the blur of neon and wail of sirens and saxophones which represent the city, epitomized in Ridley Scott's *Blade Runner* (1982).

32. Wilson, 'The Invisible Flaneur', 75–9, 86–7.

33. Ibid. 82–3, 89.

34. Compare Samuel Johnson, *London* (1738): 'And here a female atheist talks you dead.' Probably not until Dickens uses cockney does literature identify London through a specific accent. How might one relate this to the emergence in the 1990s of 'mockney', or a London accent deployed strategically by people who don't come from there?

35. The presence of women on the streets of London may feminize popular culture enough for Gay to want to differentiate an educated masculine poetry. For the variety of women on London streets, see Sean Shesgreen (ed.), *The Criers and Hawkers of London: Engravings and Drawings by Marcellus Laroon* (Palo Alto, Calif., 1990).

36. On the significance of sound to early modern urban writers, see Irving, *John Gay's London*, 154–9; on smell, see my article 'Fume and Perfume, Some Eighteenth-Century Uses of Smell', *Journal of British Studies*, 43 (2004), 444–63.

37. Cf. Pope: *The Dunciad's* mock-epic pissing contest takes place on the Thames, in the heart of London.

38. Robert Halsband (ed.), *The Letters of Lady Mary Wortley Montagu*, 3 vols. (Oxford, 1967), i. 397. (A baby is a kind of jar.) A generation later, Boswell compared the sight of London to a cabinet of curiosities.

39. Their meaning and movement cannot be captured, says de Certeau, but he has a go: 'We could mention the fleeting images, yellowish-green and metallic blue calligraphies that howl without raising their voices and emblazon themselves on the subterranean passages of the city, "embroideries" composed of letters and numbers, perfect gestures of violence painted with a pistol, Shivas made of written characters, dancing graphics whose fleeting apparitions are accompanied by the rumble of subway trains: New York graffiti.' *Practice of Everyday Life*, 102.

40. In his poem *A Journey to Exeter*, Gay celebrates a particular inn-sign as an inspiration for a new tradition of writing.
41. Public General Acts, 1715–1716, 1 & 2 Geo. 1.c.57, section VIII aimed to reduce accidents and road rage by obliging drivers to have a person on foot to guide the vehicle, thus increasing pedestrian traffic—a nice irony in the context of *Trivia*.

The Walker Beset: Gender in the Early Eighteenth-Century City

Margaret R. Hunt

The most famous of eighteenth-century fictional flâneurs, the eponymous Mr Spectator of Joseph Addison and Richard Steele's periodical of 1711–14, often sought the stimulation of the city.[1] But his London was reasonably well ordered, devoted to wholesome commerce, and growing more rational and refined by the day. It bore little resemblance to the city whose streets the walker of John Gay's *Trivia* was to tread. For the walker London is a dirty, smelly, and sinister but captivating place. Addison and Steele had dwelt little upon the way Mr Spectator got from place to place; the reader is free to surmise that he generally relied upon a coach or other non-pedestrian transport. By contrast the walker's restless quest for knowledge or novelty go along with a virtual obsession with walking the city streets. There he learns to cope at close hand, rather than from the Augustan detachment of a coach window, with a series of powerful challenges to his physical and spiritual integrity. One of the central tensions of the poem is whether the danger and pollution that are the very sinews, blood, and bowels of the living city will defeat the hero, or whether, instead, his evolving knowledge will carry him safe home, his masculinity intact.

The poem *Trivia* takes its name from a minor Roman goddess whom John Gay fancifully appoints to be patroness of streets and highways. The poem opens with an appeal to her for help with his poetry ('Thou Trivia, Goddess, aid my song') as well as for guidance in traversing the city streets (I 5). But Gay is far less sanguine about mortal women. Indeed most of these are arrayed along a narrow spectrum from suspicious to abhorrent, and London itself is figured as both feminine and dangerous. In this respect too Gay differs significantly from Addison and Steele who, if not precisely feminist, had taken a rather optimistic view of women's potential to civilize and soften men and society.[2]

In *Trivia* women, particularly women of the elite, are unequivocally emblems of luxury and corruption. The 'lazy Fair' no longer goes about on foot as her sturdier foremothers did; instead, perhaps because she is shod 'in braided Gold', she 'disdains the Street' and 'affects a limping Air' (I 109–12). When upper-class women condescend to walk at all, it is to converge upon the Mall arrayed in inappropriate clothes ('*Dress[ed] neither by Reason nor Instinct*') in order to show themselves off (*Trivia*, Index under L for Ladies). Upper-class women in the city are sickly, yet obsessed with self-display and far from modest. Their lower-class counterparts are even worse. Working women are especially enervated by the city. The 'draggled Damsel' bearing fish from Billingsgate and the 'sallow Milkmaid' exhaustedly chalking up her gains (II 9–11), both of whom the Walker encounters on an early morning ramble, proclaim their difference from their more robust, pink-cheeked country cousins. Some working women are literally executed by the city, like hapless Doll, the fruit-seller, who, plying her wares on the frozen Thames, has her head chopped off, presumably by colliding sheets of thawing river-ice (II 381–92). But the most crucial characteristic of working women is that they really only think about one thing—sex. And so one sempstress works and plays with a Belgian stove under her skirt to keep her warm—a standard symbol of overheated sexuality (II 338); other sempstresses, dangerously literate, read Alexander Pope's *The Rape of the Lock* (II 563), and a 'vain Virgin' lusts after a coachman because of his uniform (II 572–3).

In fact women of the labouring classes inspire much more revulsion in the poet than do elite women: his misogyny is of Swiftian proportions,[3] and it comes in an unsavoury mix of moralism and public-health zealotry. In *Trivia* oversexed proletarian women both personify and mediate the noxious, excremental effusions of the city; simply by existing they constitute a challenge to the health and integrity of the walker. Prostitutes with their seductive wiles, diseased bodies, and depraved souls lead the band. They ooze disquietingly from every darkened alley, like a kind of evil sweat. And they have many comrades-in-arms. There are the ballad singers whose siren song draws marks for pickpockets (III 76–80); 'sneering Ale-wives' who call after the innocent walker at night (III 132), and hucksters who, when a passerby trips and falls on their 'gaping wide, low steepy Cellars' (III 122), demand he pay for the spoiled goods. There are also fish- and shellfish-women with their noisome wares, tendency to set up stalls next to sewers, and aphrodisiac connotations (III 185–94). Gay certainly knew of the classical association of fish- and oyster-eating with sexual excess.

Lest one fail to make all the connections, one of the deities who pre-
sides over this unlovely crew is Cloacina, goddess of the sewer. In Gay's
faux-myth Cloacina takes on human form, a suitably filthy cinder girl, in
order to have down and dirty sex in a dark alley with a street scavenger,
who collects the dirtiest street refuse. The fruit of their union is then
abandoned under a huckster's stall, where he grows up nurtured on criminality. At the climax of the story, Cloacina, in a fit of maternal concern,
emerges dramatically from the Fleet Ditch, the premier sewer of London,
in order to endow her offspring with boot-black's tools and recommend
him to a life of cleaning mud and shit off the boots of his betters
(II 107–216).

It is not easy to impose order on this toxic morass, but Gay does give
it a try. The main suggestion to the walker with respect to prostitutes,
alewives, and women like them is simply to shun them, and more
specifically to avoid dark alleys at night. As Gay colourfully puts it,
beware the woman who 'leads the willing Victim to his Doom, / Through
winding Alleys to her Cobweb Room' (III 291–2). Today this sort of
advice is more often given to women: don't walk out alone at night, and,
if you do, stay in well-lighted places. But in *Trivia* it is directed to men,
and owes much to the various warnings to men in the Old Testament
book of Proverbs to shun the lustful woman whose house is death.[4] Gay
is especially indebted here to an influential late seventeenth- and early
eighteenth-century movement, generally referred to at the time and since
as the Reformation of Manners. Heavily patronized by Londoners of the
middling sort, as well as by some highly placed clergymen, the various
societies for Reformation of Manners called for better enforcement
of the laws against immorality and themselves took vigilante action
against sabbath-breakers, swearers, tipplers, homosexuals, and prostitutes.
Between about 1690 and 1720 this movement's propagandists turned
out scores of sermons and pamphlets, in tens of thousands of copies, on,
among other topics, the perils to one's health, wealth, and eternal salva-
tion of consorting with whores. Many of these use as their departure
point the woman whose house is death (as in Proverbs chapters 2, 5, 6,
and 7) and, like Gay, they favour images of the prostitute as a spider who
traps men in her web.[5]

Gay also has advice for the walker about how to deal with the other, less
poisonous, though still potentially dangerous females he is likely to come
across in the city. It is important for him to understand that even trivial
encounters with apparently harmless women can be hazardous. Thus, the
man who 'Turns oft' to pore upon the Damsel's Face' (II 102) risks injury,
because he loses the concentration needed to safely navigate the perilous

'And dextrous Damsels twirle the sprinkling Mop'
7. *A City Shower*, by Edward Penny (1764).

bustle of the street. Nor should the walker either speak to women, or ask their advice, because it would give them an opening to try to accost him or steal his valuables. There are, however, ways to make women inadvertently support the walker's larger goal of obtaining insider knowledge of the city and its surroundings. Gay wants his walker to learn to read what women do, though not what they say, as signs or markers that will help him to orient himself in time and space. Thus if a man wants to know what day of the week it is, he should take the time to observe what the women are doing. If it is Saturday, they will be cleaning their stoops; Wednesday and Friday they will be selling fish, though occasionally 'Ev'n *Sundays* are prophan'd by Mackrell Cries' (II 432). The walker can gauge whether the weather is changing by the way an old woman huddles over her kitchen hearth or by observing when women go off to flaunt themselves at the Mall. The street-cries, especially those of women hawkers ('Hark, how the Streets with treble Voices ring'), mark the onset of spring, summer, and autumn (II 427–50). And a man can tell from where the oyster-seller sets up her stall how to cross the street with the minimum of distress and damage to one's shoes: 'There may'st thou pass, with safe unmiry feet' (III 187).

Women thus become a useful natural feature of the city, akin to street signs ('Like faithful Land-marks to the walking Train' II 68), which Gay is most anxious his walker also observe. By using them as evidence, by getting them to assist passively and from a distance in the project of navigating and 'knowing' the city, one can neutralize their dangerous sensuality and elude their snares. The success of this gambit is celebrated, just as Gay is waxing eloquent on women's usefulness, by a very daring, and, for *Trivia*, uniquely permissive moment. After safely traversing the street, having properly read the 'natural signs', the walker is actually permitted to purchase some oysters from one of those natural signs, 'brown *Ostrea*', the oyster-woman (III 185). This is the only fairly positive close encounter with a woman in the entire poem and it is very charged:

> And with the sav'ry Fish indulge thy Taste:
> The Damsel's Knife the gaping Shell commands,
> While the salt Liquor streams between her Hands . . .
>
> (III 192–4)

But this interlude with an oddly commanding woman is both short-lived and followed by a peroration on bizarre and luxurious foods, such as blood sausages, frogs, snails—and raw oysters (III 195–205).

In contrast, the question that Gay seems to be asking about men is 'who will make the best allies when one is navigating the city?' It is not a simple question because men are not unproblematic in *Trivia*, though they almost never inspire the kind of anxiety that women do. One difficulty is that certain occupational groups will stain or besmear your clothes if you brush against them. Such are barbers, perfumers, and bakers (especially hazardous to the 'look' of men of the cloth), chimney-sweeps, coal-carriers, dust-men, chandlers, butchers, and millers

(II 25–44; 57–8). It is also the case that some men are prone to street violence, and Gay describes a rather impressive brawl between some colliers and a group of coachmen (III 25–50). The spectacle draws a crowd, but there seems little fear of its becoming more general. Coachmen and chairmen are a decided problem in *Trivia*. They are arrogant, they foster dependence upon non-pedestrian forms of transport, and they often cause accidents. Vigilance is essential when one shares the thoroughfares with them (III 153–84). Still these various inconveniences are of a different stamp from being lured into the house of death.

Middling or upper-class men pose fewer difficulties. The high-spirited young men who piss upon sentry boxes, possibly offending (or arousing?) the local virgins, are merely advised to find a more secluded spot in which to do their business (II 297–300). Boys who play tricks on coachmen and female pedestrians are well, just boys being boys. Beaux and fops are annoying, but Gay deals with them easily by subjecting them to traffic accidents. In *Trivia* a propensity for getting in accidents is a clear marker of flagging masculinity (II 523–38). For their part bullies are easily repelled simply by standing up to them (II 59–64).

Two groups might strike the reader as more potentially destructive of peace and security. One is petty criminals such as pickpockets and sharpsters; the other is the notorious Mohocks, a gang of upper-class hooligans who briefly gained quite a wild, indeed inflated, reputation in this period. Gay is surprisingly sanguine about the first group. Getting one's pocket picked is almost a rite of passage in *Trivia*: 'Who has not here [outside a playhouse], or Watch, or Snuff-Box lost, / Or Handkerchiefs that India's Shuttle boast?' (III 257–8). So many people are wise to the other confidence games of the city, including guinea dropping, crooked dice, and card sharping, that they have begun to die out (III 247–50). The Mohocks too are more of a menace to other people—watchmen and old women—than they are to the walker: 'I pass [over] their [the Mohocks'] desp'rate Deeds, and Mischiefs done', says the poet, mentioning only their practice of putting old women into barrels and rolling them down Snow-hill (III 326–34). The Mohocks are portrayed here as another albeit more extreme case of 'boys being boys'.[6]

Though the walker does not have to worry unduly about groups of rowdy men, he still needs allies in the city. Simply finding one's way can be a challenge, and it matters a great deal whom one approaches for directions. As has been seen, a man should not turn to women for help; they will certainly betray him.

> But do not thou, like that bold Chief [Theseus], confide
> Thy ventrous Footsteps to a female Guide;
> She'll lead thee, with delusive Smiles along,
> Dive in thy Fob [i.e. pick your pocket], and drop thee in the Throng.
>
> (II 87–90)[7]

There are men one doesn't want to rely on either, notably apprentices, fops, and link-boys. Coach- and chairmen are too compromised to have much to offer a pedestrian in need. But there are others who will do the job nicely. Sworn or licensed porters are one such group, ideal for helping one find one's way. Less trustworthy is the 'grave Tradesman', who might lead a man astray out of self-interest: he 'ne'er deceives, but when he profits by 't' (II 71–2).

The walker may get into more serious scrapes than simply getting lost, especially at night. One difficulty is what to do if one has drunk too much of an evening. The poet raises this issue immediately after telling the cautionary tale of a yeoman whose money was stolen and his health compromised by a harlot while out on a boozy spree. Should such dangers threaten the walker, he should commit his person to the night watchmen

> . . . who with friendly Light,
> Will teach thy reeling Steps to tread aright;
> For *Sixpence* will support thy helpless Arm,
> And Home conduct thee, safe from nightly Harm . . .
>
> (III 307–10)

If taken up by the night watch for other kinds of gentlemanly indiscretions one can enlist, for a bribe, the help of the local constable to get released. Finally, there are the brave firemen, who if not precisely there for the walker's personal convenience, nevertheless serve the general good by safeguarding the city through which he roams (III 362–76).

There is danger in the city and the walker must learn to recognize it before it swallows him. The city enfeebles and even, occasionally, kills women, but the hazards it poses for men and male virtue are far greater. It is notable that female virtue seems barely at risk in John Gay's city, presumably because few women have any virtue to lose. The walker is assailed by dirt, disease, injury, and noxious smells, which early modern people also thought caused disease, but he gains knowledge and stature by perseverance, by his refusal to choose the easy way, and by cautiously embracing, rather than separating himself from, the life of the streets. Of course his love affair with the pavement has strict limits. As we have seen, the walker contains the threat of pollution by carefully avoiding actual conversation with women. Women are collapsed into the background, transformed into natural signposts to mark the way. Conversely, the walker actively seeks cross-class alliances with the men who make up the urban infrastructure of transport, law and order (licensed porters, watchmen, and firemen) as well as those higher up the social scale like tradesmen, who manifestly stand to benefit from the ordered city.

It all seems quite neat. And yet, the sheer magnitude of the dangers outlined in *Trivia* makes the reader wonder whether the walker actually has the fortitude to take it in his stride. An individual clearly cannot fight the miasmic evil of the city all on his own and without expert knowledge. But are the allies he is urged to find really sufficient to save him? Can he really learn to read the signs? Can the city ever actually be redeemed? *Trivia*'s final section gives one pause. It contains a series of images in fast succession. First there is a shockingly graphic description of a street prostitute that focuses on her syphilitically toothless mouth; her hollow cheeks concealed with rouge; her come-on lines—'My noble Captain! Charmer! Love! My Dear!' (III 272–4)—and her fetish-wear (III 279). Quaker get-up was apparently in fashion in Drury Lane, the residue of decades of allegations about Quaker sexual hypocrisy.[8] This is followed by the stock tale mentioned above about an honest country yeoman despoiled, infected, and ultimately unmanned by a poxy whore. The poet addresses this 'hapless Swain':

> Canst thou forgo Roast-Beef for nauseous Pills?
> How wilt thou lift to Heav'n the Eyes and Hands,
> When the long Scroll the Surgeon's fees demands!
> Or else (ye Gods avert that worst Disgrace)
> Thy ruin'd Nose falls level with thy Face,
> Then shall thy Wife thy loathsome Kiss disdain,
> And wholesome Neighbours from thy Mug refrain.
>
> (III 299–306)

Next there is the helpful watchmen scene, swiftly followed by the Mohocks. And finally there is a highly sexualized description of a coach crashing and falling in a dark night down an unmarked gap or breach in the road into the vast sewer beneath. Here the poet conjures up something very like the *vagina dentata*, the terrifying toothed vagina of myth:[9] 'Or arched Vaults their gaping Jaws extend, / Or the dark Caves to Common-Shores descend' (III 337–8). Gay is saying here that the safety of the coach interior is only illusory, but he is also revisiting one of the central metaphors of the poem: the city pavement as a kind of skin over

the top of a heaving, pestilential sewer, one that keeps erupting into daily
life via actual open sewers, like the Fleet Ditch, fish-women, predatory
prostitutes, women stallholders, and ill-concealed potholes and gaps in
the road.

Things look bad at this point. And then suddenly there is a scene
change and a serious fire breaks out in the city. This fire is deliberately
figured as a divine judgement. The poet makes explicit reference to Nero's
Rome and to 'frightful prodigies the Skies o'erspread' (III 380), and
though they are not named, Sodom and Gomorrah, the evil cities
destroyed by divine fire in Genesis 19, also float in the mind's eye. This
apocalyptic turn again suggests Gay's indebtedness to Reformation of
Manners rhetoric. In the reformers' sermons and tracts, God almost
always preferred to punish out-of-control lust (and sabbath-breaking)
by fire, and in their view London was ripe for destruction. As one
Reformation of Manners propagandist remarked darkly in 1697, 'a City
or Nation is then in very great Danger, when it abounds with those Sins
for which other Cities and Nations have been destroyed' (this in a tract
entitled *Sodom's Vices Destructive to Other Cities and States*).[10] No doubt
memories of the Great Fire of London (1666) gave such prognostications
added force.

In *Trivia* the fire does many things. It gives rise to the only unequivocally good woman in the entire poem: the tearful, prayerful mother whose
baby the brave fireman saves from the flames (III 365–8). Symbolically, at
least, the fire does constitute a quasi-divine cleansing of the moral sink-
hole that is the city. And it offers a dramatic opportunity for one group of
male allies not just to display their heroism, but to apply a technical solution to a significant urban problem: the firemen use gunpowder to blow
up adjoining buildings so as to stop the spread of the fire (III 381–6).
They could be said to vindicate the walker's identification with the
emerging municipal law and order apparatus.[11]

It is also possible to read the fire episode as an especially hyperbolic
response to the fearful, feminine danger that lurks beneath the city. The
final few couplets of the poem liken the purposeful blowing up of buildings as a fire stop to the eruption of Mount Vesuvius:

> Her sap'd Foundations shall with Thunders shake,
> And heave and toss upon the sulph'rous Lake;
> Earth's Womb at once the fiery Flood shall rend,
> And in th'Abyss her plunging Tow'rs descend.

> (III 389–92)

One possible reading of these decidedly ambiguous lines is as a metaphorical gang-rape of majestic proportions (the Towers sent plunging by the brother-firemen-allies into the rent Womb of the Earth).[12] Alternatively they could refer to the engulfing of both the fire and the phallic towers by the dark hypersexual feminine forces that lie beneath them (the Earth's womb, which is also the Abyss).[13]

Both the gang-rape reading and the engulfment one resonate with some of the larger themes of the poem. As we have seen one of the main threats posed by Gay's city is the dissolution of masculine identity in the face of both natural and supernatural feminine forces: those women who clutch at the walker's clothes, call after him seductively, menace his health and threaten to cast him into deep pits. And yet, the feminine principle, whether mythical or not, is also at the very heart of the city's allure. Perhaps this melodramatic scene is simply an ironic attempt to show us how high the stakes really are, as well as to remind us that the contest could go either way.

NOTES

1. Joseph Addison and Richard Steele, *The Spectator 1711–14*, ed. Donald F. Bond, 5 vols. (Oxford, 1965; 1987). *The Spectator* ran from 1711–12 and then resumed publication for seven more months in 1714. The classic discussion of the flâneur, a man who saunters through the city, always an observer never quite a participant, can be found in Walter Benjamin's studies of nineteenth-century Paris and of the poet Baudelaire. See among others Walter Benjamin, *The Arcades Project*, trans. Howard Eiland and Kevin McLaughlin (Cambridge, Mass, 1999). The walker and Mr Spectator are less alienated than the nineteenth-century flâneur, but there is a clear line of descent from the former to the latter.

2. For a very positive appraisal of Addison's and Steele's view of women see Katharine M. Rogers, *Feminism in Eighteenth-Century England* (Urbana, Ill., 1982), 30.

3. John Gay knew Jonathan Swift and thanks him in the preface to '*Trivia*'. Swift's views on women especially in the 'scatological' poems of the late 1720s on have been much discussed. See especially Felicity Nussbaum, *The Brink of All We Hate: English Satires on Women, 1660–1750* (Lexington, Ky., 1984), 94–116. A more sympathetic view of Swift is to be found in Rogers, *Feminism in Eighteenth-Century England*, 58–62.

4. *Trivia* III 291–2 is essentially an epitome of Proverbs 2: 16–19; 5: 3–5; 6: 24–5 and 7: 5–27.

5. For the Reformation of Manners see Margaret R. Hunt, *The Middling Sort: Commerce, Gender, and the Family in England 1680–1780* (Berkeley and

Los Angeles, 1996), 101–3, 111–15. Reformation of Manners literature attacking prostitutes is vast. See the writings of Josiah Woodward, one of the most indefatigable propagandists of the movement, for example, *Rebuke to the Sin of Uncleanness* (1704) and *The Young Man's Monitor Shewing the Great Happiness of Early Piety: And the Dreadful Consequence of Indulging Youthful Lusts* (1718).

6. Gay's earlier work *The Mohocks: A Tragi-Comical Farce* (1712) had also implied that only whores and watchmen needed to fear them.

7. One of the points Gay may be trying to make here is that, while Theseus's Ariadne may have been trustworthy, modern women decidedly are not. This contrast between mythical female virtue (the goddess Trivia herself, for example) and modern feminine wiles appears several times in the poem, though Gay is also perfectly willing to play with mythicized vice too, as in the figure of the goddess Cloacina.

8. These verses seem to presage Jonathan Swift's notorious *A Beautiful Nymph going to Bed* (1731) about a prostitute at her toilette.

9. Sigmund Freud is generally credited with having come up with the term *vagina dentata* (the toothed vagina), to describe a rather widespread mythic image that he saw as evidence for the ubiquity of the castration fantasy; Carl Jung gave it a place in his concept of the anima. The most comprehensive psycho-mythological discussion of the *vagina dentata*, heavily indebted to Jung, is Erich Neumann, *The Great Mother: An Analysis of the Archetype*, 2nd edn. (New York, 1963).

10. Josiah Woodward, *Sodom's Vices Destructive to Other Cities and States* (1697), 3. In the same tract he remarks that 'for such, who will neither by the Mercies and Judgments of God be reclaimed from Sensuality and sordid Lusts . . . They may perhaps have a little Sunshine in the Morning, as Sodom it self had; but there is a dreadful Shower of firy Indignation coming down from God to consume his Adversaries', 22. In Woodward's *Rebuke to the Sin of Uncleanness*, 17, the same theme is sounded: 'we find in the Holy Scriptures, that Sodom and Gommorah, and other cities and their Inhabitants, were destroyed by fire from Heaven for their Uncleanness'.

11. In the early eighteenth century, private fire companies fought fires, and both the night watch and the constabulary were rotated among householders, rather than being 'professionalized'. In fact one of the aims of Reformation of Manners activists was to rationalize and professionalize the constabulary, the better to get them to use their power to suppress vice. See Hunt, *Middling Sort*, 101–15.

12. The use of the feminine possessive 'her' in 'her plunging Tow'rs' refers to the gender of the city not the towers.

13. For a particularly creative discussion of themes of sexual penetration versus sexual engulfment see Joan Cocks, *The Oppositional Imagination: Feminism, Critique, and Political Theory* (1989), 150–73.

Street Style: Dress in John Gay's *Trivia*

Aileen Ribeiro

This essay approaches dress in the poem both as reality and metaphor. The poem records the factual detail of clothing in the period from the elite to the working classes, and especially the everyday practical wear seen in the streets and public spaces of London by what Daniel Defoe called 'the middle Sort',[1] that is people like himself and the author of *Trivia*.

The poem reveals dress as a signifier of luxury, of morality, and of gentility. Demotic and everyday clothing, in particular, is linked to the freedoms that many writers saw as typical of contemporary society in England. Trade assumed new importance in the political climate created by the emergence of Britain as an important power, a status sanctified by the Treaty of Utrecht (1713) which ended the protracted wars against France. Trade, Defoe stated, created wealth. England was 'the greatest trading country in the world' and London was its 'great center'.[2] London was the centre of the textile and clothing industries, which made up the greatest part of the national wealth. It was in the capital that rich clothing and accessories were most often seen in the formal clothes of the elite, the wealthy mercers' establishments in the City and Covent Garden, and in the famous shops (like modern malls) in the Royal Exchange, and the Strand. It is probably to the New Exchange in the Strand that Gay refers when he describes how in winter

> The Sempstress speeds to 'Change with red-tipt Nose;
> The *Belgian* Stove beneath her Footstool glows,
> In half-whipt Muslin Needles useless lye,
> And Shuttle-cocks across the Counter fly.

> (II 337–40)

Luxury in 'Buildings, Furniture, Equipages and Cloaths', claimed Bernard Mandeville in his famous work *The Fable of the Bees* (1714), was not necessarily a sign of pride, but encouraged trade which thrived on the processes of emulation among all classes in society.[3] In itself, luxury was not 'enervating and effeminating',[4] as some had claimed, but Mandeville commented ironically that excessive consumerism encouraged waste, a by-product of an expanding commercial society.[5]

Too much luxury in dress and appearance, however, had implications of subservience to foreign modes, both sartorially and politically. In *Trivia* there are a number of references to the foppish fashion victim:

> You'll sometimes meet a Fop, of nicest Tread,
> Whose mantling Peruke veils his empty Head,
> At ev'ry Step he dreads the Wall to lose,
> And risques, to save a Coach, his red-heel'd Shoes . . .
>
> (II 53–6)

Such a man, with his spreading wig, his ultra-genteel deportment, and elaborately stylish dress (the red heels of his shoes indicate acquaintance with court life),[6] is the opposite in appearance to the 'middle Sort' of man with his restrained and relatively unadorned clothing.

To Gay and his contemporaries, London had become rich by trade and industry, free from over-reliance on foreign imports, and noted for simpler styles of dress manufactured from a wide range of native fabrics, mainly woollens and mixed stuffs. It was a capital re-created both by rebuilding after the Great Fire, and the development of new spaces like the square. In the city, the social theorist Richard Sennett has noted, people 'sought to create modes of speech, even of dress, which would give order to the new urban situation, and demarcate this [public] life from the private domain of family and friends'.[7] Sennett does not define these new 'modes . . . of dress', except to say that they 'suited one's body and its needs', the implication being, presumably, that they were practical and comfortable. It is an oversimplification to state that a whole new genre of clothing suitable for social interaction with strangers in public places evolved at this time, for clothing has always responded to social occasions, both public and private. But by the early eighteenth century there was more emphasis on types of dress appropriate for out-of-doors and active pursuits, for example, the greatcoat and the riding cloak. This is what *Trivia* showcases as sensible street wear for London, worlds away from the artifice and affectation of high society. Such functional garments, associated particularly with the middle class, could be regarded as representing new national sensibilities and patriotism, and compared favourably with the extremes of fashion in France, which ranged from the silken splendour of the elite to the wretchedness of the poor.

For Gay, London symbolized the vitality and freedom of the nation, as distinct from Paris where 'Slav'ry treads the Street in wooden Shoes'

(I 86). In *The Complete English Tradesman* (1726), Defoe compares the insubstantial showiness or 'fine outside' of the Frenchman to the respectable, decent costume of the middle-class Englishman.[8] By the early years of the eighteenth century, encouraged by the defeat of France, movements towards a more open and democratic society, and the growth of dissenting Protestantism, dress had increasingly become a metaphor for a sober, moral, and genteel society. *Trivia* reveals it to be a key element in the civic life of the nation.

Yet *Trivia* is as much a work of literature as social reportage. We should not necessarily equate the author with the sturdy walker of London's streets, as Gay claims in the advertisement to *Trivia*. Described rather dismissively by David Piper as 'habitually lazy',[9] Gay's preference was for an easy, pleasurable life. Jonathan Swift claimed that for Gay, a 'coach and Six horses is the utmost exercise you can bear, and this onely when you can fill it with Such company as is best Suited to your tast'.[10] Nor was Gay always an advocate of the sturdy English practicalities in dress which he praises in *Trivia*. His taste in clothes, according to his friends, was luxurious. Gay happily admitted to a delight in 'silver loops [coat/waistcoat fastenings] . . . garments blue . . . lace that edged mine hat around . . . a gorgeous sword, and eke a Knot [decoration for a sword belt]'.[11] It is not surprising that to Lewis Melville, writing in 1921, Gay's 'passion for finery' was a 'weakness', although completely unexceptional for the period, and fostered perhaps by his apprenticeship to a fashionable mercer in the Strand.[12]

What *is* worthy of comment is a recent work by David Nokes which suggests that Gay's poems 'frequently betray a transvestite fascination with women's clothing, which seems to go beyond the necessary expertise of a silk-mercer's apprentice',[13] and which he ascribes to the poet's possible homosexuality. Nokes appears to deplore Gay's 'fetishistic' obsession with the details of fashion, especially in his mock-heroic poem *The Fan* (1714),[14] but these lyrical word pictures are essential to the theme and structure of the work, and some of his finest writing. Indeed, in an essay in *The Guardian* (1713), Gay comments that dress parallels poetry in 'moving the Passions'.[15] In *Trivia*, on the other hand, Gay's passion for fashion is only allowed an occasional appearance; telling and informed though his comments are, his main concern is with the everyday clothing of ordinary people.

The longest section of the poem, Book II, describes some of the hazards encountered when 'Walking the Streets by Day'. In a city where life was lived very much out of doors, 'nothing is more remarkable than the hurries of the people' in the 'publick streets', noted Defoe in the

1720s.[16] Gay recounts the noise, confusion, and the damage that could be caused both to people and their effects in the streets. These included drunken chairmen who sometimes overturned their passengers, and the hackney coachmen 'lashing by'—an evocative phrase for the ancestors of our modern taxis as they hurtled along. Most dangerous were the carts and wagons rushing through the streets, and especially the dustcarts, whose aggressive driving often resulted in disaster for those in their path. As an incident in the class war, for example, a dustcart demolishes a 'gilded Chariot' driven by a beau—an ultra fashionable man, 'a Fop, a Spark, a Spruce-Gentleman'[17]—in an 'embroider'd Coat'. The 'lac'd Charioteer', whose lace refers here both to gold/silver braid on the suit, and to linen lace shirt and sleeve ruffles, is overturned and covered in 'Black Floods of Mire' (II 523–34).[18] Incidental damage was often caused to clothing by the implements of trade, the dustcart with its flying ashes, the chimney sweep who 'marks with sooty Stains the heedless Throng' (II 34), the chandler whose candles spoil garments with 'Tallow spots' (II 41), and the perfumer with his oils and unguents.

The prudent walker should skirt around those sweeping the streets in front of their shops, otherwise his stockings would be covered with 'spatt'ring Dirt' (II 94). The barber or his apprentice carrying powdered wigs through the city streets was a frequent sight and also someone to avoid, as was the fop with his vast wig, 'Lest from his Shoulder Clouds of Powder fly' (II 58). London was a notoriously dirty city, and apart from linen, most clothes could not be washed. Dry cleaning was rudimentary, if, for example, the walker's 'hapless Coat' were to be stained by 'Water, dash'd from fishy Stalls' (III 105–6). Water, in the form of rain, drenched wigs and spoiled clothing. Swift records in his poem *Description of a City Shower* (1710):

> Ah! Where must needy Poet seek for Aid,
> When Dust and Rain at once his Coat invade;
> His only Coat, where Dust confus'd with Rain
> Roughen the Nap, and leave a mingled Stain.[19]

In his poem Swift has a typically apocalyptic account of the result of heavy rain. It caused the 'kennels', which were drains or sometimes open sewers in the streets, to overflow.

> Sweepings from Butchers Stalls, Dung, Guts and Blood,
> Drown'd Puppies, stinking Sprats, all drench'd in Mud,
> Dead Cats and Turnip-Tops come tumbling down the Flood.[20]

Gay, less graphic in *his* description while admitting his debt to Swift here, is more concerned with advice to the walker when rain is threatened.

Prevention being more sensible than cure, the walker needs to be aware of the coming of rain, such as the 'creaking Noise' of the 'swinging Signs' (I 157–8) which hung outside shops and indicated their wares and services to a largely illiterate populace. Some of these 'Signs' took the form of images, some the objects on sale such as stockings: 'On Hosier's Poles depending Stockings ty'd, / Flag with the slacken'd Gale, from side to side' (I 165–6).

This quotation comes from Book I of *Trivia*, where Gay deals with 'the Implements for walking the Streets, and Signs of the Weather'. This section of the poem is of greatest interest to the historian of dress because of the information presented, both prescriptive and descriptive, on practical clothing for the walker of London streets. The title-page illustration depicts such 'Implements' in schematic form, like a heraldic blazon or coat of arms. There is a flapped hat at the top, with a cane on each side of it. A man's greatcoat is on the left and a woman's hooded cloak is on the right, both with an umbrella. At the bottom are two fur muffs, a fan, a square-toed masculine shoe, and a female patten. In spite of the equal attention given in the illustration to both genders, most of the detail on clothing in *Trivia* refers to men, as most likely to be walking in the streets. There were more dangers for women, especially those walking alone, and more suspicion attached to their motives for so doing.

For men, clothes and accessories that were practical and protective were of prime importance. First, the 'prudent Walker' should provide himself with sensible shoes, not of soft fine leathers like 'the *Spanish* or *Morocco* Hide' (I 29–30) with high heels and a scalloped top, but sturdy English cowhide with well-nailed soles. Such a shoe would have a long square toe (not too short in front or it would cause corns), modest heels, and would fit close at the sides. Otherwise, 'The sudden Turn may stretch the swelling Vein, / Thy cracking Joint unhinge, or Ankle sprain' (I 37–8). Good shoes of this kind had medium-height square heels and plain buckles. They were 'straights' which meant that they were symmetrical for use on either foot.[21] Men's shoes were usually black, and *Trivia* notes the importance of shoe-cleaning to preserve this colour.[22] '*Clean your Honour's Shoes*' (II 216) was a familiar cry by the 'Black Youth' (Gay's words), the shoe-cleaners with their shoe polish made of whale oil and soot, in the streets around Charing Cross and Whitehall. The practitioners of this trade (sons of the goddess Cloacina, who made dirt and mud in order to create the need for footwear to be cleaned) 'With nimble Skill the glossy Black Renew' (II 156).

Next to the shoes, the choice of outer garment was crucial, especially in bad weather: 'Nor should it prove thy less important Care, / To chuse a proper Coat for Winter's Wear' (I 41–2). Furs were impractical in the rain, and, although acceptable abroad, especially in Italy, were inappropriate in London: '. . . for who would wear / Amid the Town the Spoils of *Russia's* Bear?' (I 49–50). Perhaps they were regarded as too opulent, too 'barbaric', and too un-English.[23] The *roquelaure*, a fitted, shaped cloak, restricted the arms and hands, and the *bavaroy*, a looped coat, often embroidered, was the preserve of the fop, along with the lace-trimmed cloak.

The solution was the English greatcoat or *surtout*, a capacious collared coat made loose and full without the rigid pleats of the formal coat, and which could either be buttoned or wrapped over at the front: 'That Garment best the Winter's Rage defends, / Whose shapeless Form in ample Plaits depends' (I 55–6).[24] For Gay such a garment was a metaphor for the virtuous simplicities of his class: 'O rather give me sweet Content on Foot / Wrapt in my Vertue and a good *Surtout!*' (II 589–90).

With regard to the fabric of his coat, the sensible walker should lay aside lightweight woollens or mixed stuffs such as doily, drugget, and camlet.[25] Even frieze, a coarse napped wool, was prone to get soaked quickly in the rain, although later Gay refers approvingly to a 'double-button'd Frieze' coat (I 193). The most effective material proved to be kersey, a tightly woven and impermeable woollen cloth. Originating in Suffolk, by the early eighteenth century it was manufactured in the West Country and the North of England.

An essential implement for the cautious walker, according to *Trivia*, was the cane, which ensured a steady walk, as well as acting in a protective capacity. Canes were often luxurious objects. *Trivia* refers to beaux with amber-headed canes for 'empty Show' (I 68), that is, carried beneath the arm. But Gay stresses the need for more functionality in such an accessory, which serves to underline the middle-class status of its owner. Armed with a 'strong Cane' (I 61), the walker can summon a coach or a chair, and use it as a weapon in unruly streets, against footpads and other turbulent characters.[26] The vigorous use of the cane also ensured that the pedestrian was not beaten away from the 'Wall', the protection afforded by the inner side of the street closest to the buildings and furthest away from the traffic. Chairmen, for example, although they were supposed to keep outside the posts that marked the pavement, tended to 'press near

'When all the Mall in leafy Ruin lies'

8. *A View of the Mall from St James's Park* by Marco Ricci (c.1709–10).

the Wall' (III 154). In a period when politeness was no longer the exclusive preserve of the court and nobility, but part of decorous behaviour
based on virtue, Gay urges the walker to give the wall to the aged, the
infirm, the 'hooded Maid', and even the empty-headed fop. However
the bully with his cocked hat 'edg'd round with tarnish'd Lace' (II 60)
should not be thus accommodated. Such a swaggerer with quasi-military
airs, often erroneously claiming to have fought in the recent wars, was a
frequent trope of contemporary journalism and plays.

In bad weather, the sensible walker chose appropriate headwear. On
his head, a 'flapping Hat' with uncocked brim was better able to protect
him from wind and rain. Hats were made of felt, the matting of fibrous
materials such as fur or wool. The best fur was beaver, referred to by Gay
as 'spacious Beaver' (II 277), and finding new sources was one of the main
reasons behind the exploration of North America by the Hudson's Bay
Company, whose charter dates from 1669.[27] Such a hat 'unloop'd' (with
the sides let down to form a brim) also helped to give better cover to the
wig, which tended to drop out of curl in the rain and become 'Clotted
and strait' (I 206). At the time of *Trivia*, nearly all men wore wigs, so
as they became 'uncurl'd' in the rain, the best advice was to select 'thy
worst Wig, long us'd to Storms' (I 126), probably the oldest and least in
fashion.

Wigs were essential to the male appearance, indicating status and character. In an essay in *The Guardian* (1713), Gay refers to them as 'a kind of
Index of the Mind'. A full-bottomed wig, he claims, 'denotes the lawyer
and the Politician', whilst a man with a vast powdered wig was 'less curious in the furniture of the inward Recesses of the Skull',[28] like *Trivia*'s
'Fop of nicest [or most elegant and genteel] Tread, / Whose mantling
Peruke veils his empty Head' (II 53–4). A man of the 'middle Sort',
the kind we presume Gay's walker to be, would probably have worn a
shoulder-length bob-wig, an informal or undressed style without the
elaborate curls of the formal periwig.

Gay was a precise and perceptive recorder of fashion as well as of everyday clothing. In a period when Versailles dictated fashion for women, he
noted in *The Guardian* of 1713 the importance of France as the 'Fountain
of Dress, as Greece was of Literature'.[29] French fashions and accessories
were widely available in London, sold at expensive shops in the area near
St James's Palace, the Strand, and Covent Garden, which catered to the
elite and those aspiring to be so. According to John Macky's *A Journey
through England* (1714), Pall Mall was a highly desirable neighbourhood
because it was close to the theatres and the coffee and chocolate houses.

Even more important, it was close to St James's Palace, the main seat of royal power after the burning down of Whitehall in 1698, and to the Park 'where the best Company frequents'.[30] Pall Mall was the most refined street in London and a clear signifier of luxury. On its north side were fashionable shops—milliners, perfumers, and peruke-makers—and on the south side adjoining St James's Palace were many of the town houses of the nobility. In *Trivia* Gay exclaims: 'O bear me to the Paths of fair Pell-mell, / Safe are thy Pavements, grateful is thy Smell!' (II 257–8)

Pursuing this olfactory theme, the poet notes how 'Shops breathe Perfumes, thro' sashes Ribbons glow (II 263). This phrase could refer to the broad ribbands worn across the chest of knightly orders such as the Garter and the Thistle. It might also evoke the bright knots of silk ribbons worn on the dresses of fashionable elite women, whose gatherings could be seen through the sash-windows newly in vogue.

Gay, through his previous apprenticeship at a fashionable mercer's in the Strand, was well placed to observe the latest styles.[31] The editors of the Oxford edition of Gay's *Poetry and Prose* (1974) comment: 'To judge from Gay's many references to fashion in his works, he retained mainly happy memories of his years behind the counter or standing in the shop door watching the traffic in the Strand'.[32] When he died in 1732 his body lay in state in Exeter Exchange on the north side of the Strand, before burial in Westminster Abbey. Such a temporary place of rest, famous for its shops selling luxury goods, 'was almost as fitting as the permanent [place of rest] for one who had begun life as a silk mercer's apprentice in the same street, and had both glorified and satirized fashion in his writing'.[33]

This is an apt point, for Gay relishes the details of women's costume and accessories, even as he purports to criticize what he refers to in *The Fan* (1714) as 'the inconstant Equipage of Female Dress' (I 234). Thus he subscribes to the conventional view of the time, which compared the so-called 'perfect' and modest dress of the past with the ever-changing and immodest styles of his own time (I 199–206).[34] In *Trivia*, as in *The Fan*, Gay appears, perhaps tongue-in-cheek, to hold the view that women in this 'lavish Age' were particularly susceptible to corruption through extremes in luxury, notably dress. Pursuing the pedestrian theme of the poem, he claims that in the past women *had* to walk more, for 'Coaches and Chariots yet unfashion'd lay, / Nor late invented Chairs perplex'd the Way' (I 103–4).

Such healthy exercise gave a glowing complexion and a perfect figure through 'unartful Charms' (I 108), rather than the artificial shape created by the corset or stays. Gay bolsters his argument that women's present-day clothing made walking difficult, by exaggerating the extent of their tight-fitting, decorated shoes, intended to create the fashionable 'narrow Step', but which caused a limp. The reference to the foot 'bound' in 'braided Gold' suggests a kind of Chinese foot-binding, disabling im-mobility. Furthermore, the woman of fashion was hampered by the voluminous skirts of her dress, specifically the 'long trailing Manteau [which] sweeps the Ground' (I 110). The *manteau* or *mantua*—the name suggesting a silk from the Italian city and then by synecdoche the dress itself—was a formal gown with a long skirt held up at the back, by pins, buttons or loops, to form an elaborate 'bustle'. In *The Fan* Gay ponders on 'How to adjust the Manteau's sweeping Train' (I 236).

As a contrast to the 'proud Lady' with her ostentatiously cumbersome dress, which implies the help of a servant to arrange the mantua and to hand her in and out of her coach, Gay focuses on the middle-class 'Huswife' in her practical walking costume of hooded cloak or 'Riding-hood', umbrella, and iron-shod overshoes or pattens. Contemporary genre scenes[35] often depict the 'Riding-hood' which was usually red in colour (thus 'Little Red Riding Hood'), voluminous in cut, and with slits for the arms. It was made of sturdy wool or a strong silk/wool fabric like camlet.

Such a garment could be worn by women of all social classes, although by the time Defoe published *The Complete English Tradesman* in 1726 it had become more associated with the middle class, and with the wives and daughters of merchants and well-to-do tradesmen. The wardrobe of the wife of a prosperous grocer from Horsham in Sussex, for example, included a 'Riding-hood of English worstead-Camblet made at Norwich'.[36] This is the sense in which Gay refers to the hooded cloak in *Trivia*: 'Good Huswives all the Winter's Rage despise, / Defended by the Riding-hood's Disguise' (I 209–10). The notion of disguise here signifies modesty and practicality, as perhaps is also the case in the lines by Gay's *bête noire* John Durant Breval in his poem *The Art of Dress* (1717): 'When for the Morning Air abroad you steal, / The Cloak of Camlet may your Charms conceal'.[37] There is also the implication that the riding-hood was deceiving and dissembling, for it could disguise the class and status of the wearer, an obsessional worry in eighteenth-century English discourse. In *Trivia* Gay describes a harlot thus concealed. The hooded cloak could even hide stolen goods, as the anonymous author of *Female Folly: or, The Plague of a Woman's Riding-Hood* (1713) suggests.[38]

It has been noted that the engraved frontispiece to *Trivia* depicts the hooded cloak, which can also be seen on a small figure in the illustrated vignette to Book I. Here the pyramidal shape of the woman hints at the hooped underskirt worn beneath, a fashion which was first noted in *The Tatler* during the winter of 1709, as 'a particular Swelling in the Petticoats of several Ladies in and about this great City'.[39] Breval, in his mocking work *The Petticoat: An Heroi-Comical Poem* (1716), claims that as the author of *Trivia* had discussed the invention of the patten (and the eponymous accessory in *The Fan*) so he (Breval) would describe the origins of the petticoat. This garment in the eighteenth century was the name for the outer skirt, but Breval's main concern is the opportunity to poke fun at the hoop (a coarse linen underskirt extended by horizontal bands of whalebone), which the poem claims was invented to hide the pregnancy resulting from the nymph Chloe's affair with Thyrsis:

> The stiffen'd Canvas, now, the Nymph displays,
> The stiffen'd Canvas, now, the Touch obeys;
> Now Ribs of Whale, with artful Care she bends,
> And Each in their adapted Place extends:
> The Whalebones spread the swelling Canvas wide,
> And stretch'd their stubborn Lengths from Side to Side.[40]

By the time of *Trivia*, the hoop was quite large. In his poem *The Art of Dress* (1717) Breval claimed it was inspired by the 'Roman Cupola' of St Paul's cathedral.[41] Gay's intention, perhaps conveyed to the illustrator of *Trivia*, was not to exaggerate the size of the hoop, but to suggest a modest version appropriate for the female walker.

Such a woman, whether a 'walking Maid' (I 218) or a 'frugal Dame' (I 281), found that the protection of 'th' *Umbrella's* oily Shed' (I 211) was an added necessity in rainy weather. Umbrellas were waxed or oiled to keep out the rain. Swift in his *Description of a City Shower* refers to the 'tuck'd-up Semptress', with skirts hitched up as a protective device in bad weather, walking 'with hasty Strides / While Streams run down her oil'd Umbrella's Sides'.[42] Until the mid-eighteenth century, when the umbrella for men was introduced into England by Jonas Hanway, it was almost exclusively a feminine accessory. A correspondent in *The Female Tatler* (1709) wondered sarcastically if 'the young Gentleman borrowing the Umbrella belonging to Wills Coffee House of the Mistress' would also like to borrow the maid's pattens so that he might be 'dry from Head to Foot'.[43]

The patten was an overshoe with a wooden sole raised on an iron ring, protecting the fabric or leather shoe from the mud and rain of the streets. Randle Holme's *Academy of Armory* (1688) has a comprehensive

description: 'The Patten is . . . a thing of Wood like a Shooe sole, with
Straps over it, to tye over the Shooe, having an iron at the bottom, to raise
the Wearer thereof from the Dirt, by means whereof clean Shooes may
be preserved though they go in foul Streets . . .'[44] Such a practical form
of footwear was singled out for praise by Gay, for pattens were worn by
middle-class and working women, as distinct from the fashionable elite
who rarely walked in the streets. In a lyrical and wonderfully inventive
account of the origin of the patten—a famous episode in *Trivia*—Gay
describes how Vulcan, the god of fire, courted 'the bloomy Maiden' Patty,
the daughter of a 'goodly Yeoman' from Lincolnshire, by making her iron
overshoes. 'Above the Mire her shelter'd Steps to raise, / And bear her
safely through the Wintry Ways' (I 273–4). As a result: 'The Patten now
supports each frugal Dame, / Which from the blue-ey'd *Patty* takes the
Name' (I 281–2).

Book III of *Trivia*, 'Of Walking the Streets by Night' is more sombre in
tone, for London outside the hours of daylight presented most danger,
and the walker needed 'constant Vigilance' (III 111). The main problem
was theft, 'the archetypal Augustan crime',[45] as reflected in contemporary journalism, the paintings and engravings of Hogarth, and such
novels as Defoe's *Moll Flanders*. On the streets, small and expensive items
like watches and snuff-boxes were easy prey, especially when people left
the theatre, as *Trivia* warned:

> I need not strict enjoyn the Pocket's Care,
> When from the crouded *Play* thou lead'st the Fair;
> Who has not here, or Watch, or Snuff-Box lost,
> Or Handkerchiefs that *India's* Shuttle boast?
>
> (III 255–8)

The handkerchief was often a luxury accessory, made of silk or printed
cotton from India, or fine linen from Flanders. Gay comments that a
well-known ploy was for ballad singers or 'Syrens' to attract a crowd while
their confederates stole 'Cambrick Handkerchiefs' from unsuspecting
bystanders (III 79–82). Wigs, too, being expensive, were highly prized,
especially those made of blonde hair, and thieves were even audacious
enough to steal them from their wearers' heads.

> Nor is thy Flaxen Wigg with Safety worn;
> High on the Shoulder, in a Basket born,
> Lurks the sly Boy; whose Hand to Rapine bred,
> Plucks off the curling Honours of thy Head.
>
> (III 55–8)

Clothing and accessories, which provided a quarter of the nation's annual expenditure,[46] were expensive commodities in proportion to other goods and services, and by the lower classes in particular they were regarded as a portable form of property. Stealing these items was the most common type of theft, as the Old Bailey Proceedings record. A rough survey of cases brought to court in 1716, the year when *Trivia* was published, reveals the theft of shirts, coats, greatcoats, mantuas, petticoats, stays, calico gowns, aprons, riding hoods, shoes, canes, and wigs. The sentences for those found guilty were often severe.[47]

Another kind of theft which Gay warns his readers to beware was that of virtue, due to the temptations posed by prostitutes who loitered in Drury Lane and the maze of streets off the Strand. Such 'Night-Walkers', claimed John Macky, made it impossible 'to walk the Streets, and especially about the Play-Houses, without being picked up by this Sort of Vermine'.[48] The category of 'prostitute' covered a multitude of sinners, from the piteous and ragged creatures at the very bottom of the social ladder, to the 'elegant' 'London Curtezan' from Laroon's *Cries of London*, in her mantua, lace-trimmed petticoat, and beribboned headdress. The harlot described in *Trivia* wears a spurious imitation of fashion, but without stays, the most basic signifier of female respectability.

> No stubborn Stays her yielding Shape embrace;
> Beneath the Lamp her tawdry Ribbons glare,
> The new-scower'd Manteau, and the slattern Air;
> High-draggled Petticoats her Travels show,
> And hollow Cheeks with artful Blushes glow . . .
>
> (III 268–72)

Such a woman revealed her status by her tawdry clothing—cheap and gaudy ribbons, a mantua 'new-scower'd' (second-hand and refurbished), her skirts ('High-draggled') lifted up as she walked the streets—and her painted face ('artful Blushes'). She is Protean in disguise, though on the surface only, sometimes wearing a hooded cloak ('Riding-hood'), or a scarf ('muffled Pinner') (III 275–6). Holding an 'empty Bandbox' for collars, she may pretend to be on an errand from one of the fashionable milliner's shops in the Strand (III 277–8). Sometimes 'Her Fan will pat thy Cheek', a grotesque parody of an elegant gesture of intimacy (III 283). Other favourite sartorial incarnations for prostitutes were mourning[49] and Quaker dress, both of which might have added an extra frisson to a sexual encounter: 'Nay, she will oft' the Quaker's Hood prophane, / And trudge demure the Rounds of *Drury-Lane*'

(III 279–80). It was a widely held belief that Quakers were hypocrites, whose sanctity was feigned, and whose simplicity in costume—for women, a plain dark woollen dress and plain linen collar and cap—was just as contrived as high fashion. *The Female Tatler* (1709) has a description at an India goods shop in London of 'a couple of quality Quakers'. Their 'clothes were costly without making any show, and though they abominate profane pinners and topknots, yet by the disposition of their locks and the artful crimping of their hoods upon wires, they showed themselves equally vain, and that they had taken as much pains to be particular as other ladies do to appear like the rest of the world'.[50]

Trivia celebrates all aspects of life—even the nasty and brutish—of the bustling metropolis, an increasingly popular theme with artists and writers by the early eighteenth century. The title of one of Gérard de Lairesse's chapters in his *The Art of Painting* (1707) is 'The Nature of City-like Subjects; which daily afford plentiful matter for a modern Painter'.[51] In *Trivia* Gay paints word pictures of 'City-like Subjects'—the bustling markets, the street Cries, the frozen Thames, the changing seasons, and the trades and pastimes of London. *Trivia* is not so much a microcosm of the social structure of the capital, as a practical guide, a lively description, a literary discourse, and a moral homily. To these ends, Gay uses dress to depict those who walk, work, and play in London.

NOTES

1. Daniel Defoe, *The Review*, vol. 6, no. 40 (7 July 1709), 158.

2. Daniel Defoe, *The Complete English Tradesman* (1726), 369. He also noted the importance of tradesmen: 'Their wealth at this time out-does that of the like rank of any nation in Europe' (380). Gay's line in *Trivia*: 'Now Industry awakes her busy Sons' (II 21) is partly inspired by similar thoughts of London as the capital of trade.

3. Bernard Mandeville, *The Fable of the Bees, or Private Vices, Publick Benefits* (1714), 90–1, and *passim*. The success of trade enabled more people from more social classes to wear better clothes in order to make a good impression: 'People where they are not known, are generally honour'd according to their Cloaths and other Accoutrements they have about them' (103).

4. Mandeville, *Fable*, 96. Typical of the numerous anti-luxury publications is Erasmus Jones, *Luxury, Pride, and Vanity, The Bane of the British Nation* (1735) and J. Philemerus (pseud.), *Of Luxury, more particularly with respect to Apparel* (1736). For useful surveys of the luxury debate in the eighteenth century see John Sekora, *Luxury: The Concept in Western Thought from Eden to Smollett* (Baltimore, 1977), and Maxine Berg and Elizabeth Eger (eds.),

Luxury in the Eighteenth Century: Debates, Desires, and Delectable Goods (Basingstoke, 2003).

5. Mandeville, *Fable*, unpaginated preface. He notes how 'dirty Streets are a necessary Evil' of London. On the subject of waste see Stephen Copley and Ian Haywood, 'Luxury, Refuse, and Poetry: John Gay's *Trivia*' in Peter Lewis and Nigel Wood (eds.), *John Gay and the Scriblerians* (1988), 62–82.

6. Red-heeled shoes were first worn by Louis XIV and his courtiers at Versailles.

7. Richard Sennett, *The Fall of Public Man* (1986), 18.

8. Defoe, *Complete English Tradesman*, 319.

9. David Piper, *Catalogue of Seventeenth-Century Portraits in the National Portrait Gallery 1625–1714* (Cambridge, 1963), 134.

10. John Gay, *Poetry and Prose*, ed. Vinton A. Dearing and Charles E. Beckwith (Oxford, 1974) ii. 548.

11. From the prologue to Gay's poem *The Shepherd's Week* (1714). A letter from Pope (1713) to Swift refers to Gay spending money on 'buttons and loops for his coat'. Both quotations are in Lewis Melville, *Life and Letters of John Gay* (1921), 8–9.

12. There is some confusion as to whether Gay was apprenticed to a draper or a mercer (see David Nokes, *John Gay: A Profession of Friendship* (Oxford, 1995), 35), although these categories were often blurred with regard to small shops. The New Exchange in the Strand was noted in particular for its shops selling luxury goods such as millinery, a term that included not only hats and headdresses, but a wide range of lace, linen, gloves, hoops, and silks, which the mercer sold. Robert Campbell's guide to the trades and professions of London, *The London Tradesman* (1747), distinguishes the 'Woollen-Draper', who sells mainly woollen fabrics, or mixed cloths of wool and silk, from the mercer, who 'deals in Silks, Velvets, Brocades, and an innumerable Train of expensive Trifles for the Ornament of the Fair Sex'. The mercer 'must dress neatly, and affect a Court Air' and as he 'traficks most with the Ladies, [he] has a small Dash of their Effeminacy in his Constitution' (197). Given Gay's preference for the minutiae of women's dress, it seems more plausible that he worked for a mercer at the New Exchange in the Strand.

13. Nokes, *John Gay*, 48.

14. Nokes remarks on what he terms Gay's 'fetishistic fascination with the details of feminine underwear' (49) in regard to such lines in *The Fan* (1714) as: 'How the strait Stays the slender Waste constrain, / How to adjust the Manteau's sweeping Train? / What Fancy can the Petticoat surround, / With the Capacious Hoop of Whalebone bound' (I 235–8). But stays were essential to create the fashionable shape, and the 'Petticoat' was the outer skirt, not an item of underwear.

15. Gay, *Poetry and Prose*, ii. 460.

16. Daniel Defoe, *A Tour through the Whole Island of Great Britain*, ed. P. N. Furbank and W. R. Owens (New Haven, 1991), 160, 162.

17. Nicholas Bailey, *Universal Etymological English Dictionary* (1721).

18. Such incidents as decribed in *Trivia* feature frequently in contemporary journalism and plays. In Susannah Centlivre's *The Beau's Duel: or A Soldier for the Ladies* (1702), the foppish Sir William Mode complains of a 'dirty Dray-man' who bedaubs his new suit which had cost him £50 (Act II, Scene i).

19. *The Tatler*, 238 (17 October 1710), lines 27–30.

20. Ibid., lines 61–3.

21. Shoes were 'straights' until the end of the eighteenth century. The best shoes came from Northampton; see Defoe, *Complete English Tradesman*, 401.

22. An advertisement in *The Tatler* 193 (1–4 July 1710) commends 'Spanish blacking' for men's shoes, claiming that it did not stain the hands or stockings, nor produce a 'noisom Stink'.

23. This dislike of wearing fur may also be due to an embryonic sense of what we might call the animal rights movement, or at least an acknowledgement of the part played by animals in what Pope calls the 'vast chain of being'. In his *Essay on Man* (1733) he writes of 'the fur that warms a monarch warm'd a bear' (III 44). The anonymous author of *England's Vanity* (1683) refers to the way in which 'we . . . rob and spoil all Creatures . . . to cover our backs and to adorn our bodies withal; from some we take their wool, from many their Skins, from diverse their Furrs' (132).

24. An alternative variant to line 56 reads: 'Whose ample Form without one Plait depends'. Seemingly contradictory, either line makes sense in contemporary terms, for 'plait' has two meanings. The greatcoat has loose folds ('ample Plaits'), and lacks the stiffened side pleats (or plaits) which denoted the formal, less practical coat.

25. Doily was a light woollen stuff; drugget and camlet were sometimes mixed with linen or silk. Doily was named after a well-known linen-draper's shop in the Strand, and was, according to Eustace Budgell, cheap and genteel. See *The Spectator*, 283 (24 January 1712). In *Trivia*, Gay specifically refers to 'the Camlet's cockled Grain' (I 46), that is, a watered stuff of wool/silk, with a wavy surface. See Defoe, *Complete English Tradesman*, for a discussion of native manufactures of woollens and stuffs (393–403 and *passim*).

26. Canes could also provide some defence against the bands of street marauders known as Mohocks. In *Trivia* Gay refers to these men—'Who has not trembled at the *Mohock's* Name?' (III 326)—about whom in 1712 he had published *The Mohocks: A Tragi-Comical Farce*.

27. Previously, most beaver came from the Baltic, but supplies were in decline by this time. On the hat trade, see David Corner, 'The Tyranny of Fashion: The Case of the Felt-Hatting Trade in the Late Seventeenth and Eighteenth Centuries', in N. B. Harte (ed.), *Fabrics and Fashions: Studies in the Economic and Social History of Dress*, Textile History, 22 (1991), 153–78.

28. Gay, *Poetry and Prose*, ii. 461.

29. Ibid.

30. John Macky, *A Journey through England* (1714), 107.
31. As well as the New Exchange, there were also Exeter Exchange and Middle Exchange in the Strand. Defoe noted: 'He that sets up in the Strand or near the Exchange, is likely to sell more rich silks, more fine hollands, more fine broad-cloths, more fine toys and trinkets, than one of the same trade, setting up in the skirts of the town.' See Defoe, *Complete English Tradesman*, 101. The 'Exchange' in this context is the original trading place in the City of London, the Royal Exchange rebuilt after the Great Fire of 1666.
32. Gay, *Poetry and Prose*, i. 2. We can't say if this was the case or not, but certainly Gay learned much information on fashion during this early part of his life, which he later put to good use.
33. Gay, *Poetry and Prose*, i. 15.
34. See also John D. Breval's satirical verse *The Art of Dress* (1717), which he claims is the first work wherein dress is 'wholly the Subject', the theme of which is the supposed simplicity of female appearance in the past. Women 'Guiltless of Pride, in DRESS took no delight' (line 6).
35. For example, Joseph van Aken's *Covent Garden Market*, *c.*1730 (Museum of London) and Pieter Angillis's *Vegetable Seller in Covent Garden*, *c.*1726 (Yale Center for British Art, New Haven).
36. Defoe, *Complete English Tradesman*, 403. See also Ursula Priestley, 'The Marketing of Norwich Stuffs, *c.*1660–1730', in Harte (ed.), *Fabrics and Fashions*, 193–209. Red riding hoods were much prized for their practicality and warmth. They feature among the stolen goods in the *Old Bailey Proceedings* (**www.oldbaileyonline.org**). For example, on 13 January 1716, one Deborah Green from Shadwell in the East End of London was tried and acquitted for the theft of a 'worsted Camblet Riding Hood, value 10s.' (t17160113–42).
37. Breval, *The Art of Dress*, lines 313–14.
38. Anonymous, *Female Folly: or, The Plague of a Woman's Riding-Hood* (1713), 2. The author notes that such a garment can hide the 'bad Cloathing' of prostitutes, and concludes that it is only suitable wear for Quakers.
39. *The Tatler*, 113 (27–9 December 1709).
40. Breval, *The Petticoat: An Heroi-Comical Poem* (1716), lines 264–9.
41. Breval, *Art of Dress*, line 205. This was not an original comment, having first been made by Steele in *The Tatler*, 116 (3–5 January 1710).
42. Swift in *The Tatler*, 288 (17 October 1710), lines 37–8.
43. Quoted in Aileen Ribeiro, 'Men and Umbrellas in the Eighteenth Century', *Journal of the Royal Society of Arts*, 5362 (September 1986), 654. There is some semantic confusion in the use of the word umbrella, which we understand as providing protection from rain. But it derives from the Italian 'ombrella', as in providing shade, and Nicholas Bailey's *Universal Etymological English Dictionary* (1721) describes an 'umbrello' as 'a sort of Skreen that is held over the Head for preserving from the Sun or Rain'. In

Trivia Gay makes a comparison between the oriental splendours of the 'umbrella' as protecting '*Persian* Dames' from the sun (I 213), or as an accessory of state held over the head of 'Eastern Monarchs' (I 216).

44. Randle Holme, *An Academy of Armoury* (Chester, 1688), Book III: 14.

45. Pat Rogers, *The Augustan Vision* (1978), 99.

46. Harte, 'The Economics of Clothing in the Late Seventeenth Century', in Harte (ed.), *Fabrics and Fashions*, 278.

47. *Old Bailey Proceedings* (**www.oldbaileyonline.org**). Note two examples from 1716: Edward Spencer was tried on 11 April for stealing a periwig worth 35*s*. and a cane valued at 2*s*. He was sentenced to death (t17160411–21). On 17 May, Martha Green was tried for the theft of '1 Poplin Mantua Gown and Petticoat, value 20*s*., another petticoat value 8*s*., 1 Pair of Stays 15*s*.' and 'Burnt in the Hand', i.e., branded (t17160517–19). 'The Goods were found in Rag Fair', a famous second-hand clothes fair in Rosemary Lane near the Tower of London. Another well-known place for second-hand clothes, generally of a superior quality, was Monmouth Street, off Charing Cross Road, which Gay refers to in *Trivia* (II 548).

48. Macky, *A Journey*, 195.

49. *The Spectator*, 410 (20 June 1712) describes a woman of dubious virtue 'dressed in a black tabby Mantua and petticoat, without Ribbonds; her Linnen striped Muslin, and the whole in an agreeable Second-Mourning; decent Dresses being often affected by the Creatures of the Town, at once consulting Cheapness and Modesty'.

50. Fidelis Morgan (ed.), *The Female Tatler* (1992), 136. See also Susan Centlivre's play *The Beau's Duel: or A Soldier for the Ladies* (1702) for similar attitudes towards female Quakers.

51. Gérard de Lairesse, *The Art of Painting*, trans. John Fritsch (1738), 137.

Gay's *Trivia*: Walking the Streets of Rome

Susanna Morton Braund

Before embarking on his poem, Gay makes a triple declaration of his classical framework, first, in the title, *Trivia*, the Latin name meaning 'Crossroads' given to the goddess Hecate;[1] second, in his epigraph, a quotation from Virgil's *Eclogues*; and third, in the further two-line quotation from Virgil which concludes his 'Advertisement'. In this essay I shall explore the significance of Gay's classical framework, intertexts, and allusions. Since *Trivia* is a work of satire, we might expect to be overwhelmed by echoes of the works of the Roman satirists Horace and Juvenal. These we can identify, for sure, but more significant is Gay's deployment of epic allusions to Homer, Virgil, and Ovid, and still more significant is his self-presentation as an expert, in obvious imitation of the Roman didactic poets Lucretius (*De Rerum Natura*) and Virgil (*Georgics*). My analysis of *Trivia*'s classical antecedents will reveal that Gay moves freely between all the genres of Latin poetry which use the hexameter—epic in its heroic and didactic forms, pastoral, and satire—in a way which suggests that he was aware of their generic interconnectedness.[2] My essay, then, has a twofold aim. First, to demonstrate to students and scholars of English literature the depth and breadth of Gay's classical learning, not simply by identifying his allusions (which is done competently by Dearing and Beckwith and other scholars[3]), but by exploring how he uses classical material to structure his poem and bolster his voice of authority. Second, to demonstrate to students and scholars of classical literature that Gay had some special insights into the classical poetry which he uses in this poem. It is my contention that in walking the literal streets of London, Gay shows that he knows how to walk the poetic streets of Rome.

TRIVIA AS PASTORAL?

A puzzle is set up right away. Gay subtitles his poem 'The Art of Walking the Streets of London', which clearly announces his didactic pose, but immediately offers as epigraph a line from Virgil's pastoral poetry, the opening line of *Eclogue* 9, *Quo te Moeri pedes? An, quo via ducit, in Urbem?* ('Where are you off to, Moeris? Are you following the path, headed to the city?') The difference between Virgil's pastoral *Eclogues* and his didactic epic *Georgics*, which takes agriculture and not pastoralism as its theme, is too often elided. Clearly, these two genres of poetry share a focus on rural themes, but here I must emphasize the differences between them. In scale, in subject matter, in philosophy, and especially in voice, Virgil's *Eclogues* are worlds apart from his *Georgics*. Especially in voice: Bakhtinian dialogism is the predominant mode in Virgil's pastoral, while in his *Georgics* he presents a monologic philosophizing voice of authority.[4] So why use an epigraph from the *Eclogues* for what has already been announced as a didactic poem? And, more, why use an epigraph from a genre that concerns itself with the lives, loves, and losses of rustic herdsmen for a poem whose topic is walking the streets of the metropolis?

The answer, I suggest, is that Gay chose his epigraph with great care. Virgil inherited the genre of pastoral from the Greek poet Theocritus who worked at the court of Ptolemy in Alexandria in the third century BCE. Theocritus was part of a poetic movement, headed by his contemporary the scholar-poet Callimachus, that rejected the bombast of trite epic themes in favour of newly crafted miniature genres of poetry. These privileged previously invisible themes, such as the psychology of women, the experience of children, and the daily lives of insignificant members of society. In this environment, Theocritus appears to have invented the genre of pastoral, appropriating the dactylic hexameter in which epic was written for his tiny miniatures (which we call *Idylls*, appropriately enough) dealing with fleeting and mundane events in the lives of rustic herdsmen. When Virgil took up this genre, early in his poetic career, he introduced an element that was barely present in Theocritus's work: he explored the relationship between city and countryside, especially how city life intrudes upon the lives of country folk. So in *Eclogue* 2, a reworking of Theocritus' spurned lovers in *Idylls* 3 and 11, his herdsman Corydon experiences the fever of a love unrequited by the boy Alexis who, significantly, lives in the city. And *Eclogues* 1 and 9 lament the land dispossessions which resulted from the civil wars of Virgil's time, which meant that decisions made in Rome displaced rural herdsmen from their ancestral acres. This is the context of Gay's quotation from Virgil: it is the opening line of *Eclogue* 9, a poem which marks the dominance of city over country. The pastoral herdsmen, instead of relaxing and singing in the pastoral shade, are on the road, walking towards the city. What is

'Let Persian *Dames th'* Umbrella *'s Ribs display'*
9. Printer's emblem from *Trivia,* second edition (1716).

more, they are doing so in fear and trepidation, with no confidence that their old rustic way of life will ever be theirs again. It seems to me that Gay has understood Virgil's agenda precisely and has taken this line as his epigraph because it explicitly directs attention away from the country, conceived as an idyllic setting, and towards the city, with its potential for danger and destruction. In other words, Gay declares that *Trivia* will be a didactic piece by announcing it as an 'Art', then by his choice of epigraph immediately hints that this 'Art' will offer a negative perspective of his topic, 'the streets of London'.

This agenda is taken one step further in the lines from Virgil that close Gay's 'Advertisement'. This quotation comes from *Eclogue* 3, which starts out as an exchange of insults between two foul-mouthed yokels: *Non tu, in Triviis, Indocte, solebas / Stridenti, miserum, stipula, disperdere Carmen?* ('Wasn't it you that was always mangling your wretched song on your screeching pipe at the crossroads, you ignoramus?') This quotation is not only an aggressively satirical pre-emptive strike against those who might criticize Gay's poem. It also replays a moment from Dryden's *Discourse Concerning Satire*, as the commentators Dearing and Beckwith observe, where Dryden asserts that Virgil possessed a satirical edge. I believe Gay is reusing this to indicate the satirical agenda of his poem, too.[5] So, in his very opening materials, Gay has already woven together three different genres of Latin poetry which use the hexameter: didactic epic,[6] pastoral, and satire.

TRIVIA AS SATIRE?

Later I shall explore the modes of authority afforded Gay by his deployment of classical material, but first I shall deal with the interrelationship between *Trivia* and Roman satire. Satire is incontestably 'an urban genre'.[7] So much is self-evident from any consideration of the settings and targets of satire: the crowded metropolis abounds in material for a satirist in a way in which the dullness of country living never can, except perhaps in the hands of an ironist like Jane Austen.[8] The genre of verse satire was an invention by the Romans which took definitive shape in the hands of Lucilius, an aristocrat writing in the second half of the second century BCE, at the time when Rome was establishing itself as the dominant power in the Mediterranean and when, presumably, there was a marked influx of foreign people, goods and customs which threatened the traditional concept of what it was to be truly Roman, the concept of the farmer-soldier. Though we have only fragments of Lucilius' poems, it is absolutely clear that his satires were immersed in city life and full of criticisms of behaviour that fell short of Roman ideals. One of the longer fragments to survive[9] depicts a vivid street scene full of swindlers:

> But as it is, from morning to night, on holiday and workday,
> the whole people and senators too all alike
> are bustling about the forum and nowhere leave off;
> they all devote themselves to one and the same pursuit and expertise—
> to be able to swindle successfully, to fight cunningly,
> to compete in flattery, to pretend to be an upright citizen,
> to lay ambushes as if everyone were everyone's enemies.

Writing nearly a century later, Horace in his satirical poetry (two books of *Satires* and two books of *Epistles*, all in hexameters) takes up the themes established by Lucilius, in a series of poems which mock the inconsistency, pomposity, and inconveniences of life in the city of Rome, though with a satiric persona that is much more mild and indirect than Lucilius' fierceness. Another 150 years on, in the early decades of the second century CE, the satirist Juvenal produced poems that shaped the subsequent conception of the genre of European satire. His early poems take as their central topic the degradation of the city of Rome. *Satires* 1 and 3, in particular, are indignant rants that pillory Rome as a thoroughly un-Roman place. These poems offer Gay a major source of inspiration in *Trivia*.

Satire 1 takes the form of the satirist's self-justification for writing satire, which is based upon the corruption he claims to see all around him as he stands at the crossroads, notebook in hand (1. 63–4). The poem is often referred to as a Rogue's Gallery, but it should be remembered that the coterie of undesirables is found on the streets, not the page or wall. The satirist explicitly situates himself at the crossroads, watching a veritable procession of criminals as they pass by. This position on the street supplies an important hint to Gay which he develops with aplomb. Take, for example, the concluding lines of *Trivia* Book II, where Gay praises the walker by expressing satirical scorn towards those who prefer other modes of transportation (II 569–90). His strategy of pointing the finger at a variety of reprobates as they pass by is drawn precisely from Juvenal

> Who is so tolerant
> of the injustices of Rome, who so hardened, that they can contain themselves
> when along comes the lawyer Matho in his brand new litter,
> filling it up all by himself?—when behind him comes the man who informed
> on his powerful friend, the man who will soon grab any scraps left
> from the carcass of the nobility . . .
>
> (*Satire* 1. 30–5)[10]

As he strips away their pretentious finery and exposes their immorality and criminality, Gay's catalogue is full of demonstratives that do the same duty as Juvenal's long list of 'when's: 'See, yon' bright Chariot . . . This Coach . . . Here the brib'd Lawyer, sunk in Velvet sleeps . . . There flames a Fool . . . That other, with a clustering Train behind . . . This next . . .'.[11] Gay's final flourish is to claim 'Vertue' for the walker:

> O rather give me sweet Content on Foot,
> Wrapt in my Vertue, and a good *Surtout*!
>
> (II 589–90)

in phraseology that seems to me to replay Juvenal's sad musing towards the end of his catalogue, *probitas laudatur et alget* (*Satire* 1. 74: 'Honesty is praised—and left in the cold'). In other words, it is not difficult to demonstrate that Juvenal's first *Satire* was a major inspiration for Gay.

Satire 3, which famously inspired Samuel Johnson's poem *London* (1738), is even more important for understanding the classical backdrop to *Trivia*. Juvenal's poem is presented as a conversation with his friend Umbricius which takes place outside the city-gates while Umbricius' possessions are being loaded into a wagon. *Satire* 3 is another catalogue, put into the mouth of the disillusioned Umbricius who has decided to quit the city for a Greek resort on the Bay of Naples, which he implies is more Roman than the city of Rome itself (he calls Rome 'Greek', *Graecam Vrbem*, 3. 61). Juvenal's Umbricius complains that though he is an honest and honourable native-born Roman, he has been displaced by unprincipled cheats, by foreigners, especially Greeks, and by rich Romans, who all compete in the rat-race alongside men of modest means like himself. In the course of this rant, he includes an overview of the perils of city life which is organized as a twenty-four-hour sequence, starting with the impossibility of getting a good night's sleep, through the hazards of the day's business on the streets, and ending with the risks of walking home at night.

There are numerous explicit echoes and reworkings of material from *Satire* 3 in Gay's *Trivia*, many of which are well documented by scholars. Of these, I shall confine myself to one short sequence about traffic, although it would be easy to adduce parallels on the topics of fires (*Trivia* III 353–92 and *Satire* 3. 190–222, which both deploy references to Virgil's *Aeneid*)[12] and night-time attacks by bullies (*Trivia* III 321–34 and *Satire* 3. 278–301). Juvenal includes a section on the terrible traffic congestion in Rome, which generates noise, dirt, delay, danger, and even death, at lines 232–67. Particularly vivid is the picture of the carts with their large loads

> A long fir log
> judders as its wagon gets closer and another cart
> trundles a whole pine tree. They wobble threateningly way above the crowds.
> After all, if the axle that's transporting rocks from Liguria
> collapses and spills an upturned mountain on top of the masses,
> what will be left of the bodies?
>
> (*Satire* 3. 254–9)

Juvenal goes on to present the pathetic picture of a casualty of this traffic accident sitting on the banks of the River Styx in mock-epic terms borrowed from Virgil's description of Aeneas' visit to the Underworld in *Aeneid* 6.[13] It seems to me that Gay has this sequence in mind when he presents in mock-epic terms and tone the dangers of traffic in the narrow streets:

Though Expedition bids, yet never stray
Where no rang'd Posts defend the rugged Way.
Here laden Carts with thundering Waggons meet,
Wheels clash with Wheels, and bar the narrow Street;
The lashing Whip resounds, the Horses strain,
And Blood in anguish bursts the swelling Vein.

(II 227–32)

These lines include a calque, or word-for-word translation, taken from ancient martial epic in the phrase 'Wheels clash with Wheels', an effect that serves to mark the gulf between his theme and the original epic context of battle in full progress.

The corpus of Roman satire, then, provides plenty of inspiration for a critique of city life. Juvenal in particular offers a focus on the streets of Rome with which Gay clearly connects. But there is a crucial difference: in *Trivia*, the walker is in locomotion, moving through the city, actively engaged in delivering advice to those less experienced in the hazards of the London streets. There is nothing exactly like this in Roman satire. There are only two 'journey' poems in extant Roman satire, both in Horace's first book of *Satires*: the fifth poem, describing a journey from Rome to Brindisi, and the ninth, a stroll through Rome, but neither does what Gay does in *Trivia*. Horace *Satires* 1. 5 is filled with mundane details, that perform a clever concealment of a complex and delicate political agenda.[14] In *Satires* 1. 9, a poem often known as 'The Pest', Horace's stroll through Rome becomes an episode of torture as he strives in vain to rid himself of a social climber. Both poems use a journey format but in neither does Horace really interact with his location. In Juvenal's *Satire* 1, the satirist's self-situation on the street inspires Gay, but he has none of the dynamism or the authority of Gay's walker. Similarly, *Satire* 3 has a stationary setting in a grove outside the city gates and Umbricius' observations on city life are essentially passive and often conceived from the victim's perspective. It seems to me that Gay is quite original in the dynamics of his poem. Though he is clearly indebted to depictions of the city provided by Roman satire, his focus upon walking is a significant, independent development.

TRIVIA AS EPIC?

It is no secret that the central classical intertext behind Gay's *Trivia* is Virgil's didactic epic, *Georgics*, the two-thousand-line disquisition, organized into four books, which represents itself as advice to farmers (Book 1, soils; Books 2, plants; Book 3, large domesticated animals; Book 4, bees) but which really tackles a much larger theme, the relationship between humans and the environment. Dearing and Beckwith's commentary on *Trivia* helpfully proposes parallels: a few examples here will show Gay's familiarity with the Latin poem. Two exclamations of happiness by Gay borrow from celebrated passages from *Georgics* 2. First, as Dearing and Beckwith observe, Gay's eight lines on 'The Happiness of *London*' (III 145–52) seem to nod at Virgil's celebration of Italy at *Georgics* 2. 136–76, a passage which commences with a negative enumeration of the things from which Italy is free.[15] Again, in the section of Book II which Gay entitles 'The Happiness of Walkers', his emotional apostrophe, 'O ye associate Walkers, O my friends, / Upon your State what happiness attends!' (II 501–2), clearly reworks the opening lines of *Georgics* 2. 458–74, *o fortunatos nimium, sua si bona norint, / agricolas!* ('O happy farmers! too happy, if they knew their blessings'). And in his description of the fire that devastates the city (III 377–80), Gay explicitly draws an analogy with the terrible omens that heralded the assassination of Julius Caesar, a topic treated at length by Virgil towards the end of *Georgics* 1.

More significant than these individual parallels is how epic texts, in particular Virgil's *Georgics*, shape the persona assumed by Gay. Didactic epic is predicated upon authority and expertise. This feature distances didactic epic from satire and pastoral, which share the hexameter metre, and brings it closer to heroic epic, a genre which usually deploys an omniscient impersonal narrator and which offers a total, or totalizing, worldview. The speaker of didactic epic—or, in *Trivia*, didactic mock-epic —sets himself up as an authority, with information, exhortations, and warnings to deliver. His is a dominating personality and his technique is persuasion, which can take many forms. These many forms emerge from authorial personae in classical didactic epic, from the archaic Greek poet Hesiod's *Theogony* and *Works and Days*, through the verse fragments of Greek philosophers such as Parmenides and Empedocles and the third century BCE scientist Aratus, to the magisterial Latin poem *De Rerum Natura* written in the 50s BCE by Lucretius to articulate the Epicurean materialist philosophy and, finally, to Virgil's *Georgics*, published in 29 BCE. In these poems the voice of authority asserts facts, offers logical proofs, argues by analogy, appeals to the evidence of the senses, deploys fables, maxims, and personal anecdotes, and even resorts occasionally to satire, in the *reductio ad absurdum*. Many of these strategies of persuasion appear in Gay's poem. I shall now point out how Gay uses classical learning and literature to bolster his authoritative stance.

One of the most striking manifestations of Gay's strategy is his deployment of classical material to cap a topic and provide punctuation before introducing a new topic. There are numerous examples in *Trivia* of material from Greek mythology and Roman history used as a flourish towards the end of a section. My first case is very marked. Towards the end of Book I, Gay, operating in a markedly Lucretian mode, warns against belief in superstitions and urges instead that attention be paid to the weather prognostications offered by nature (I 175–208). In a grandiose comparison, Gay invites us to view the uncurling of the incautious person's wig in the rain as the collapse of a Fury's snaky hair when tamed by the song of Orpheus or as the appearance of a sea-god's beard as he emerges from the deep to gaze at a nymph:

> So fierce *Alecto*'s snaky Tresses fell,
> When *Orpheus* charm'd the rig'rous Pow'rs of Hell.
> Or thus hung *Glaucus*' Beard, with briny Dew
> Clotted and strait, when first his am'rous View
> Surpris'd the bathing Fair; the frighted Maid
> Now stands a Rock, transform'd by *Circe*'s Aid.
>
> (I 203–8)

The reference to the taming of Alecto's snake-hair evokes Virgil's narrative of Orpheus and Eurydice at *Georgics* 4. 453–527, where he describes how Orpheus cast a spell over all the occupants of Hell, including the Furies. The story of Glaucus' pursuit of the nymph Scylla and her metamorphosis into a monstrous rock by the goddess Circe is taken directly from Ovid's *Metamorphoses* (13. 900–14. 74), a narrative in which Ovid draws attention to Glaucus' beard (13. 960). Gay could assume his readership's familiarity with Ovid's mythological epic;[16] what is curious here is that he extends the allusion beyond the specific point of comparison— the water streaming from Glaucus' beard as he emerges from the sea— and offers a potted version of the entire narrative. This may be designed to resemble the extended similes that occur from time to time in Greek and Roman epic, where the destination is far removed from the point of departure. It may, too, be a clever segue by Gay into his next section, where he offers advice specifically to female walkers. References to the Fury Alecto, to the unnamed 'Maid', and to Circe not only punctuate the previous section with an exaggerated classical flourish but also prepare for the new focus upon apparel suitable for female walkers, a topic which will occupy the rest of Book I.

Similar explanations offer themselves for the numerous other classical flourishes which Gay deploys. For example, when imagining the city of London as a place where it is easy to get lost, he not surprisingly turns to the most famous image of the labyrinth in classical mythology. Offering advice on asking directions, Gay presents the analogy of Theseus finding his way out of the Cretan labyrinth:

> Thus hardy *Theseus*, with intrepid Feet,
> Travers'd the dang'rous Labyrinth of *Crete*;
> But still the wandring Passes forc'd his Stay,
> Till *Ariadne*'s Clue unwinds the Way.

> (II 83–6)

The classical reference seems designed to enhance the speaker's authority by displaying his knowledge and to flatter those among his readership who would knowingly nod in recognition. There are many such references: another, an image from *Iliad* 8. 133–6, marks the end of a short section on ballad singers when the crowd flows back from an approaching coach or cart as if 'Jove' were deploying his thunderbolts on the battlefield at Troy (*Trivia* III 85–6). In the next section (III 95–100), about what to do if the crowd separates you from your walking companion, Gay produces a bumper climax consisting of two classical similes which refer to different night-time episodes in the *Aeneid*: Aeneas searching for his missing wife Creusa in *Aeneid* 2 and the valiant but fatal night raid of the lovers Nisus and Euryalus in *Aeneid* 9.[17]

The occasional footnotes that Gay inserts also seem designed to enhance his authority in the same kind of way, through their display of learning. A typical example appears early on, at I 149, where Gay cites two lines from *Georgics* 1, which he has rendered into his poem as:

> Not that their Minds with greater Skill are fraught,
> Endu'd by Instinct, or by Reason taught.

Although his debt to Virgil's *Georgics* must already be apparent, it is curious that he flags the relationship so explicitly here. Another learned footnote appears early in Book II, where he glosses *Cloacina* at line 115 with a three-line footnote in which he cites two ancient sources, Lactantius and Minucius Felix, as evidence for his assertions about the image of the goddess found in the sewer.

My favourite deployment of classical material in *Trivia* concerns the myth of Oedipus. There are not, after all, so many stories in classical literature which feature the meeting of three ways. One of those is the story of Oedipus, who in the earliest recorded incident of road rage killed a man in a vehicle who would not give way to him. That man turned out to be his father, of course, and the incident forms part of the story of Oedipus' fulfilment of the oracle's prophecy that he would kill his father and sleep with his mother. Oedipus goes on to blind himself and to pronounce a curse upon the children he has produced by incest. Gay makes delightful use of the story for his poem about the 'meeting of three ways'. He cleverly inscribes Oedipus into one of several sections which deal with the etiquette of 'keeping the Wall' (III 205–24). Gay strongly urges the walker to stay close to the wall, especially in wet weather, but above all to avoid a quarrel on this point, offering Oedipus' fate as a cautionary tale

> O think on *Oedipus'* detested State,
> And by his Woes be warn'd to shun thy Fate.
> Where three Roads join'd, he met his Sire unknown;
> (Unhappy Sire, but more unhappy Son!)
> Each claim'd the Way, their Swords the Strife decide,
> The hoary Monarch fell, he groan'd and dy'd!
> Hence sprung the fatal Plague that thinn'd thy Reign,
> Thy cursed Incest! and thy Children slain!
> Hence wert thou doom'd in endless Night to stray
> Through *Theban* Streets, and cheerless groap thy Way.
>
> (III 215–24)

He has wittily inserted this into Book III, which deals with walking the city at night, to make a connection with Oedipus' self-inflicted blindness and thereby to demonstrate again his learnedness.

Maintaining an authoritative voice runs the risk of tedium; the author of didactic epic does well to introduce sufficient variation[18] to avoid that reproach. This is easier in mock-epic than in serious epic, because bathos is readily generated thanks to the tension between its epic form and its non-epic content. The gap between the two elements of comparison when the walker is urged, for example, to avoid becoming embroiled in an Oedipus-like quarrel lighten the tone and create welcome *variatio*. But there are other strategies too that the author of mock-epic didactic shares with authors of serious didactic epic.

The key for the critic is to examine the building-blocks of the poem with a view to identifying shifts between miscellaneous advice and extended elaborated examples. In scholarship on didactic poetry, such elaborated examples are sometimes unhelpfully called 'digressions', a label which begs more questions than it solves. However, I think the notion can be useful to flag up how Gay's elaborated material often relies on classical sources. Some examples will demonstrate.

Gay announces the theme of Book I as 'Of the Implements for walking the Streets, and Signs of the Weather'. The long section on the signs of the weather is the more straightforward, in terms of classical influence. Gay's extensive discussion (I 121–208) of the 'sure Prognosticks' that will help his listener 'learn to know the Skies' (I 122)—a line rebounding in Lucretian flavour, incidentally—is heavily indebted to a lengthy passage from *Georgics* 1. 351–463, a fact to which Gay himself draws our attention by including in his footnote to I 149 the two Latin lines that he here translates (as discussed above). But much more interesting is the extensive narrative of the invention of the patten with which Gay concludes Book I (I 223–82).

In 'An Episode of the Invention of Pattens' Gay pauses to invoke his Muse in mock-epic ingratiation before embarking on this episode:

> But, O! forget not, Muse, the *Patten*'s Praise,
> That female Implement shall grace thy Lays;
> Say from what Art Divine th' Invention came,
> And from its Origine deduce the Name.
>
> (I 219–22)

Sounds like lofty, learned stuff. What actually follows is the story of a god's seduction of a virgin beauty. Now this is precisely the type of story that dominates the opening two books of Ovid's *Metamorphoses*: Apollo pursues Daphne, Jupiter pursues Io, Pan pursues Syrinx, Jupiter pursues Europa, and so on and so on. But Gay's god is not the gloriously handsome Apollo or the all-powerful Jupiter, but instead the limping, grimy blacksmith god, Vulcan. And his beloved is not one of Ovid's nymphs, but a lowly milkmaid called Patty, the daughter of a country yeoman from Lincolnshire. This episode takes us well away from London, well away from any city in fact, into a country scene in which Vulcan improvises a forge in 'a lonely Hut' (I 251), where he devises 'a new Machine' (I 272) to secure his seduction, namely, a raised shoe that will keep her lungs from shaking 'with dropping Rheums' (I 277). Gay closes his first book with a neat two-line explanation of the origin of the word 'patten' from 'blue-ey'd *Patty*', just as Ovid often rounds off an elaborate mythological narrative with a perfunctory explanation of the origin of a plant.

Evidently, the two longest building-blocks in Book I of *Trivia* are founded upon easily identifiable sources in classical literature. It is no great surprise to find Gay deploying Virgil's weather-lore; it is more un-expected to find the Ovidian god-seduces-mortal narrative pattern from the opening books of the *Metamorphoses* deployed to shape this 'episode' on the origin of this type of women's shoe.

The next extended building-block in *Trivia* is the passage at II 99–216, which Gay explicitly introduces as 'digressive Song' (II 104) designed to refresh his Muse in her state of fatigue—although, in a fine piece of metapoetics, he will criticize it as excessively long once he has finished it (II 217–20)! The narrative tells of the amatory liaison between the goddess Cloacina with 'a mortal Scavenger' (II 118), which Gay intro-duces as analogous to Jupiter's 'Amours' with mortal women (II 107–14), reprising precisely the theme from Ovid's *Metamorphoses* discussed above. Gay proceeds to narrate the ensuing birth of a boy, his early years as 'a Beggar's Brat' (II 142) and the goddess's request to the other gods that her son be endowed with 'some beneficial Art' (II 152). Her request is successful and the gods contribute all the requisites for the boy to become a shoe-shiner (II 157–68). At this moment, as the boy laments his orphaned lot, his mother miraculously appears to him and presents him with his brush, soot, oil, and tripod. As Dearing and Beckwith assert, this episode 'parallels Virgil's account of how the art of engendering bees from the putrid blood of cattle was discovered' in *Georgics* 4. Gay has devised a banal version of the relationship between Virgil's nymph Cyrene and her shepherd son Aristaeus: when he laments the loss of his bees, his mother appears to him to instruct him on what he must do to recreate his hive and his livelihood. Both in *Georgics* 4 and in *Trivia*, we may sense that the author is taking us away from the matter in hand, but in both cases the final connection justifies the narrative meander: Aristaeus revives his hive of bees by following his mother's instructions and Cloacina's son takes up the profession of blacking shoes, to the benefit of 'the walking Croud' (II 154).

That Gay has *Georgics* 4 in mind in *Trivia* is demonstrated by one fur-ther interaction with Virgil's narrative of Aristaeus' loss of his bees. This episode is particularly notable for its incorporation, as an inset narrative, of the story of Orpheus and Eurydice, which runs like this. After Eurydice's death from a snake bite as she flees the amorous advances of Aristaeus, Orpheus journeys into the Underworld to reclaim her. Just as he seems to have succeeded, he ignores the instruction forbidding him to look round and she is lost again, this time for ever. In his grief, Orpheus spurns the company of women and soon meets his own death, torn apart by enraged maenads. The story ends with the image of Orpheus' torn-off head still singing as it is carried away on the river Hebrus. It is this image which Gay deploys to round off his account (II 381–98) of the 'doleful Fate' (II 375) met on the ice by the matron Doll:

> The cracking Crystal yields, she sinks, she dyes,
> Her Head, chopt off, from her lost Shoulders flies:
> Pippins she cry'd, but Death her Voice confounds,
> And Pip-Pip-Pip along the Ice resounds.

(II 389–92)

Gay goes on to spend six lines making the analogy with Orpheus explicit, even mentioning the river's name.

TRIVIA: THE MEETING OF THE GENRES

What conclusion are we to draw about this blending of classical genres in Gay's *Trivia*? He seems to move with ease between reminiscences and evocations of the heroic epics of Homer and Virgil, of the mythological epic of Ovid, of the didactic epics by Hesiod, Lucretius, and Virgil, of Virgil's pastoral poetry, and of Juvenal's satire. It is my contention that Gay was aware of the interrelationships between all these classical genres and that as he shifts in matter and tone he reflects the intricate relatedness of the ancient genres.[19]

All these poems had as their invariable metre the dactylic hexameter. Epic poetry was used to articulate an authoritative view of the world, whether that was the world of heroic achievements familiar from the *Iliad* or the *Aeneid*, or the world considered from the philosophical or religious perspectives of didactic epic. The grand form of epic later generated two offshoots, pastoral and satire, both of which subvert or invert essential qualities of epic poetry. Pastoral, first in Greek and then in Latin, proved a medium for the exploration of small, insignificant lives in poems on a miniature scale. Satire, a Roman invention, hijacked the metre of epic to become a vehicle for the exposure of the worse, distinctly unheroic, side of human nature in a grim form of Bakhtinian carnival.[20] Both offshoots introduced a new set of literal and emotional vocabulary into the metre of epic. Pastoral provided botanical details of the countryside along with the language of love and loss. Satire incorporated the detailed observation of city life with its glitter and dirt, pomposity and deception and rage. Satire also at times invoked the idealism of the world of pastoral in order to intensify the depravity of Rome.

Gay seems to be sensible of these complex dynamics. He chooses for his poem a grand metre, a grand scale, and a grand topic: the metropolis of London. Within this framework he brings things down to earth by taking our attention to ground level—precisely, to our feet (Book I: see my appended 'Foot Note'). He offers advice for safe passage through the city by day (Book II) and by night (Book III), weaving together a catalogue of dangers and criminals drawn from the pages of satire, but at times he represents those dangers and criminals in terms borrowed from epic battle scenes, with occasional relief provided by rustic scenes of love and seduction, such as might seem to belong to the world of pastoral, or Ovid's mythological epic. He does all of this while maintaining the voice of authority associated with didactic epic. And he covertly and overtly invites comparison with 'the best poem of the best poet', as Virgil's *Georgics* has been called. In the end, one can only gasp at the audacity of Gay's wit. This is a poet who had mastered 'The Art of Walking the Streets of London' and who had also mastered the art of reading the poems of Rome.

A FOOT NOTE

I said above that Gay brings things down to earth through his emphatic focus upon walking. This seems to me an extreme case of the Bakhtinian theory that genres such as comedy and satire tend to concern themselves with the lower bodily strata, through the themes of sex and food and excretion.[21] After all, the lowest element of the body—the lowest bodily stratum—is literally the foot. In *Trivia*, Gay takes his satirical impulse down to the most basic level possible: an exploration of the experience of physical contact between foot and ground. This is especially noticeable in Book 1, which begins and ends with shoes. The opening display of learning addresses the appropriate choice of footwear for the season (I 23–40), before moving on to coats and canes, and the first book concludes with an extended account of the invention of the shoe he calls the 'Patten' (I 219–82), which Gay fancifully ascribes to Vulcan, the god of blacksmithery (who was also, curiously, lame, though Gay does not make this explicit), as a gift to the maid he is courting.

Gay's focus upon feet and footwear leads me to a speculation on the structure of his poem. Its division into three books might, of course, just be a learned joke on *Trivia*, literally 'three ways'. But when we consider the programme he articulates at the start of Book I we find a twofold division into day and night (I 1–6):

> Through Winter Streets to steer your Course aright,
> How to walk clean by Day, and safe by Night,
> How jostling Crouds, with Prudence, to decline,
> When to assert the Wall, and when resign,
> I sing: Thou *Trivia*, Goddess, aid my Song,
> Thro spacious Streets conduct thy Bard along.

This division corresponds to the avowed topics of Books II and III, which are comparable in length at 590 and 416 lines respectively. So what is the function of the signally shorter first book (282 lines)? I suggest that Gay's initial disquisition on the bodily experience of walking is no mere preliminary. Rather, with his emphasis upon the Bakhtinian physicality of foot-ground contact, Gay is inviting us to appreciate his literally bathetic approach to his subject.[22] He wants us never to forget that this poem, whatever its blend of satire and instruction, is essentially about walking. In other words, Book I of *Trivia* is the most assertive foot note ever composed.

NOTES

My essay is dedicated to the memory of Jonathan Walters, sometime classicist, youth adviser, and travel writer, my dear gay, punk, anarchist friend who died in August 2004, who knew the streets of London better than anyone else I know, and who would really appreciate being the dedicatee of a poem by Gay.

1. For the Greeks and Romans, the goddess Hecate was generally associated with the transition between the world of the living and the world of the dead. This must explain her association with black magic and probably accounts for her being worshipped at crossroads, which were viewed as numinous places.

2. This is a different point from discussions of Gay's generic playfulness, as discussed by Clare Brant in this volume. The hexameter was a dactylic metre consisting of six metrical units; in Greek and then in Latin literature, it was the most prestigious metre, and hence the metre used for heroic and didactic epic. Later, the genres of pastoral and satire appropriate the metre of epic to create a counterpoint between form and content that the poets deploy for effect. Pastoral revels in putting the metre used for the narration of heroic deeds into the mouth of humble herdsmen, whose concerns are

insignificant and mundane in comparison. Satire revels in talking about food and sex and dirt and crimes in the metre of heroic epic.

3. A good case is Dianne S. Ames, 'Gay's *Trivia* and the Art of Allusion', *Studies in Philology*, 75 (1978), 199–222.

4. I use the phrase 'Bakhtinian dialogism' to denote texts in which the speakers produce discourse that is open and unfinalizable, in contrast with 'monologic' texts which restrict or ignore the idea of any opposition or dissent from the views expressed. For a neat definition of Bakhtinian dialogism in this sense see Gary Saul Morson, 'Dialogue, Monologue, and the Social' in Gary Saul Morson (ed.), *Bakhtin: Essays and Dialogues on his Work* (1986), 83–4.

5. To say this is not to rule out Clare Brant's interpretation of the epigraph in her essay in this volume.

6. I use this term through my dissatisfaction with the modern label 'didactic poetry', which is often used to distinguish works such as Virgil's *Georgics* and Lucretius' *De Rerum Natura* from epics such as the *Aeneid*. The term 'didactic poetry' does not correspond to any category the ancients used. The first century CE professor Quintilian, for example, lists Lucretius as an author of epic in *Institutes of Oratory* (10. 1. 87).

7. Matthew Hodgart, *Satire* (New York, 1969), 129.

8. Clare Brant suggests that some English poets did manage to combine the pastoral and satirical modes—for example, George Crabbe in *The Village* (1783)—but this combination seems to be absent from Greco-Roman literature.

9. Lines 1145–51. I use the line numbering established by Warmington in his edition for the Loeb Classical Library: *Remains of Old Latin vol. III: Lucilius, The XII Tables*, trans. E. H. Warmington (Cambridge, Mass., 1979).

10. The translations from Juvenal are adapted from my prose translation for the Loeb Classical Library: *Juvenal and Persius*, ed. and trans. Susanna Morton Braund (Cambridge, Mass., 2004).

11. Clare Brant observes that Pope also uses these 'Here . . . There' directives, especially in his *Imitations of Horace* (1734–8), e.g., *Epistle* I.1, lines 77–80.

12. Margaret Hunt in her essay in this volume offers another perspective on Gay's fire in terms of biblical overtones and a persuasive reading of the poem in terms of gender.

13. Discussed in detail in Susanna Morton Braund, 'City and Country in Roman Satire', in Susanna Morton Braund (ed.), *Satire and Society in Ancient Rome* (Exeter, 1989), 34–6.

14. Brilliantly unravelled by I. M. LeM. DuQuesnay in 'Horace and Maecenas: The Propaganda Value of *Sermones* I', in Tony Woodman and David West (eds.), *Poetry and Politics in the Age of Augustus* (Cambridge, 1984), 19–58.

15. The fact that Gay here, and here only, refers to London as '*Augusta*' (for *Augusta Trinobantum*, under Roman occupation) seems a deliberate invitation to think of matters Roman.

16. Ovid, alongside Virgil, held prime position in the reception of Latin poetry into later European culture. He was widely read and adapted throughout the Middle Ages and was the favourite Latin poet of the Renaissance. Any cultured person could be expected to be familiar with Ovid's retelling of the ancient Greek myths.

17. Further cases include references to Scylla and Charybdis (III 183–4) and the intrepid Roman general Regulus (III 334).

18. The Latin term is *variatio*.

19. Cf. Bliss Carnochan, 'Gay's *Trivia* and the Ways of Walking', in Peter E. Firchow and Hermann J. Real (eds.), *Perennial Satirist: Essays in Honour of Bernfried Nugel* (Münster, 2005), 7–28.

20. See Mikhail Bakhtin, *Rabelais and his World*, trans. H. Iswolsky (Bloomington, Ind., 1984); for useful discussion relating to classical literature, see Peter I. Barta et al. (eds.), *Carnivalizing Difference: Bakhtin and the Other* (2001), especially Paul Allen Miller, 'The Otherness of History in Rabelais' Carnival, or Why Bakhtin Got it Right the First Time', 141–64.

21. Bakhtin, *Rabelais and his world*.

22. The word 'bathetic' derives from the Greek word *bathos*, meaning 'lowness', as opposed to elevation.

THE POEM

'Be sure observe the Signs, for Signs remain
Like faithful Land-marks to the walking Train.'
10. *The Curds and Whey Seller, Cheapside*, anonymous (*c*.1730).

TRIVIA:

OR, THE
ART of *WALKING*
THE
STREETS of LONDON

By Mr. *GAY.*

Quo te Mœri pedes? An, quo via ducit, in Urbem?
Virg.

ADVERTISEMENT.

*T*HE *World, I believe, will take so little Notice of me, that I need not take much of it. The Criticks may see by this Poem, that I walk on Foot, which probably may save me from their Envy. I should be sorry to raise that Passion in Men whom I am so much obliged to, since they allowed me an Honour hitherto only shown to better Writers: That of denying me to be the Author of my own Works. I am sensible this must be done in pure Generosity; because whoever writ them, provided they did not themselves, they are still in the same Condition.*

Gentlemen, If there be any thing in this Poem, good enough to displease you, and if it be any Advantage to you to ascribe it to some Person of greater Merit; I shall acquaint you for your Comfort, that among many other Obligations, I owe several Hints of it to Dr Swift. And if you will so far continue your Favour as to write against it, I beg you to oblige me in accepting the following Motto.

—Non tu, in *Triviis,* Indocte, solebas
Stridenti, miserum, stipulâ, disperdere Carmen?

TRIVIA.

BOOK I.

*Of the Implements for walking the Streets, and
Signs of the Weather.*

Through Winter Streets to steer your Course aright,
How to walk clean by Day, and safe by Night,
How jostling Crouds, with Prudence, to decline,
When to assert the Wall, and when resign,
I sing: Thou *Trivia*, Goddess, aid my Song,　　　　　　5
Thro' spacious Streets conduct thy Bard along;
By thee transported, I securely stray
Where winding Alleys lead the doubtful Way,
The silent Court, and op'ning Square explore,
And long perplexing Lanes untrod before.　　　　　　10
To pave thy Realm, and smooth the broken Ways,
Earth from her Womb a flinty Tribute pays;
For thee, the sturdy Pavior thumps the Ground,
Whilst ev'ry Stroke his lab'ring Lungs resound;
For thee, the Scavinger bids Kennels glide　　　　　　15
Within their Bounds, and Heaps of Dirt subside.
My youthful Bosom burns with Thirst of Fame,
From the great Theme to build a glorious Name,
To tread in Paths to ancient Bards unknown,
And bind my Temples with a *Civic* Crown;　　　　　　20
But more, my Country's Love demands the Lays,
My Country's be the Profit, mine the Praise.

　　When the *Black Youth* at chosen Stands rejoice,
And *clean your Shoes* resounds from ev'ry Voice;
Who late their miry Sides Stage-Coaches show,　　　　　　25
And their stiff Horses thro' the Town move slow;
When all the *Mall* in leafy Ruin lies,
And Damsels first renew their Oyster Cries:
Of Shoes.　Then let the prudent Walker Shoes provide,
Not of the *Spanish* or *Morocco* Hide;　　　　　　30
The wooden Heel may raise the Dancer's Bound,
And with the 'scallop'd Top his Step be crown'd:

Let firm, well-hammer'd Soles protect thy Feet
Thro' freezing Snows, and Rains, and soaking Sleet.
Should the big Laste extend the Shoe too wide,   35
Each Stone will wrench th'unwary Step aside:
The sudden Turn may stretch the swelling Vein,
Thy cracking Joint unhinge, or Ankle sprain;
And when too short the modish Shoes are worn,
You'll judge the Seasons by your shooting Corn.   40

Nor should it prove thy less important Care,   *Of Coats*
To chuse a proper Coat for Winter's Wear.
Now in thy Trunk thy *Doily* Habit fold,
The silken Drugget ill can fence the Cold;
The Frieze's spongy Nap is soak'd with Rain,   45
And Show'rs soon drench the Camlet's cockled Grain.
True *Witney* Broad-cloath with it's Shag unshorn,
Unpierc'd is in the lasting Tempest worn:
Be this the Horse-man's Fence; for who would wear
Amid the Town the Spoils of *Russia*'s Bear?   50
Within the *Roquelaure*'s Clasp thy Hands are pent,
Hands, that stretch'd forth invading Harms prevent.
Let the loop'd *Bavaroy* the Fop embrace,
Or his deep Cloak be spatter'd o'er with Lace.
That Garment best the Winter's Rage defends,   55
Whose shapeless Form in ample Plaits depends;
By * various Names in various Counties known,
Yet held in all the true *Surtout* alone:
Be thine of *Kersey* firm, though small the Cost,
Then brave unwet the Rain, unchill'd the Frost.   60

If the strong Cane support thy walking Hand,   *Of Canes.*
Chairmen no longer shall the Wall command;
Ev'n sturdy Car-men shall thy Nod obey,
And rattling Coaches stop to make thee Way:
This shall direct thy cautious Tread aright,   65
Though not one glaring Lamp enliven Night.
Let Beaus their Canes with Amber tipt produce,
Be theirs for empty Show, but thine for Use.

* A Joseph, *A Wrap-Rascal*, &c.

In gilded Chariots while they loll at Ease,
And lazily insure a Life's Disease;   70
While softer Chairs the tawdry Load convey
To Court, to *White's*, Assemblies, or the Play;
Rosie-complexion'd Health thy Steps attends,
And Exercise thy lasting Youth defends.
Imprudent Men Heav'ns choicest Gifts prophane.   75
Thus some beneath their Arm support the Cane;
The dirty Point oft checks the careless Pace,
And miry Spots thy clean Cravat disgrace:
O! may I never such Misfortune meet,
May no such vicious Walkers croud the Street,   80
May Providence o'er-shade me with her Wings,
While the bold Muse experienc'd Dangers sings.

    Not that I wander from my native Home,
And tempting Perils foreign Cities roam.
Let *Paris* be the Theme of *Gallia's* Muse,   85
Where Slav'ry treads the Streets in wooden Shoes;
Nor do I rove in *Belgia's* frozen Clime,
And teach the clumsy Boor to skate in Rhyme,
Where, if the warmer Clouds in Rain descend,
No miry Ways industrious Steps offend,   90
The rushing Flood from sloping Pavements pours,
And blackens the Canals with dirty Show'rs.
Let others *Naples* smoother Streets rehearse,
And with proud *Roman* Structures grace their Verse,
Where frequent Murders wake the Night with Groans,   95
And Blood in purple Torrents dies the Stones;
Nor shall the Muse through narrow *Venice* stray,
Where *Gondola's* their painted Oars display.
O happy Streets to rumbling Wheels unknown,
No Carts, no Coaches shake the floating Town!   100
Thus was of old *Britannia's* City bless'd,
E'er Pride and Luxury her Sons possess'd;
Coaches and Chariots yet unfashion'd lay,
Nor late invented Chairs perplex'd the Way:
Then the proud Lady trip'd along the Town,   105
And tuck'd up petticoats secur'd her Gown,
Her rosie Cheek with distant Visits glow'd

And Exercise unartful Charms bestow'd;
But since in braided Gold her Foot is bound,
And a long trailing Manteau sweeps the Ground,   110
Her Shoe disdains the Street; the lazy Fair,
With narrow Step affects a limping Air.
Now gaudy Pride corrupts the lavish Age,
And the Streets flame with glaring Equipage;
The tricking Gamester insolently rides,   115
With *Loves* and *Graces* on his Chariots Sides;
In sawcy State the griping Broker sits,
And laughs at Honesty, and trudging Wits;
For you, O honest Men, these useful Lays
The Muse prepares; I seek no other Praise.   120

      When Sleep is first disturb'd by Morning Cries;   *Of the*
From sure Prognosticks learn to know the Skies,   *Weather.*
Lest you of Rheums and Coughs at Night complain;
Surpriz'd in dreary Fogs, or driving Rain.
When suffocating Mists obscure the Morn,   125
Let thy worst Wig, long us'd to Storms, be worn;
This knows the powder'd Footman, and with Care,
Beneath his flapping Hat, secures his Hair.
Be thou, for ev'ry Season, justly drest,
Nor brave the piercing Frost with open Breast;   130
And when the bursting Clouds a Deluge pour,
Let thy Surtout defend the drenching Show'r.

      The changing Weather certain Signs reveal.   *Signs of*
E'er Winter sheds her Snow, or Frosts congeal,   *cold*
You'll see the Coals in brighter Flame aspire,   *Weather.*
And Sulphur tinge with blue the rising Fire: 135
Your tender Shins the scorching Heat decline,
And at the Dearth of Coals the Poor repine;
Before her Kitchin Hearth, the nodding Dame
In Flannel Mantle wrapt, enjoys the Flame;   140
Hov'ring, upon her feeble Knees she bends,
And all around the grateful Warmth ascends.

      Nor do less certain Signs the Town advise,   *Signs of*
Of milder Weather, and serener Skies.   *fair*
                                                                        Weather.

The Ladies gayly dres'd, the *Mall* adorn   145
With various Dyes, and paint the sunny Morn;
The wanton Fawns with frisking Pleasure range,
And chirping Sparrows greet the welcome Change:
* Not that their Minds with greater Skill are fraught,
Endu'd by Instinct, or by Reason taught,   150
The Seasons operate on every Breast;
'Tis hence that Fawns are brisk, and Ladies drest.
When on his Box the nodding Coachman snores,
And dreams of fancy'd Fares; when Tavern Doors
The Chairmen idly croud; then ne'er refuse   155
To trust thy busy Steps in thinner Shoes.

Signs of   But when the swinging Signs your Ears offend
rainy   With creaking Noise, then rainy Floods impend;
Weather. Soon shall the Kennels swell with rapid Streams,
And rush in muddy Torrents to the *Thames.*   160
The Bookseller, whose Shop's an open Square,
Foresees the Tempest, and with early Care
Of Learning strips the Rails; the rowing Crew
To tempt a Fare, cloath all their Tilts in Blue:
On Hosier's Poles depending Stockings ty'd,   165
Flag with the slacken'd Gale, from side to side;
Church-Monuments foretell the changing Air;
Then *Niobe* dissolves into a Tear,
And sweats with secret grief; you'll hear the Sounds
Of whistling Winds, e'er Kennels break their Bounds;   170
Ungrateful Odours Common-shores diffuse,
And dropping Vaults distil unwholesom Dews,
E'er the Tiles rattle with the smoaking Show'r,
And Spouts on heedless Men their Torrents pour.

Superstition All Superstition from thy Breast repel.   175
to be   Let cred'lous Boys, and prattling Nurses tell,
avoided. How, if the Festival of *Paul* be clear,
Plenty from lib'ral Horn shall strow the Year;
When the dark Skies dissolve in Snows or Rain,
The lab'ring Hind shall yoke the Steer in Vain;   180

---

   * *Haud equidem credo quia sit divinitus illis, Ingenium, aut rerum fator prudential major.*
Virg. Georg.I.

But if the threatning Winds in Tempests roar,
Then War shall bathe her wasteful Sword in Gore.
How, if on *Swithin*'s Feast the Welkin lours,
And ev'ry Penthouse streams with hasty Show'rs,
Twice twenty Days shall Clouds their Fleeces drain,   185
And wash the Pavements with incessant Rain.
Let not such vulgar Tales debase thy Mind;
Nor *Paul* nor *Swithin* rule the Clouds and Wind.

If you the Precepts of the Muse despise,
And slight the faithful Warnings of the Skies,   190
Others you'll see, when all the Town's afloat,
Wrapt in th'Embraces of a *Kersey* Coat,
Or double-button'd Freize; their guarded Feet
Defie the muddy Dangers of the Street,
While you, with Hat unloop'd, the Fury dread   195
Of Spouts high-streaming, and with cautious Tread
Shun ev'ry dashing Pool, or idly stop,
To seek the kind Protection of a Shop.
But Bus'ness summons; Now with hasty Scud
You jostle for the Wall, the spatter'd Mud   200
Hides all thy Hose behind; in vain you scow'r,
Thy Wig, alas! uncurl'd, admits the Show'r.
So fierce *Alecto*'s snaky Tresses fell,
When *Orpheus* charm'd the rig'rous Pow'rs of Hell.
Or thus hung *Glaucus*' Beard, with briny Dew   205
Clotted and strait, when first his am'rous View
Surpris'd the bathing Fair; the frighted Maid
Now stands a Rock, transform'd by *Circe*'s Aid.

Good Huswives all the Winter's Rage despise,
Defended by the Riding-hood's Disguise;   210
Or underneath th'*Umbrella*'s oily Shed,
Safe thro' the Wet on clinking Pattens tread.
Let Persian Dames th'*Umbrella*'s Ribs display,
To guard their Beauties from the sunny Ray;
Or sweating Slaves support the shady Load,   215
When Eastern Monarchs shew their State abroad;
Britain in Winter only knows its Aid,
To guard from chilly Show'rs the walking Maid.
But, O! forget not, Muse, the *Patten*'s Praise,

Imple-
ments
proper for
female
Walkers.

That female Implement shall grace thy Lays;   220
Say from what Art Divine th'Invention came,
And from its Origine deduce the Name.

*An
Episode
of the
Invention
of Pattens*
        Where *Lincoln* wide extends her fenny Soil,
A goodly Yeoman liv'd grown white with Toil;
One only Daughter blest his nuptial Bed,   225
Who from her infant Hand the Poultry feed:
Martha (her careful Mother's Name) she bore,
But now her careful Mother was no more.
Whilst on her Father's Knee the Damsel play'd,
Patty he fondly call'd the smiling Maid;   230
As Years increas'd, her ruddy Beauty grew,
And *Patty*'s Fame o'er all the Village flew.

        Soon as the blushing Morning warms the Skies,
And in the doubtful Day the Woodcock flies,
Her cleanly Pail the pretty Huswife bears,   235
And singing to the distant Field repairs:
And when the Plains with ev'ning Dews are spread,
The milky Burthen smoaks upon her Head.
Deep, thro' a miry Lane she pick'd her Way,
Above her Ankle rose the chalky Clay.   240

        Vulcan, by chance the bloomy Maiden spies,
With Innocence and Beauty in her Eyes,
He saw, he lov'd; for yet he ne'er had known
Sweet Innocence and Beauty meet in One.
Ah *Mulciber*! recall thy nuptial Vows,   245
Think on the Graces of thy *Paphian* Spouse,
Think how her Eyes dart inexhausted Charms,
And canst thou leave her Bed for *Patty*'s Arms?

        The *Lemnian* Pow'r forsakes the Realms above,
His Bosom glowing with terrestrial Love: 250
Far in the Lane, a lonely Hut he found,
No Tenant ventur'd on th'unwholesome Ground.
Here smoaks his Forge, he bares his sinewy Arm,
And early Strokes the sounding Anvil warm;
Around his Shop the steely Sparkles flew,   255
As for the Steed he shap'd the bending Shoe.

When blue-ey'd Patty near his Window came,
His Anvil rests, his Forge forgets to flame.
To hear his soothing Tales, she feigns Delays;
What Woman can resist the Force of Praise? 260

At first she coyly ev'ry Kiss withstood,
And all her Cheek was flush'd with modest Blood:
With headless Nails he now surrounds her Shoes,
To save her Steps from Rains and piercing Dews;
She lik'd his soothing Tales, his Presents wore, 265
And granted Kisses, but would grant no more.
Yet Winter chill'd her Feet, with Cold she pines,
And on her Cheek the fading Rose declines;
No more her humid Eyes their Lustre boast,
And in hoarse Sounds her melting Voice is lost. 270

This *Vulcan* saw, and in his heav'nly Thought,
A new Machine Mechanick Fancy wrought,
Above the Mire her shelter'd Steps to raise,
And bear her safely through the Wintry Ways.
Strait the new Engine on his Anvil glows, 275
And the pale Virgin on the Patten rose.
No more her Lungs are shook with drooping Rheums,
And on her Cheek reviving Beauty blooms.
The God obtain'd his Suit, though Flatt'ry fail,
Presents with Female Virtue must prevail. 280
The Patten now supports each frugal Dame,
Which from the blue-ey'd *Patty* takes the Name.

BOOK II.

Of Walking the Streets by Day.

THUS far the Muse has trac'd in useful Lays,
The proper Implements for Wintry Ways;
Has taught the Walker, with judicious Eyes,
To read the various Warnings of the Skies.
Now venture, Muse, from Home to range the Town, 5
And for the publick Safety risque thy own.

The
Morning
For Ease and for Dispatch, the Morning's best:
No Tides of Passengers the Street molest.
You'll see a draggled Damsel, here and there,
From *Billingsgate* her fishy Traffick bear;   10
On Doors the sallow Milk-maid chalks her Gains;
Ah! How unlike the Milk-maid of the Plains!
Before proud Gates attending Asses bray,
Or arrogate with solemn Pace the Way;
These grave Physicians with their milky Chear,   15
The love-sick Maid, and dwindling Beau repair;
Here rows of Drummers stand in martial File,
And with their Vellom-Thunder shake the Pile,
To greet the new-made Bride. Are Sounds like these,
The proper Prelude to a State of Peace?   20
Now Industry awakes her busy Sons,
Full charg'd with News the breathless Hawker runs:
Shops open, Coaches roll, Carts shake the Ground,
And all the Streets with passing Cries resound.

What
Trades
prejudical
to
Walkers.
If cloath'd in Black, you tread the busy Town,   25
Or if distinguish'd by the rev'rend Gown,
Three Trades avoid; oft' in the mingling Press,
The *Barber*'s Apron soils the sable Dress;
Shun the *Perfumer*'s Touch with cautious Eye,
Nor let the *Baker*'s Step advance too nigh: 30
Ye Walkers too that youthful Colours wear,
Three sullying Trades avoid with equal Care;
The little *Chimney-sweeper* skulks along,
And marks with sooty Stains the heedless Throng;
When *Small-coal* murmurs in the hoarser Throat,   35
From smutty Dangers guard thy threaten'd Coat:
The *Dust-man*'s Cart offends thy Cloaths and Eyes,
When through a Street a Cloud of Ashes flies;
But whether Black, or lighter Dyes are worn,
The *Chandler*'s Basket, on his Shoulder born,   40
With Tallow spots thy Coat; resign the Way,
To shun the surly *Butcher*'s greasy Tray,
Butchers, whose Hands are dy'd with Blood's soul Stain,
And always foremost in the Hangman's Train.

Let due Civilities be strictly paid. 45
The Wall surrender to the hooded Maid;
Nor let thy sturdy Elbow's hasty Rage
Jostle the feeble Steps of trembling Age:
And when the Porter bends beneath his Load,
And pants for Breath; clear thou the crouded Road. 50
But above all, the groaping Blind direct,
And from the pressing Throng the Lame protect.
You'll sometimes meet a Fop, of nicest Tread,
Whose mantling Peruke veils his empty Head,
At ev'ry Step he dreads the Wall to lose, 55
And risques, to save a Coach, his red-heel'd Shoes;
Him, like the *Miller*, pass with Caution by,
Lest from his Shoulder Clouds of Powder fly.
But when the Bully, with assuming Pace,
Cocks his broad Hat, edg'd round with tarnish'd Lace, 60
Yield not the Way; defie his strutting Pride,
And thrust him to the muddy Kennel's side;
He never turns again, nor dares oppose,
But mutters coward Curses as he goes.

If drawn by Bus'ness to a Street unknown, 65
Let the sworn Porter point thee through the Town;
Be sure observe the Signs, for Signs remain,
Like faithful Land-marks to the walking Train.
Seek not from Prentices to learn the Way,
Those fabling Boys will turn thy Steps astray; 70
Ask the grave Tradesman to direct thee right,
He ne'er deceives, but when he profits by't.

Where fam'd Saint *Giles*'s ancient Limits spread,
An inrail'd Column rears its lofty Head,
Here to sev'n Streets, sev'n Dials count the Day, 75
And from each other count the circling Ray.
Here oft the Peasant, with enquiring Face,
Bewilder'd, trudges on from Place to Place;
He dwells on ev'ry Sign, with stupid Gaze,
Enters the narrow Alley's doubtful Maze, 80
Trys ev'ry winding Court and Street in vain,
And doubles o'er his weary Steps again.

To whom to give the Wall.

To whom to refuse the Wall.

Of whom to enquire the Way.

Thus hardy *Theseus*, with intrepid Feet,
Travers'd the dang'rous Labyrinth of *Crete*;
But still the wandring Passes forc'd his Stay,   85
Till *Ariadne's* Clue unwinds the Way.
But do not thou, like that bold Chief, confide
Thy ventrous Footsteps to a female Guide;
She'll lead thee, with delusive Smiles along,
Dive in thy Fob, and drop thee in the Throng.   90

Useful   When waggish Boys the stunted Beesom ply,
Precepts. To rid the slabby Pavement; pass not by
E'er thou hast held their Hands; some heedless Flirt
Will over-spread thy Calves with spatt'ring Dirt.
Where Porters Hogsheads roll from Carts aslope,   95
Or Brewers down steep Cellars stretch the Rope,
Where counted Billets are by Carmen tost;
Stay thy rash Steps, and walk without the Post.

What though the gath'ring Mire thy feet besmear,
The Voice of Industry is always near.   100
Hark! The Boy calls thee to his destin'd Stand,
And the Shoe shines beneath his oily Hand.
Here let the Muse, fatigu'd amid the Throng,
Adorn her Precepts with digressive Song;
Of shirtless Youths the secret Rise to trace,   105
And show the Parent of the sable Race.

Like mortal Man, great *Jove* (grown fond of Change)
Of old was wont this nether World to range
To seek Amours; the Vice the Monarch lov'd
Soon through the wise etherial Court improv'd,   110
And ev'n the proudest Goddess now and then
Would lodge a Night among the Sons of Men;
To vulgar Deitys descends the Fashion,
Each, like her Betters, had her earthly Passion.
Then * *Cloacina* (Goddess of the Tide   115

* Cloacina *was a Goddess whose Image* Tatius (*a King of the* Sabines) *found in the common Sewer, and not knowing what Goddess it was, he called it* Cloacina *from the Place in which it was found, and paid to it divine Honours.* Lactant 1.20. Minuc. Fel. Octo. p. 232.

Whose sable Streams beneath the City glide)
Indulg'd the modish Flame; the Town she rov'd,
A mortal Scavenger she saw, she lov'd;
The muddy Spots that dry'd upon his Face,
Like Female Patches, heighten'd ev'ry Grace: 120
She gaz'd; she sigh'd. For Love can Beauties spy
In what seems Faults to ev'ry common Eye.

    Now had the Watchman walk'd his second Round;
When *Cloacina* hears the rumbling Sound
Of her brown Lover's Cart, for well she knows   125
That pleasing Thunder: Swift the Goddess rose,
And through the Streets pursu'd the distant Noise,
Her Bosom panting with expected Joys.
With the Night-wandring Harlot's Airs she past,
Brush'd near his Side, and wanton Glances cast;   130
In the black Form of Cinder-Wench she came,
When Love, the Hour, the Place had banish'd Shame;
To the dark Alley Arm in Arm they move:
O may no Link-Boy interrupt their Love!

    When the pale Moon had nine Times fill'd her Space,   135
The pregnant Goddess (cautious of Disgrace)
Descends to Earth; but sought no Midwife's Aid,
Nor midst her Anguish to *Lucina* pray'd;
No cheerful Gossip wish'd the Mother Joy,
Alone, beneath a Bulk she dropt the Boy.   140

    The Child through various Risques in Years improv'd,
At first a Beggar's Brat, Compassion mov'd;
His Infant Tongue soon learnt the canting Art,
Knew all the Pray'rs and Whines to touch the Heart.

    O happy unown'd Youths, your Limbs can bear   145
The scorching Dog-star, and the Winter's Air,
While the rich Infant, nurs'd with Care and Pain,
Thirsts with each Heat, and coughs with ev'ry Rain!

    The Goddess long had mark'd the Child's Distress,
And long had sought his Suff'rings to redress;   150

She prays the Gods to take the Fondling's Part,
To teach his Hands some beneficial Art
Practis'd in Streets; the Gods her Suit allow'd,
And made him useful to the walking Croud,
To cleanse the miry Feet, and o'er the Shoe   155
With nimble Skill the glossy Black renew.
Each Power contributes to relieve the Poor:
With the strong Bristles of the mighty Boar
Diana forms his Brush; the God of Day
A Tripod gives, amid the crouded Way   160
To raise the dirty Foot, and ease his Toil;
Kind *Neptune* fills his Vase with fetid Oil
Prest from th'enormous Whale; the God of Fire,
From whose Dominion smoaky Clouds aspire,
Among these gen'rous Presents joins his Part,   165
And aids with Soot the new japanning Art:
Pleas'd she receives the Gifts; she downward glides,
Lights in *Fleet-ditch*, and shoots beneath the Tides.

      Now dawns the Morn, the sturdy Lad awakes,
Leaps from his Stall, his tangled Hair he shakes,   170
Then leaning o'er the Rails, he musing stood,
And view'd below the black Canal of Mud,
Where common Sewers a lulling Murmur keep,
Whose Torrents rush from *Holborn*'s fatal Steep:
Pensive through Idleness, Tears flow'd apace,   175
Which eas'd his loaded Heart, and wash'd his Face;
At length he sighing cry'd; That Boy was blest,
Whose Infant Lips have drain'd a Mother's Breast;
But happier far are those, (if such be known)
Whom both a Father and a Mother own: 180
But I, alas! hard Fortune's utmost Scorn,
Who ne'er knew Parent, was an Orphan born!
Some Boys are rich by Birth beyond all Wants,
Belov'd by Uncles, and kind good old Aunts;
When Time comes round, a Christmas-box they bear,   185
And one Day makes them rich for all the Year.
Had I the Precepts of a Father learn'd,
Perhaps I then the Coachman's Fare had earn'd,
For lesser Boys can drive; I thirsty stand

And see the double Flaggon charge their Hand,   190
See them puff off the Froth, and gulp amain,
While with dry Tongue I lick my Lips in vain.

   While thus he fervent prays, the heaving Tide
In widen'd Circles beats on either Side;
The Goddess rose amid the inmost Round,   195
With wither'd Turnip Tops her Temples crown'd;
Low reach'd her dripping Tresses, lank, and black
As the smooth Jet, or glossy Raven's Back;
Around her Waste a circling Eel was twin'd,
Which bound her Robe that hung in Rags behind.   200
Now beck'ning to the Boy; she thus begun,
Thy Prayers are granted; weep no more, my Son:
Go thrive. At some frequented Corner stand,
This Brush I give thee, grasp it in thy Hand,
Temper the Soot within this Vase of Oil,   205
And let the little Tripod aid thy Toil;
On this methinks I see the walking Crew
At thy Request support the miry Shoe,
The Foot grows black that was with Dirt imbrown'd,
And in thy Pocket gingling Half-pence sound.   210
The Goddess plunges swift beneath the Flood,
And dashes all around her Show'rs of Mud:
The Youth strait chose his Post; the Labour ply'd
Where branching Streets from *Charing-cross* divide;
His treble Voice resounds along the *Meuse*,   215
And *White-hall* echoes—*Clean your Honour's Shoes.*

   Like the sweet Ballad, this amusing Lay
Too long detains the Walker on his Way;
While he attends, new Dangers round him throng;
The busy City asks instructive Song.   220

   Where elevated o'er the gaping Croud,
Clasp'd in the Board the perjur'd Head is bow'd,
Betimes retreat; here, thick as Hail-stones pour,
Turnips, and half-hatched Eggs, (a mingled Show'r)
Among the Rabble rain: Some random Throw   225
May with the trickling Yolk thy Cheek o'erflow.

Of narrow Streets.

Though Expedition bids, yet never stray
Where no rang'd Posts defend the rugged Way.
Here laden Carts with thundering Waggons meet,
Wheels clash with Wheels, and bar the narrow Street;   230
The lashing Whip resounds, the Horses strain,
And Blood in anguish bursts the swelling Vein.
O barb'rous Men, your cruel Breasts asswage,
Why vent ye on the gen'rous Steed your Rage?
Does not his Service earn your daily Bread?   235
Your Wives, your Children, by his Labours fed!
If, as the *Samian* taught, the Soul revives,
And shifting Seats, in other Bodies lives;
Severe shall be the brutal Coachman's Change,
Doom'd, in a *Hackney* Horse, the Town to range: 240
Carmen, transform'd the groaning Load shall draw,
Whom other Tyrants, with the Lash, shall awe.

The most inconvenient Streets to Walkers.

Who would of *Watling-street* the Dangers share,
When the broad Pavement of *Cheap-side* is near?
Or who * that rugged Street would traverse o'er,   245
That stretches, O *Fleet-ditch*, from thy black Shore
To the *Tow'rs* moated Walls? Here Steams ascend
That, in mix'd Fumes, the wrinkled Nose offend.
Where Chandlers Cauldrons boil, where fishy Prey
Hide the wet Stall, long absent from the Sea;   250
And where the Cleaver chops the Heifer's Spoil,
And where huge Hogsheads sweat with trainy Oil,
Thy breathing Nostril hold; but how shall I
Pass, where in Piles † *Cornavian* Cheeses lye;
Cheese, that the Table's closing Rites denies,   255
And bids me with th'unwilling Chaplain rise.

The Pell-mell celebrated.

O bear me to the Paths of fair Pell-mell,
Safe are thy Pavements, grateful is thy Smell!
At distance, rolls along the gilded Coach,
Nor sturdy Carmen on thy Walks encroach;   260
No Lets would bar thy Ways, were Chairs deny'd,

* Thames-street.   † Cheshire *anciently so called.*

The soft Supports of Laziness and Pride;
Shops breathe Perfume, thro' Sashes Ribbons glow,
The mutual Arms of Ladies, and the Beau.
Yet still ev'n Here, when Rains the Passage hide,   265
Oft the loose Stone spirts up a muddy Tide
Benath thy careless Foot; and from on high,
Where Masons mount the Ladder, Fragments fly;
Mortar, and crumbled Lime in Show'rs descend,
And o'er thy Head destructive Tiles impend.   270

But sometimes let me leave the noisie Roads,
And silent wander in the close Abodes
Where Wheels ne'er shake the Ground; there pensive stray,
In studious Thought, the long uncrouded Way.
Here I remark each Walker's diff'rent Face,   275
And in their Look their various Bus'ness trace.
The Broker here his spacious Beaver wears,
Upon his Brow sit Jealousies and Cares;
Bent on some Mortgage, to avoid Reproach,
He seeks bye Streets, and saves th'expensive Coach.   280
Soft, at low Doors, old Letchers tap their Cane,
For fair Recluse, that travels *Drury-lane.*
Here roams uncomb'd, the lavish Rake, to shun
His *Fleet-street* Draper's everlasting Dun.

The Pleasure of walking through an Alley.

Careful Observers, studious of the Town,   285
Shun the Misfortunes that disgrace the Clown.
Untempted, they contemn the Jugler's Feats,
Pass by the *Meuse,* nor try the * Thimble's Cheats
When Drays bound high, they never cross behind,
Where bubbling Yest is blown by Gusts of Wind: 290
And when up *Ludgate-hill* huge Carts move slow,
Far from the straining Steeds, securely go,
Whose dashing Hoofs, behind them, fling the Mire,
And mark, with muddy Blots, the gazing 'Squire.
The *Parthian* thus his Jav'lin backward throws,   295
And as he flies, infests pursuing Foes.

Inconveniences that attend those who are unacquainted with the Town.

* *A Cheat, commonly practic'd in the Streets, with three Thimbles and a little Ball.*

The thoughtless Wits shall frequent Forfeits pay,
Who 'gainst the Centry's Box discharge their Tea.
Do thou some Court, or secret Corner seek,
Nor flush with Shame the passing Virgin's Cheek.   300

Precepts   Yet let me not descend to trivial Song,
vulgarly   Nor vulgar Circumstance my Verse prolong;
known.   Why should I teach the Maid when Torrents pour,
Her Head to shelter from the sudden Show'r?
Nature will best her ready Hand inform,   305
With her spread Petticoat to fence the Storm.
Does not each Walker know the warning Sign,
When Wisps of Straw depend upon the Twine
Cross the close Street: that then the Pavior's Art
Renews the Ways, deny'd to Coach and Cart?   310
Who knows not, that the Coachman lashing by,
Oft', with his Flourish, cuts the heedless Eye;
And when he takes his Stand, to wait a Fare,
His Horses Foreheads shun the Winter's Air?
Nor will I roam, when Summer's sultry Rays   315
Parch the dry Ground, and spread with Dust the Ways;
With whirling Gusts, the rapid Atoms rise,
Smoak o'er the Pavement, and involve the Skies.

Frosty   Winter my Theme confines; whose nitry Wind
Weather. Shall crust the slabby Mire, and Kennels bind;   320
She bids the Snow descend in slaky Sheets,
And in her hoary Mantle cloath the Streets.
Let not the Virgin tread these slipp'ry Roads,
The gath'ring Fleece the hollow Patten loads;
But if thy Footsteps slide with clotted Frost,   325
Strike off the breaking Balls agains the Post.
On silent Wheel the passing Coaches roll;
Oft' look behind and ward the threatening Pole.
In harden'd Orbs the School-boy moulds the Snow,
To mark the Coachman with a dextrous Throw.   330
Why do ye, Boys, the Kennel's Surface spread,
To tempt with faithless Pass the Matron's Tread?
How can ye laugh, to see the Damsel spurn,
Sink in your Frauds and her green Stocking mourn?

At *White's*, the harness'd Chairman idly stands,   335
And swings, around his Waste, his tingling Hands:
The Sempstress speeds to '*Change* with red-tipt Nose;
The *Belgian* Stove beneath her Footstool glows,
In half-whipt Muslin Needles useless lye,
And Shuttle-cocks across the Counter fly.   340
These Sports warm harmless; why then will you prove,
Deluded Maids, the dang'rous Flame of Love?

    Where *Covent-garden's* famous Temple stands,   *The*
That boasts the Work of *Jones'* immortal Hands;   *Dangers*
Columns, with plain Magnificence appear,   345   *of Foot-*
And graceful Porches lead along the Square: *ball.*
Here oft' my Course I bend, when lo! from far,
I spy the Furies of the Foot-ball War:
The 'Prentice quits his Shop, to join the Crew,
Encreasing Crouds the flying Game pursue.   350
Thus, as you roll the Ball o'er snowy Ground,
The gath'ring Globe augments with ev'ry Round;
But whither shall I run? the Throng draws nigh,
The Ball now Skims the Street, now soars on high;
The dextrous Glazier strong returns the Bound,   355
And gingling Sashes on the Pent-house sound.

    O roving Muse, recal that wond'rous Year,   *An*
When Winter reigned in bleak *Britannia's* Air;   *Episode*
When hoary *Thames*, with frosted Oziers crown'd,   *of the*
Was three long Moons in icy Fetters bound.   360   *great*
The Waterman, forlorn along the Shore,   *Frost.*
Pensive reclines upon his useless Oar,
Sees harness'd Steeds desert the stony Town;
And wander Roads unstable, not their own:
Wheels o'er the harden'd Waters smoothly glide,   365
And rase with whiten'd Tracks the slipp'ry Tide.
Here the fat Cook piles high the blazing Fire,
And scarce the Spit can turn the Steer entire.
Booths sudden hide the *Thames*, long Streets appear,
And num'rous Games proclaim the crouded Fair.   370
So when a Gen'ral bids the martial Train
Spread their Encampment o'er the spatious Plain;

Thick-rising Tents a Canvas City build,
And the loud Dice resound thro' all the Field.
'Twas here the Matron found a doleful Fate: 375
In Elegiac Lay the Woe relate,
Soft, as the Breath of distant Flutes, at Hours,
When silent Ev'ning closes up the Flow'rs;
Lulling, as falling Water's hollow noise;
Indulging Grief, like *Philomela*'s Voice.   380

    Doll ev'ry day had walk'd these treach'rous Roads;
Her Neck grew warpt beneath autumnal Loads
Of various Fruit; she now a Basket bore,
That Head, alas! shall Basket bear no more.
Each Booth she frequent past, in quest of Gain,   385
And Boys with pleasure heard her shrilling Strain.
Ah Doll! All Mortals must resign their Breath,
And Industry it self submit to Death!
The cracking Crystal yields, she sinks, she dyes,
Her Head, chopt off, from her lost Shoulders flies: 390
Pippins she cry'd, but Death her Voice confounds,
And Pip-Pip-Pip along the Ice resounds.
So when the *Thracian* Furies *Orpheus* tore,
And left his bleeding Trunk deform'd with Gore,
His sever'd Head floats down the silver Tide,   395
His yet warm Tongue for his lost Consort cry'd;
Eurydice, with quiv'ring Voice, he mourn'd,
And *Heber*'s Banks *Eurydice* return'd.

A Thaw.   But now the western Gale the Flood unbinds,
And black'ning Clouds move on with warmer Winds,   400
The wooden Town its frail Foundation leaves,
And *Thames*' full Urn rolls down his plenteous Waves:
From ev'ry Penthouse streams the fleeting Snow,
And with dissolving Frost the Pavements flow.

How to   Experienc'd Men, inur'd to City Ways,   405
know the Need not the Calendar to count their Days.
Days of When through the Town, with slow and solemn Air,
the Week. Led by the Nostril, walks the muzled Bear;
Behind him moves majestically dull,

The Pride of *Hockley-hole*, the surly Bull;   410
Learn hence the Periods of the Week to name,
Mondays and *Thursdays* are the Days of Game.

When fishy Stalls with double Store are laid;
The golden-belly'd Carp, the broad-finn'd Maid,
Red-speckled Trouts, the Salmon's silver Joul,   415
The jointed Lobster, and unscaly Soale,
And luscious 'Scallops, to allure the Tastes
Of rigid Zealots to delicious Fasts;
Wednesdays and *Fridays* you'll observe from hence,
Days, when our Sires were doom'd to Abstinence.   420

When dirty Waters from Balconies drop,
And dextrous Damsels twirl the sprinkling Mop,
And cleanse the spatter'd Sash, and scrub the Stairs,
Know *Saturday's* conclusive Morn appears.

Successive Crys the Season's Change declare,   425   *Remarks*
And mark the Monthly Progress of the Year.   *on the*
Hark, how the Streets with treble Voices ring,   *Cries*
To sell the bounteous Product of the Spring!   *of the*
Sweet-smelling Flow'rs, and Elders early Bud,   *Town.*
With Nettle's tender Shoots, to cleanse the Blood: 430
And when *June's* Thunder cools the sultry Skies,
Ev'n *Sundays* are prophan'd by Mackrell Cries.

Wallnutts the *Fruit'rer's* Hand, in Autumn, stain,
Blue Plumbs, and juicy Pears augment his Gain;
Next Oranges the longing Boys entice,   435
To trust their Copper-Fortunes to the Dice.

When Rosemary, and Bays, the Poet's Crown,   *Of*
Are bawl'd, in frequent Cries, through all the Town,   *Christmas.*
Then judge the Festival of *Christmas* near,
Christmas, the joyous Period of the Year.   440
Now with bright Holly all your Temples strow,
With Laurel green, and sacred Mistletoe.
Now, Heav'n-born *Charity*, thy Blessings shed;
Bid meagre Want uprear her sickly Head:

Bid shiv'ring Limbs be warm; let Plenty's Bowle,   445
In humble roofs, make glad the needy Soul.
See, see, the Heav'n-born Maid her Blessings shed.
Lo! meagre Want uprears her sickly Head;
Cloath'd are the Naked, and the Needy glad,
While selfish Avarice alone is sad.   450

Precepts
of Charity. Proud Coaches pass, regardless of the Moan,
Of Infant Orphans, and the Widow's Groan;
While Charity still moves the Walker's Mind,
His lib'ral Purse relieves the Lame and Blind.
Judiciously thy Half-pence are bestow'd,   455
Where the laborious Beggar sweeps the Road
Whate'er you give, give ever at Demand,
Nor let Old-Age long stretch his palsy'd Hand.
Those who give late, are importun'd each Day,
And still are teaz'd, because they still delay.   460
If e'er the Miser durst his Farthings spare,
He thinly spreads them through the publick Square,
Where, all beside the Rail, rang'd Beggars lie,
And from each other catch the doleful Cry;
With Heav'n, for Two-pence, cheaply wipes his Score,   465
Lifts up his Eyes, and hasts to beggar more.

Where the brass Knocker, wrapt in Flannel Band,
Forbids the Thunder of the Footman's Hand;
Th'Upholder, rueful Harbinger of Death
Waits, with Impatience, for the dying Breath;   470
As Vultures, o'er a Camp, with hov'ring Flight,
Snuff up the Carnage of the Fight.
Here cans't thou pass, unmindful of a Pray'r,
That Heav'n in Mercy may thy Brother spare?

Come, *F**** sincere, experienc'd Friend,   475
Thy Briefs, thy Deeds, and ev'n thy Fees suspend;
Come, let us leave the *Temple's* silent Walls,
Me Bus'ness to my distant Lodging calls:
Through the long *Strand* together let us stray,
With thee conversing, I forget the Way.   480
Behold that narrow Street, which steep descends,

Whose Building to the slimy Shore extends;
Here *Arundell's* fam'd Structure rear'd its Frame,
The Street alone retains an empty Name:
Where *Titian's* glowing Paint the Canvas warm'd, 485
And *Raphael's* fair Design, with Judgment, charm'd,
Now hangs the Bell-man's Song, and pasted here,
The colour'd Prints of *Overton* appear.
Where Statues breath'd, the Work of *Phidias'* Hands,
A wooden Pump, or lonely Watch-house stands.
There *Essex* stately Pile adorn'd the Shore, 490
There *Cecil's, Bedford's, Viller's,* now no more.
Yet *Burlington's* fair Palace still remains;
Beauty within, without Proportion reigns.
Beneath his Eye declining Art revives, 495
The Wall with animated Picture lives;
There *Hendel* strikes the Strings, the melting Strain
Transports the Soul, and thrills through ev'ry Vein;
There oft' I enter (but with cleaner Shoes)
For *Burlington's* belov'd by ev'ry Muse. 500

    O ye associate Walkers, O my friends,
Upon your State what Happiness attends!
What, though no Coach to frequent Visit rolls,
Nor for your Shilling Chairmen sling their Poles;
Yet still your Nerves rheumatic Pains defye, 505
Nor lazy Jaundice dulls your Saffron Eye;
No wasting Cough discharges Sounds of Death,
Nor wheezing Asthma heaves in Vain for Breath;
Nor from your restless Couch is heard the Groan
Of burning Gout, or sedentary Stone. 510
Let others in the jolting Coach confide,
Or in the leaky Boat the *Thames* divide;
Or, box'd within the Chair, contemn the Street,
And trust their Safety to another's Feet,
Still let me walk; for oft' the sudden Gale 515
Ruffles the Tide, and shifts the dang'rous Sail,
Then shall the Passenger, too late, deplore
The whelming Billow, and the faithless Oar;
The drunken Chairman in the Kennel spurns,
The Glasses shatters, and his Charge o'erturns. 520

The Happiness of Walkers.

Who can recount the Coach's various Harms?
The Legs disjointed, and the broken Arms?

   I've seen a Beau, in some ill-fated Hour,
When o'er the Stones choak'd Kennels swell the Show'r,
In gilded Chariot loll; he with Disdain   525
Views spatter'd Passengers, all drenched in Rain;
With Mud fill'd high, the rumbling Cart draws near,
Now rule thy prancing Steeds, lac'd Charioteer!
The *Dustman* lashes on with spiteful Rage,
His pond'rous Spokes thy painted Wheel engage,   530
Crush'd is thy Pride, down falls the shrieking Beau,
The slabby Pavement crystal Fragments strow,
Black Floods of Mire th'embroider'd Coat disgrace,
And Mud enwraps the Honours of his Face.
So when dread *Jove*, the Son of *Phoebus* hurl'd,   535
Scarr'd with dark Thunder, to the nether World;
The headstrong Coursers tore the silver Reins,
And the Sun's beamy Ruin gilds the Plains.

   If the pale Walker pants with weak'ning Ills,
His sickly Hand is stor'd with friendly Bills: 540
From hence, he learns the seventh-born Doctor's Fame,
From hence, he learns the cheapest Tailor's Name.

   Shall the large Mutton smoak upon your Boards?
Such, *Newgate's* copious Market best affords;
Would'st though with mighty Beef augment thy Meal?   545
Seek *Leaden-hall*; Saint *James's* sends thee Veal.
Thames-street gives Cheeses; *Covent-garden* Fruits;
Moor-fields old Books; and *Monmouth-street* old Suits.
Hence may'st thou well supply the Wants of Life,
Support thy Family, and cloath thy Wife.   550

   Volumes, on shelter'd Stalls, expanded lye,
And various Science lures the learned Eye;
The bending Shelves with pond'rous Scholiasts groan,
And deep Divines to modern Shops unknown:
Here, like a Bee that on industrious Wing,   555
Collects the various Odours of the Spring,

Walkers, at leisure, Learning's Flow'rs may spoil,
Nor watch the Wasting of the Midnight Oil,
May Morals snatch'd from *Plutarch's* tatter'd Page,
A mildew'd *Bacon*, or *Stagyra's* Sage.   560
Here saunt'ring 'Prentices o'er *Otway* weep,
O'er *Congreve* smile, or over *D*** sleep;
Pleas'd Sempstresses the *Lock's* fam'd *Rape* unfold,
And † *Squirts* read *Garth*, 'till *Apozems* grow cold.

    O *Lintott*, let my Labours obvious lie,   565
Rang'd on thy Stall, for ev'ry curious Eye;
So shall the Poor these Precepts *gratis* know,
And to my Verse their future Safeties owe.

    What Walker shall his mean Ambition fix,
On the false Lustre of a Coach and Six?
Let the vain Virgin, lur'd by glaring Show,   570
Sigh for the Liv'rys of th'embroider'd Beau.

    See, yon' bright Chariot on its Harness swing,
With *Flanders* Mares, and on an arched Spring,
That Wretch, to gain an Equipage and Place,   575
Betray'd his Sister to a lewd Embrace.
This Coach, that with the blazon'd 'Scutcheon glows,
Vain of his unknown Race the Coxcomb shows.
Here the brib'd Lawyer, sunk in Velvet, sleeps;
The starving Orphan, as he passes, weeps;   580
There flames a Fool, begirt with tinselled Slaves,
Who wastes the Wealth of a whole Race of Knaves.
That other, with a clustering Train behind,
Owes his new Honours to a sordid Mind.
This next in Court Fidelity excels,   585
The Publick rifles, and his Country sells.
May the proud Chariot never be my fate,
If purchas'd at so mean, so dear a Rate;
O rather give me sweet Content on Foot,
Wrapt in my Vertue, and a good *Surtout*!   590

    † *The Name of an* Apothecary *in the Poem of the* Dispensary.

BOOK III.

Of Walking the Streets by Night.

*O T*RIVIA, Goddess, leave these low Abodes,
    And traverse o'er the wide Ethereal Roads,
Celestial Queen, put on thy Robes of Light,
Now *Cynthia* nam'd, fair Regent of the Night.
At Sight of thee, the Villain sheaths his Sword,   5
Nor scales the Wall, to steal the wealthy Hoard.
Oh! May thy Silver Lamp in Heav'n's high Bow'r
Direct my Footsteps in the Midnight Hour.

The   When Night first bids the twinkling Stars appear,
Evening.   Or with her cloudy Vest inwraps the Air,   10
Then swarms the busie Street; with Caution tread,
Where the Shop-Windows falling threat thy Head;
Now Lab'rers home return, and join their Strength
To bear the tott'ring Plank, or Ladder's Length;
Still fix thy Eyes intent upon the Throng,   15
And as the Passes open, wind along.

Of the   Where the fair Columns of Saint *Clement* stand,
Pass of   Whose straiten'd Bounds encroach upon the *Strand*;
St.   Where the low Penthouse bows the Walker's Head,
Clements. And the rough Pavement wounds the yielding Tread;   20
Where not a Post protects the narrow Space,
And strung in Twines, Combs dangle in thy Face;
Summon at once thy Courage, rouze thy Care,
Stand firm, look back, be resolute, beware.
Forth issuing from steep Lanes, the *Collier*'s Steeds   25
Drag the black Load; another Cart succeeds,
Team follows Team, Crouds heap'd on Crouds appear,
And wait impatient, 'till the Road grow clear.
Now all the Pavement sounds with trampling Feet,
And the mixt Hurry barricades the Street.   30
Entangled here, the Waggon's lengthened Team
Crack the tough Harness; Here a pond'rous Beam
Lies over-turn'd athwart; For Slaughter fed,
Here lowing Bullocks raise their horned Head.

Now Oaths grow loud, with Coaches Coaches jar,   35
And the smart Blow provokes the sturdy War;
From the high Box they whirl the Thong around,
And with the twining Lash their Shins resound:
Their Rage ferments, more dang'rous Wounds they try,
And the Blood gushes down their painful Eye.   40
And now on Foot the frowning Warriors light,
And with their pond'rous Fists renew the fight;
Blow answers Blow, their Cheeks are 'smear'd with Blood,
'Till down they fall, and grappling roll in Mud.
So when two Boars, in wild * *Ytene* bred,   45
Or on *Westphalia's* fatt'ning Chest-nuts fed,
Gnash their sharp Tusks, and rous'd with equal Fire,
Dispute the Reign of some luxurious Mire;
In the black Flood they wallow o'er and o'er,
'Till their arm'd Jaws distill with Foam and Gore.   50

    Where the Mob gathers, swiftly shoot along,   *Of Pick-*
Nor idly mingle in the noisy Throng.   *Pockets.*
Lur'd by the Silver Hilt, amid the Swarm,
The subtil Artist will thy Side disarm.
Nor is thy Flaxen Wigg with Safety worn;   55
High on the Shoulder, in the Basket born,
Lurks the sly Boy; whose Hand to Rapine bred,
Plucks off the curling Honours of the Head.
Here dives the skulking Thief, with practis'd Slight,
And unfelt Fingers make thy Pocket light.   60
Where's now thy Watch, with all its Trinkets, flown?
And thy late Snuff-Box is no more thy own.
But lo! his bolder Thefts some Tradesman spies,
Swift from his Prey the scudding Lurcher flies;
Dext'rous he scapes the Coach, with nimble Bounds,   65
While ev'ry honest Tongue *Stop Thief* resounds.
So speeds the wily Fox, alarm'd by Fear,
Who lately filch'd the Turkey's callow Care;
Hounds following Hounds, grow louder as he flies,
And injur'd Tenants joyn the Hunter's Cries.   70
Breathless he stumbling falls: Ill-fated Boy!

    * New Forest *in* Hampshire, *anciently so call'd.*

Why did not honest Work thy Youth employ?
Seiz'd by rough Hands, he's dragg'd amid the Rout,
And stretch'd beneath the Pump's incessant Spout:
Or plung'd in miry Ponds, he gasping lies,   75
Mud choaks his Mouth, and plaisters o'er his Eyes.

Of Ballad-Singers.   Let not the Ballad-Singer's shrilling Strain
Amid the Swarm thy list'ning Ear detain:
Guard well thy Pocket; for these *Syrens* stand,
To aid the Labours of the diving Hand;   80
Confed'rate in the cheat, they draw the Throng,
And *Cambrick* Handkerchiefs reward the Song.
But soon as Coach or Cart drives rattling on,
The Rabble part, in Shoals they backward run.
So *Jove's* loud Bolts the mingled War divide,   85
And *Greece* and *Troy* retreats on either side.

Of walking with a Friend.   If the rude Throng pour on with furious Pace,
And hap to break thee from a Friend's Embrace,
Stop short; nor struggle thro' the Croud in vain,
But watch with careful Eye the passing Train.   90
Yet I (perhaps too fond) if chance the Tide
Tumultuous, bears my Partner from my Side,
Impatient venture back; despising Harm,
I force my Passage where the thickest swarm.
Thus his lost Bride the *Trojan* sought in vain   95
Through Night, and Arms, and Flames, and Hills of Slain.
Thus *Nisus* wander'd o'er the pathless Grove,
To find the brave Companion of his Love,
The pathless Grove in vain he wanders o'er:
Euryalus alas! is now no more.   100

Of inadvertent Walkers.   That Walker, who regardless of his Pace,
Turns oft' to pore upon the Damsel's Face,
From Side to Side by thrusting Elbows tost,
Shall strike his aking Breast against the Post;
Or Water, dash'd from fishy Stalls, shall stain   105
His hapless Coat with Spirts of scaly Rain.
But if unwarily he chance to stray,

Where twirling Turnstiles intercept the Way,
The thwarting Passenger shall force them round,
And beat the Wretch half breathless to the Ground.   110

    Let constant Vigilance thy Footsteps guide;   *Useful*
And wary Circumspection guard thy Side;   *Precepts.*
Then shalt thou walk unharm'd the dang'rous Night,
Nor need th'officious Link-Boy's smoaky Light.
Thou never wilt attempt to cross the Road,   115
Where Alehouse Benches rest the Porter's Load,
Grievous to heedless Shins; No Barrow's Wheel,
That bruises oft' the Truant School-Boy's Heel,
Behind thee rolling, with insidious Pace,
Shall mark thy Stocking with a miry Trace.   120
Let not thy vent'rous Steps approach too nigh,
Where gaping wide, low steepy Cellars lie;
Should thy Shoe wrench aside, down, down you fall,
And overturn the scolding Huckster's Stall,
The scolding Huckster shall not o'er thee moan,   125
But Pence exact for Nuts and Pears o'erthrown.

    Though you through cleanlier Allies wind by Day,   *Safety*
To shun the Hurries of the publick Way,   *first of*
Yet ne'er to those dark Paths by Night retire;   *all to be*
Mind only Safety, and contemn the Mire.   *consider'd.*   130
The no impervious Courts thy haste detain,
Nor sneering Ale-Wives bid thee turn again.

    Where *Lincoln's-Inn*, wide Space, is rail'd around   *The*
Cross not with vent'rous Step; there oft' is found   *Danger*
The lurking Thief, who while the Day-light shone,   135   *of crossing*
Made the walls eccho with his begging Tone: *a Square*
That Crutch which late Compassion mov'd, shall wound   *by Night.*
Thy bleeding Head, and fell thee to the Ground.
Though thou art tempted by the Link-man's Call,
Yet trust him not along the lonely Wall;   140
In the Mid-way he'll quench the flaming Brand,
And share the Booty with the pilf'ring Band.
Still keep the publick Streets, where oily Rays
Shot from the Crystal Lamp, o'erspread the Ways.

The
Happiness
of
London.
  Happy *Augusta*! Law-defended Town!   145
Here no dark Lanthorns shade the Villain's Frown;
No *Spanish* Jealousies thy Lanes infest,
Nor *Roman* Vengeance stabs th'unwary Breast;
Here *Tyranny* ne'er lifts her purple Hand,
But Liberty and Justice guard the Land;   150
No *Bravos* here profess the bloody Trade,
Nor is the Church the Murd'rer's Refuge made.

  Let not the Chairman, with assuming Stride,
Press near the Wall, and rudely thrust thy Side:
The Laws have set him Bounds; his servile Feet   155
Should ne'er encroach where Posts defend the Street.
Yet who the Footman's Arrogance can quell,
Whose Flambeau gilds the Sashes of *Pell-mell*?
When in long Rank a Train of Torches flame,
To light the Midnight Visits of the Dame?   160
Others, perhaps by happier Guidance led,
May where the Chairmen rests, with Safety tread;
Whene'er I pass, their Poles unseen below,
Make my Knee tremble with the jarring Blow.

Of
crossing
the
Street.
  If Wheels bar up the Road, where Streets are crost, 165
With gentle Words the Coachman's Ear accost:
He ne'er the Threat, or harsh Command obeys,
But with Contempt the spatter'd Shoe surveys.
Now man with utmost Fortitude thy Soul,
To cross the Way where Carts and Coaches roll;   170
Yet do not in thy hardy Skill confide,
Nor rashly risque the Kennel's spacious Stride;
Stay till afar the distant Wheel you hear,
Like dying Thunder in the breaking Air;
Thy Foot will slide upon the miry Stone,   175
And passing Coaches crush thy tortur'd Bone,
Or Wheels enclose the Road; on either Hand
Pent round with Perils, in the midst you stand,
And call for Aid in vain; the Coachman swears,
And Carmen drive, unmindful of thy Prayers.   180
Where wilt thou turn? ah! whither wilt thou fly?

On ev'ry side the pressing Spokes are nigh.
So Sailors, while *Charybdis'* Gulphs they shun,
Amaz'd, on *Scylla's* craggy Dangers run.

Be sure observe where brown *Ostrea* stands,   185   *Of*
Who boasts her shelly Ware from *Wallfleet* Sands;   *Oysters.*
There may'st thou pass, with safe unmiry Feet,
Where the rais'd Pavement leads athwart the Street.
If where the *Fleet-Ditch* with muddy Current flows,
You chance to roam; where Oyster-Tubs in Rows   190
Are rang'd beside the Posts; there stay thy Haste,
And with the sav'ry Fish indulge thy Taste:
The Damsel's Knife the gaping Shell commands,
While the salt Liquor streams between her Hands.

The Man had sure a Palate cover'd o'er   195
With Brass or Steel, that on the rocky Shore
First broke the oozy Oyster's pearly Coat,
And risqu'd the living Morsel down his Throat.
What will not Lux'ry taste? Earth, Sea, and Air
Are daily ransacked for the Bill of Fare.   200
Blood stuff'd in Skins is *British* Christian's Food,
And *France* robs Marshes of the croaking Brood;
Spungy *Morells* in strong *Ragousts* are found,
And in the *Soupe* the slimy Snail is drown'd.

When from high Spouts the dashing Torrents fall,   205   *Observa-*
Ever be watchful to maintain the Wall;   *tions*
For should'st thou quit thy Ground, the rushing Throng   *concerning*
Will with impetuous Fury drive along;   *keeping*
All press to gain those Honours thou hast lost,   *the Wall.*
And rudely shove thee far without the Post.   210
Then to retrieve the Shed you strive in vain,
Draggled all o'er, and soak'd in Floods of Rain.
Yet rather bear the Show'r, and Toils of Mud,
Than in the doubtful Quarrel risque thy Blood.
O think on *Œdipus'* detested State,   215
And by his Woes be warn'd to shun thy Fate.

Where three Roads join'd, he met his Sire unknown;
(Unhappy Sire, but more unhappy Son!)
Each claim'd the Way, their Swords the Strife decide,
The hoary Monarch fell, he groan'd and dy'd!   220
Hence sprung the fatal Plague that thinn'd thy Reign,
Thy cursed Incest! and thy Children slain!
Hence wert thou doom'd in endless Night to stray
Through *Theban* Streets, and cheerless groap thy Way.

Of a   Contemplate, Mortal, on thy fleeting years;   225
Funeral.   See, with black Train the Funeral Pomp appears!
Whether some Heir attends in sable State,
And mourns with outward Grief a Parent's Fate;
Or the fair Virgin, nipt in Beauty's Bloom,
A Croud of Lovers follow to her Tomb.   230
Why is the Herse with 'Scutcheons blazon'd round,
And with the nodding Plume of Ostrich crown'd?
No: The Dead know it not, nor Profit gain;
It only serves to prove the Living vain.
How short is Life! how frail is human Trust!   235
Is all this Pomp for laying Dust to Dust?

Of   Where the nail'd Hoop defends the painted Stall,
avoiding   Brush not thy sweeping Skirt too near the Wall;
Paint.   Thy heedless Sleeve will drink the colour'd Oil,
And Spot indelible thy Pocket soil.   240
Has not wise Nature strung the Legs and Feet
With firmest Nerves, design'd to walk the Street?
Has she not given us Hands, to groap aright,
Amidst the frequent Dangers of the Night?
And think'st thou not the double Nostril meant,   245
To warn from oily Woes by previous Scent?

Of various   Who can the various City Frauds recite,
Cheats   With all the petty Rapines of the Night?
formerly   Who now the *Guinea-Dropper*'s Bait regards,
in practice. Trick'd by the Sharper's Dice, or Juggler's Cards?   250
Why shou'd I warn thee ne'er to join the Fray,
Where the Sham-Quarrel interrupts the Way?
Lives there in these our Days so soft a Clown,

Brav'd by the Bully's Oaths, or threat'ning Frown?
I need not strict enjoyn the Pocket's Care,   255
When from the crouded *Play* thou lead'st the Fair;
Who has not here, or Watch, or Snuff-Box lost,
Or Handkerchiefs that *India*'s Shuttle boast?

O! may thy Virtue guard thee through the Roads
Of *Drury*'s mazy Courts, and dark Abodes,   260
The Harlots' guileful Paths, who nightly stand,
Where *Katherine-street* descends into the *Strand*.
Say, vagrant Muse, their Wiles and subtil Arts,
To lure the Stranger's unsuspecting hearts;
So shall our Youth on healthful Sinews tread,   265
And City Cheeks grow warm with rural Red.

An Admonition to Virtue.

'Tis She who nightly strowls with saunt'ring Pace,
No stubborn Stays her yielding Shape embrace;
Beneath the Lamp her tawdry Ribbons glare,
The new-scower'd Manteau, and the slattern Air;   270
High-draggled Petticoats her Travels show,
And hollow Cheeks with artful Blushes glow;
With flatt'ring Sounds she sooths the cred'lous Ear,
My noble Captain! Charmer! Love! my Dear!
In Riding-hood, near Tavern-Doors she plies,   275
Or muffled Pinners hide her livid Eyes.
With empty Bandbox she delights to range,
And feigns a distant Errand from the *Change*;
Nay, she will oft' the Quaker's Hood prophane,
And trudge demure the Rounds of *Drury-Lane*.   280
She darts from Sarsnet Ambush wily Leers,
Twitches thy Sleeve, or with familiar Airs,
Her Fan will pat thy Cheek; these Snares disdain,
Nor gaze behind thee, when she turns again.

How to know a Whore.

I knew a Yeoman, who for thirst of Gain,   285
To the great City drove from *Devon*'s Plain
His num'rous lowing Herd; his Herds he sold,
And his deep leathern Pocket bagg'd with Gold;
Drawn by a fraudful Nymph, he gaz'd, he sigh'd;
Unmindful of his Home, and distant Bride,   290

A dreadful Example.

She leads the willing Victim to his Doom,
Through winding Alleys to her Cobweb Room.
Thence thro' the Street he reels, from Post to Post,
Valiant with Wine, nor knows his Treasure lost.
The vagrant Wretch th'assembled Watchmen spies,   295
He waves his Hanger, and their Poles defies;
Deep in the *Round-House* pent, all Night he snores,
And the next Morn in vain his Fate deplores.
Ah hapless Swain, unus'd to Pains and Ills!
Canst thou forgo Roast-Beef for nauseous Pills?   300
How wilt thou lift to Heav'n the Eyes and Hands,
When the long Scroll the Surgeon's fees demands!
Or else (ye Gods avert that worst Disgrace)
Thy ruin'd Nose falls level with thy Face,
Then shall thy Wife thy loathsome Kiss disdain,   305
And wholesome Neighbours from thy Mug refrain.

Of   Yet there are Watchmen, who with friendly Light,
Watchmen. Will teach thy reeling Steps to tread aright;
For *Sixpence* will support thy helpless Arm,
And Home conduct thee, safe from nightly Harm;   310
But if they shake their Lanthorns, from afar,
To call their Breth'ren to confed'rate War,
When Rakes resist their Pow'r; if hapless you
Should chance to wander with the scow'ring Crew;
Though Fortune yield thee Captive, ne'er despair,   315
But seek the Constable's consid'rate Ear;
He will reverse the Watchman's harsh Decree,
Mov'd by the Rhet'rick of a Silver Fee.
Thus would you gain some fav'rite Courtier's Word;
Fee not the petty Clarks, but bribe my Lord.   320

Of Rakes.   Now is the Time that Rakes their Revells keep;
Kindlers of Riot, Enemies of Sleep.
His scatter'd Pence the flying * *Nicker* flings,
And with the Copper Show'r the Casement rings.

---

* *Gentlemen, who delighted to break Windows with* Half-Pence.

Who has not heard the *Scowrer's* Midnight Fame? 325
Who has not trembled at the *Mohock's* Name?
Was there a Watchman took his hourly Rounds,
Safe from their Blows, or new-invented Wounds?
I pass their desp'rate Deeds, and Mischiefs done,
Where from *Snow-hill* black steepy Torrents run; 330
How Matrons, hoop'd within the Hogshead's Womb,
Were tumbled furious thence, the rolling Tomb
O'er the Stones thunders, bounds from Side to Side.
So *Regulus* to save his Country dy'd.

Where a dim Gleam the paly Lanthorn throws 335 *A*
O'er the mid' Pavement; heapy Rubbish grows, *necessary*
Or arched Vaults their gaping Jaws extend, *Caution*
Or the dark Caves to Common-Shores descend. *in a dark*
Oft' by the Winds, extinct the Signal lies, *Night.*
Or smother'd in the glimm'ring Socket dies, 340
E'er Night has half roll'd round her Ebon Throne;
In the wide Gulph the shatter'd Coach o'erthrown,
Sinks with the snorting Steeds; the Reins are broke,
And from the cracking Axle flies the Spoke.
So when fam'd *Eddystone's* far-shooting Ray, 345
That led the Sailor through the stormy Way,
Was from its rocky Roots by Billows torn,
And the high Turret in the Whirlewind born,
Fleets bulg'd their Sides against the craggy Land,
And pitchy Ruines blacken'd all the Strand. 350

Who then through Night would hire the harness'd Steed,
And who would chuse the rattling Wheel for Speed?

But hark! Distress with screaming Voice draws nigh'r, *A Fire.*
And wakes the slumb'ring Street with Cries of Fire.
At first a glowing Red enwraps the Skies, 355
And born by Winds the scatt'ring Sparks arise;
From Beam to Beam, the fierce Contagion spreads;
The spiry Flames now lift aloft their Heads,
Through the burst Sash a blazing Deluge pours,
And splitting Tiles descend in rattling Show'rs. 360
Now with thick Crouds th'enlighten'd Pavement swarms,

The Fire-man sweats beneath his crooked Arms,
A leathern Casque his vent'rous Head descends,
Boldly he climbs where thickest Smoak ascends;
Mov'd by the Mother's streaming Eyes and Pray'rs,   365
The helpless Infant through the Flame he bears,
With no less Virtue, than through hostile Fire,
The *Dardan* Hero bore his aged Sire.
See forceful Engines spout their levell'd Streams,
To quench the Blaze that runs along the Beams;   370
The grappling Hook plucks Rafters from the Walls,
And Heaps on Heaps the smoaky Ruine falls.
Blown by strong Winds the fiery Tempest roars,
Bears down new Walls, and pours along the Floors:
The Heaven's are all a-blaze, the Face of Night   375
Is cover'd with a sanguine dreadful Light;
'Twas such a Light involv'd thy Tow'rs, O *Rome*,
The dire Presage of mighty *Cæsar*'s Doom,
When the Sun veil'd in Rust his mourning Head,
And frightful Prodigies the Skies o'erspread.   380
Hark! the Drum thunders! Far, ye Crouds, retire:
Behold! the ready Match is tipt with Fire,
The nitrous Store is laid, the smutty Train
With running Blaze awakes the barrell'd Grain;
Flames sudden wrap the Walls; with sullen Sound,   385
The shatter'd Pile sinks on the smoaky Ground.
So when the Years shall have revolv'd the Date,
Th'inevitable Hour of *Naples*' Fate,
Her sap'd Foundations shall with Thunders shake,
And heave and toss upon the sulph'rous Lake;   390
Earth's Womb at once the fiery Flood shall rend,
And in th'Abyss her plunging Tow'rs descend.

Consider, Reader, what Fatigues I've known,
The Toils, the Perils of the wintry Town;
What Riots seen, what bustling Crouds I bor'd,   395
How oft' I cross'd where Carts and Coaches roar'd;
Yet shall I bless my Labours, if Mankind
Their future Safety from my Dangers find.
Thus the bold Traveller, inur'd to Toil,

Whose Steps have printed *Asia*'s desert Soil,   400
The barb'rous *Arabs* Haunt; or shiv'ring crost
Dark *Greenland*'s Mountains of eternal Frost;
Whom Providence, in length of Years, restores
To the wish'd Harbour of his native Shores;
Sets forth his Journals to the publick View,   405
To caution, by his Woes, the wandring Crew.

    And now compleat my gen'rous Labours lye,
Finish'd and ripe for Immortality.
Death shall entomb in Dust this mould'ring Frame,
But never reach th'eternal Part, my Fame.   410
When *W** and *G***, mighty Names, are dead;
Or but at *Chelsea* under Custards read;
When Criticks crazy Bandboxes repair,
And Tragedies, turn'd Rockets, bounce in Air;
High-rais'd on *Fleetstreet* Posts, consign'd to Fame,   415
This Work shall shine, and Walkers bless my Name.

FINIS

INDEX.

A.

B.

C.

D.

M.

N.

O.

P.

T.

V.

W.

Y.

† Entries added in 1730

POEM NOTES

Note on the Poem Text

The first edition of *Trivia* had two impressions. The one for subscribers, who paid a guinea for each copy, had generous margins and illustrative plates at the head of each of the poem's three books. Pope wrote to a friend on 10 January 1716 that the poem was on the brink of publication; on 26 January, the trade impression was published. There was a second edition in London in 1716, and one in Dublin from which a second Dublin edition was set in 1727, in which *Trivia* was followed by *Rural Sports*. The second London edition provided the text that appeared in Gay's *Poems* (1720), the third London edition of *Trivia* (1730), and the *Poems* of 1730 (published in Dublin) and 1731.

The text used below is taken from the first edition, but includes corrections issued with it and the passages Gay added to the second edition. Gay revised the poem for the second and third London editions, the *Poems* of 1720 when he dropped all but one side notes, and *Poems* 1731. Readers will find full variants and more information in John Gay, *Poetry and Prose*, ed. Vinton A. Dearing and Charles E. Beckwith, (Oxford, 1974), 2 vols.

Notes to the Poem

The following notes are indebted to those by Dearing and Beckwith. Their edition in turn draws on notes supplied by W. H. Williams in his edition of *Trivia* (1922).

Title *Trivia*: a pun. Its primary sense is Tri-via, three roads (pronounced with a long *i*); the secondary sense, a possible but not common usage, is trivia (pronounced with a short *i*), meaning trifles.

Epigraph *Quo te Mœri pedes? An, quo via ducit, in Urbem*: Virgil, Eclogue IX 1 'Whither afoot, Moeris? Is it, as the path leads, to town?' (trans. H. R. Fairclough, Loeb Classical Library, 1916); 'Where are you footing it, Moeris? to town? This trackway leads there' (trans. C. Day Lewis, 1940, repr. Oxford World's Classics, 1983). Moeris is a farmer, coming to town on foot.

Advertisement *denying me to be the Author of my own Works*: Gay refers obliquely to insinuations by Colley Cibber, playwright, actor and later protagonist of Pope's *Dunciad*, that Gay's 1715 farce, *The What D'Ye Call It*, was mostly written by Pope. Attribution was complicated in the early eighteenth century, not least by satirists who chose anonymity to escape prosecution.
   I owe several Hints of it to Dr. Swift: two poems by Swift, 'A Description of the Morning', published in *Tatler* No. 9, 30 April 1709, and 'A Description of a City Shower', in *Tatler* No. 238, 17 October 1710, provide antecedents for *Trivia*.
   Non tu: 'Was it not you, master Dunce, who at the cross-roads used to murder a sorry tune on a scrannel straw?' (Fairclough) Virgil, *Eclogues* III 26–7.

BOOK I

4   *When to assert the Wall*: walking on the inside of the street, next to the wall, was safest.

5   *I sing*: Thou Trivia aid my song: an imitation of classical invocations, for instance Virgil, *Georgics* I 40–2.

7   *transported*: transport in the period means both literal and figurative movement, i.e., to be carried away by emotion.

13   *Pavior*: paver, one who paves or lays pavements.

15   *Scavinger*: a street cleaner. Not just a person who does dirty work, but also one who labours for the public good (*OED*).
    Kennel: surface drain of a street, a gutter (*OED*).

19 *to ancient Bards unknown*: Gay glances here at a big debate at the time, as to whether ancient writers were the only model of literary excellence.

20 *bind my Temples*: the garland of laurels for poets.

21–2 a burlesque of Virgil's patriotic dedication in *Georgics* II, 174–5. 'Lays' means songs; more words rhyme with it than with 'poem', hence its popularity.

27 *Mall*: an avenue of trees at the north side of St James's Park.

28 *Oyster Cries*: the calls of those selling oysters, renewed around September.

30 *Morocco*: Dearing and Beckwith note this is the first reference to Morocco leather cited by *OED*.

32 *'scalloped top*: wavy-shaped around the ankle.

35 *Laste*: a cobbler's last is a wooden model of the foot, on which shoemakers shape boots or shoes.

40 *shooting Corn*: horny parts of the feet register changes in weather.

43 *Doily*: woollen material used for summer clothing. Named after a draper whose warehouse stood on the west side of Catherine St where it joined the Strand; he also gave his name to decorative pierced cloths or doileys.

44 *Drugget*: a thin material, half silk, half wool.

45 *Frieze*: fabric covered with a nap, which makes cotton downy.

46 *Camlet's cockled grain*: woven worsted, with a ribbed texture. Gay's details of fabrics and their textures may be attributed to his apprenticeship to a linen-draper.

47 *Witney Broad-cloath*: a heavy woollen material. Witney, a town in Oxfordshire, was famous for its wool products.

    Shag: rough, shaggy texture or surface.

49 *Horse-man's Fence*: parry, barrier or defence. Those wearing fur coats were often abused as foreigners.

51 *Roquelaure*: a knee-length coat, favoured by the first Duc de Roquelaure (1656–1738).

53 *loop'd Bavaroy*: a cloak or overcoat, with a knot of ribbons or braid, or fastened by loops. For anxieties about fops, see Philip Carter, 'Men about Town: Representations of Foppery and Masculinity in Early Eighteenth-Century Urban Society', in Hannah Barker and Elaine Chalus (eds.), *Gender in Eighteenth-Century England* (1997).

54 *deep*: expensive.

57–8 *Joseph, Wrap-Rascal, Surtout*: all names for loose overcoats.

59 *Kersey*: coarse narrow cloth, woven from long wool and usually ribbed (*OED*), possibly named for Kersey in Suffolk.

62 *Chairmen*: men who carried sedan chairs.

63 *Car-men*: drivers of work vehicles.

66 *Lamp*: lamps with magnifying lenses, which were lit between Michaelmas and Lady Day (29 September–25 April) between 6 p.m. and midnight, from the third day after a full moon to the sixth day after a new moon.

69 *Chariot*: a light, four-wheeled carriage with back seats and a coach box.

72 *White's, Assemblies*: White's was a chocolate house on St James's Street Public assemblies were receptions to which no invitation was needed.

78 *Cravat*: a handkerchief, usually linen, lace or silk, tied round the neck. Named after Croatian mercenaries in the seventeenth century who wore linen scarves (*OED*).

85–6 *Gallia*: France. Wooden shoes were a stock image expressing English ideas of French poverty and oppression at the time.

87 *Belgia*: the Netherlands. Usually the Dutch were represented as clean: thus Lady Mary Wortley Montagu, in 1716, on Rotterdam, 'Here is neither Dirt nor Beggary to be seen. One is not shock'd with those loathsome Cripples so common in London, nor teiz'd with the Importunitys of idle Fellows and Wenches that chuse to be nasty and lazy.' *Letters* (ed. R. Halsband), 3 vols. (Oxford, 1965), i. 249.

95 *frequent Murders*: another stock image of Naples as a city of assassins.

102 *Luxury*: a preoccupying concept in eighteenth-century social critiques. See John Sekora, *Luxury: The Concept in Western Thought, Eden to Smollett* (Baltimore, 1977) and Maxine Berg and Elizabeth Eger (eds.), *Luxury in the Eighteenth Century: Debates, Desires and Delectable Goods* (2003).

104 *late invented Chairs*: 'A closed vehicle to seat one person, borne on two poles by two bearers, one in front and one behind' (*OED*), sedan chairs were introduced into England in 1634, probably from Italy.

110 *Manteau*: a loose upper garment worn by women instead of a straight-bodied gown (*OED*).

111 *the . . . Fair*: women, often referred to in polite discourse as 'the fair' or 'the sex'.

114 *Equipage*: a word of many meanings—relevant senses here are a carriage and horses with attendant servants, and articles denoting rank or status (*OED*).

116 *Loves and Graces*: pictorial devices on the side of a coach.

117 *Broker*: Dearing and Beckwith suggest Gay means a pawnbroker.

121 *Morning Cries*: the cries of street sellers advertising their wares. Illustrated by Marcellus Laroon in *The Cryes of the Citye of London, Drawne after the Life* (1711). *Spectator* 251 complained, comically, 'Vocal Cries are of a

much larger Extent, and indeed so full of Incongruities and Barbarisms, that we appear a distracted City, to Foreigners, who do not comprehend the Meaning of such Enormous Outcries.' Donald Bond (ed.), *The Spectator*, 5 vols. (Oxford, 1965), ii. 475.

122 *Prognosticks*: Compare Virgil, *Georgics* I 351–463 on signs of the weather, and Swift, 'A Description of a City Shower', 1–2.

128 *flapping Hat*: with the brim not looped up, for greater protection against bad weather.

136 *Sulphur*: naturally present in coal in the form of pyrites.

138 *Dearth*: scarcity, especially of provisions; a time of scarcity (*OED*).

140 *Flannel Mantle*: flannel is an open woollen stuff; a mantle is a long sleeveless cloak of varying length (*OED*).

147 *Fawns*: young deer, here in St James's Park.

149 *Not that their Minds with greater Skill are fraught*: compare Virgil, *Georgics* I 415–16: 'Not, methinks, that they have wisdom from on high, or from Fate a larger foreknowledge of things to be' (Fairclough).

157 *Signs*: shop signs. Gay borrows the pun from Virgil, *Georgics* I 351.

161 *open Square*: this bookseller has no shop, but hangs his wares on railings around a square.

163 *rowing Crew*: Thames watermen.

164 *Tilts*: awnings over passenger boats. Smaller boats had no coverings.

168 *Niobe*: Niobe, queen of Thebes, made the mistake of vaunting her children above those of Latona, mother of Apollo and Diana. For this Apollo slew her children, and Niobe was changed to a rock, from which a trickle of tears forever flowed. The story was told by Ovid in *Metamorphoses* VI 165–312.

171 *Common-shores*: sewers.

177 *the Festival of Paul*: 25 January, feast of the conversion of St Paul.

180 *Hind*: a farm servant, an agricultural labourer.

183 *Swithin's Feast*: 15 July. Tradition says if rain falls on St Swithin's Day, rain will fall for forty days.
Welkin: a poetic word for sky.

184 *Penthouse*: in 1716, a penthouse meant a structure with a sloping roof, attached to a main building; it could apply to a canopy, a ledge over a door, a covered way, or projecting eaves. *OED* cites Defoe, *Robinson Crusoe*: 'It cast off the Rains like a Penthouse'.

203 *Alecto*: one of the Furies. Virgil describes the Furies as having snakes twined in their hair, *Georgics* IV 454–527.

204 *Orpheus*: poet and musician, Orpheus charmed even beasts and inanimate objects by the beauty of his songs. Hades, or Pluto, allowed him to descend to the underworld to bring back his dead wife Eurydice, on condition he did not look back. (He did.)

205 *Glaucus*: a sea-god who fell in love with Scylla when he saw her bathing. The enchantress Circe was jealous and changed her to a rock.

210 *Riding-hood*: on the fashion for hoods, see *Spectator* 265. Riding-hoods could cover the face as well as head.

211 *Umbrella*: used in hot countries to protect against the sun (note its etymology, from Latin *umbra*, shade) and as a symbol of rank.

212 *Patten*: an overshoe with a wooden sole on an iron ring (see Fig. 6).

223 *fenny*: a fen is a low-lying area of marshy ground, either covered with water or subject to inundation. Lincolnshire is famous for its fens.

227 *Martha*: a proverbial name for a good housewife, taken from the Bible, Luke 10: 38–42.

234 *Woodcock*: *scolopax rustica*, a bulky wading bird with short legs, much eaten in the eighteenth century. Appropriate here not just because it inhabits marshes, but because it was used figuratively to refer to a person easy to snare or to dupe.

241 *Vulcan*: the Roman god of fire and craftsmanship.

245 *Mulciber*: another name for Vulcan, implying his power to soften metals (used thus by Milton in *Paradise Lost*).

246 *Paphian Spouse*: Venus, to whom Vulcan was married. Paphos, in south-west Cyprus, is where, according to legend, Aphrodite (the Greek version of Venus) rose from the sea.

249 *Lemnian Pow'r*: Vulcan. The island of Lemnos in the Aegean Sea was where Vulcan fell after being thrown off Mount Olympus by his father, Jupiter, for defending his mother Juno in a quarrel.

260 *the Force of Praise*: a cliché of much early eighteenth-century writing about women, who supposedly found compliments irresistible.

280 *Presents*: another cliché of the time—that women could be seduced by presents if flattery failed. See Felicity Nussbaum, *The Brink of All We Hate: English Satires on Women 1660–1750* (Lexington, Ky., 1984).

BOOK II

1 *Thus far*: an echo of the beginning of the second *Georgic*, where Virgil reviews where the poem has got to and will go next.

9 *draggled*: made wet, limp, and dirty by trailing; often with reference to women's skirts.

10 *Billingsgate*: officially established as a fish market by an Act of Parliament in 1698, Billingsgate market was situated in the streets around Lower Thames Street. (The market moved into a waterfront building in 1859 and relocated to Docklands in 1984.)

11 *sallow*: sickly yellow. It was commonplace to describe town people as less healthy than country folk.

Gains: a note of deliveries of milk would be marked on doors, then erased when the bill was paid.

13 *Asses*: asses' milk was prescribed for sickly people; it helped patients put on weight. The asses were milked at customers' doors.

17 *Drummers*: drummers and players of other instruments visited the houses of newly married couples the morning after the wedding, and had to be paid to go away.

18 *Vellom-Thunder*: referring to the drum's covering of skin or vellum.

22 *Hawker*: one who sells. Laroon's *Cryes* (1711) include a man calling 'London's *Gazette* here'.

26 *rever'nd Gown*: clergy typically wore a black gown over a cassock.

26–30 *three Trades avoid*: the barber and perfumer used powder, the baker used flour.

33 *little Chimney-sweeper*: a boy sent up inside chimneys to clean them.

35 *Small-coal*: coal in small pieces or charcoal, used to start coal fires. 'Small Coal' was included in Laroon's *Cryes*.

40–1 *chandler*: chandlers sold candles, and sometimes other household goods. Expensive candles were made of beeswax, cheap ones of animal fat.

54 *mantling Peruke*: a large spreading wig, more usually referred to in England as a periwig. Gay's choice of an Anglicized French word, perruque, implies imported modishness. Comic contrasts between full wigs and empty heads were common in early eighteenth-century satire.

56 *red-heel'd Shoes*: compare *The Guardian*, No. 149 (2 vols., 1714, ii. 243) 'A *Dancing Master* of the lowest Rank seldom fails of the Scarlet Stocking and the Red Heel; and shows a particular respect to the *Leg* and *Foot*, to which he owes his Substance'.

59 *Bully*: the modern sense of bully, a cowardly tyrant, is present, but also included is an early modern sense of bully as a gallant or pimp—hence his finery.

66 *sworn Porter*: a porter who belonged to the Fellowship or Society of Porters. They were all freemen of London.

67 *Signs*: London shop signs were usually pictures, sometimes elaborate, without words. People not used to the conventions could easily be

mystified or misled by them. (Two survivals to the present day are a red and white striped pole, for a barber, and three brass balls, for a pawnbroker.)

69–70 *Prentices*: apprentices were commonly associated with mischief, disorderly behaviour, and riot.

72 *deceives . . . profits*: an odd remark for Gay to make. One might note a modern evolution of trust, in terms of asking a policeman for directions.

73 *fam'd Saint Giles*: the parish of St Giles was a mixed one—home to cheap tenements rented by porters, hawkers, needlewomen, prostitutes, and, in winter, gypsies.

74–5 *Column . . . sev'n Dials*: in 1690 Thomas Neal bought the land now known as Seven Dials, erecting a large sundial and designing a street system based on a six-pointed star (the seventh street was added later). Dickens described it as 'this complicated part of London' in *Sketches by Boz* (1836, ch. 5): 'The stranger who finds himself in 'the Dials' for the first time . . . at the entrance of seven obscure passages, uncertain which to take, will see enough around him to keep his curiosity and attention awake for no inconsiderable time'.

83–6 *Theseus . . . Ariadne*: Theseus, son of King Aegeus, volunteered to be one of seven youths and seven maidens sacrificed to the Minotaur, a bull-like monster kept in a labyrinth by King Minos of Crete. Minos's daughter, Ariadne, gave him a ball of thread to unwind as he passed through the labyrinth, by which means he was able to return safely after killing the Minotaur. One version of the myth has Theseus later abandoning Ariadne, which makes Gay's next lines about female duplicity more misogynist.

90 *Dive in thy Fob*: reach into a watch pocket. Dive was a cant term for pickpocketing. Gay calls one of the characters in *The Beggar's Opera* Jenny Diver.

91–2 *waggish Boys the stunted Beesom ply*: apprentices, associated with pranks, were commonly required to sweep the areas in front of their masters' shops. Compare Swift, 'A Description of the Morning', ll. 9–10: 'The Youth with Broomy Stumps began to trace / The Kennel-Edge, where Wheels had worn the Place.'

92 *slabby*: thick and sticky. Etymologically from Scandinavian words for mud and wet filth.

95 *Hogsheads*: large casks, each holding 52½ gallons. Deliveries of beer into cellars below street-level posed risks for pedestrians.

97 *counted Billets*: logs of firewood, counted out as they were thrown off carts.

98 *without the Post*: outside the line of posts that divided the walking area from the roadway.

99–220 This long digression, added in 1730, parallels and parodies Virgil's account at the end of the *Georgics*, of how Aristaeus, a shepherd, seeks help in discovering why his bees have all died. He appeals to his mother, the river goddess Cyrene, for help, visiting her watery domain. She tells him he must overpower Proteus, a creature of many shapes, who will then tell him the cause. Aristaeus learns from Proteus he has offended Orpheus and must propitiate him by sacrifices. When these are made, bees emerge from the bellies of rotting oxen. What Gay particularly makes use of is the plaintive appeal of a son to a powerful mother.

100 *Industry*: Hogarth described his series of twelve prints, *Industry and Idleness* (1747) as 'Modern Moral Subjects'.

102 *oily*: shoes were blacked with a mixture of soot and whale oil.

104 *digressive Song*: as Addison wrote in *An Essay on the Georgics* (1711), 'the Poet must take care not to encumber his Poem with too much Business; but sometimes to relieve the Subject with a Moral Reflection, or let it rest awhile for the sake of a pleasant and pertinent Digression.'

106 *Parent of the sable race*: in Christian thought, traditionally Ham, one of the three sons of Noah.

115 n. Gay's references are Book 1 ch. XX of the *Divine Institutes* of Lactantius (*c*.250–*c*.317AD) and ch. XXV of the *Octavius* by Minucius Felix (fl. *c*.200AD). Although Gay's note is typically Scriblerian in its parody of erudition, both authors were admired in the early eighteenth century as models of Christian piety and Roman eloquence, and had been translated into English.

117 *modish*: fashionable.

120 *Patches*: artificial beauty-spots or moles, usually made of black taffeta or silk, sometimes in intricate designs.

131 *Cinder-Wench*: a woman whose occupation was to rake live coals from ashes, for selling on.

134 *Link-Boy*: a lad who carried a torch of pitch and flax for public hire.

138 *Lucina*: the name given to Juno as goddess of childbirth; literally, 'she who brings light', hence not invoked by Cloacina in this black passage of the poem.

139 *Gossip*: a godmother or female friend who attended a birth.

140 *Bulk*: stall in front of a shop, which provided a rough bed or shelter for poor people.

142 *Beggar's Brat*: a boy employed by a beggar to increase sympathy.

143 *canting Art*: the peculiar form of speech and body language used by beggars. As one account from 1735 puts it, 'the greatest profligate of them flies to religion for aid, and assists his cant with a doleful tone and a study'd dismality of gestures'. See Tim Hitchcock, 'The Rhetoric of Rags', ch. 5, *Down and Out in Eighteenth-Century London* (2004).

146 *Dog-star*: Sirius, brightest star in the constellation Canis Major, which rises in August, and since Egyptian times associated with summer heat.

147 *rich Infant*: it was common in eighteenth-century thought to associate poverty with health.

149–68 As Dearing and Beckwith note, 'Here Gay introduces a parody of the sea-nymph Thetis' successful appeal to Hephaestus for armour for her son Achilles to replace that taken by the Trojans from Patroclus (Iliad XVIII. 380–617).'

151 *Fondling*: foundling. During winter walks in central London in the 1720s, Thomas Coram was so appalled by the number of abandoned children on the streets that he campaigned to establish a Foundling Hospital. It opened in 1741; Hogarth was one of its first governors.

159 *Diana . . . the God of Day*: in Greek religion, Diana was the goddess of hunting and Apollo was particularly associated with tripods.

166 *the new japanning Art*: highly polished lacquer work, usually with black background and gold decoration. Originally imported from the East, it was manufactured in England from the late seventeenth century. Pope mentions japanned tea-trays in *The Rape of the Lock* (1714): 'On shining Altars of Japan, they raise / The silver Lamp . . .' (III 107–8).

168 *Fleet-ditch*: the lower end of the Fleet River, which ran to the Thames. In Gay's time it was an open sewer. Gay's invocation of filthy waterways parodies Virgil's descriptions of the pure waters that lead Aristaeus to his mother Cyrene's watery bower.

174 *Holborn's fatal Steep*: fatal because the street formed a main part of the route for condemned criminals being taken from Newgate Prison to execution at Tyburn (near what is now Marble Arch). Holborn, still a major thoroughfare, becomes steeper at its east end.

177–82 *he sighing cry'd*: the Bootboy's lament echoes that of Aristaeus in Virgil's *Georgics*, IV 321–4.

185 *Christmas-box*: it was customary to pass round a box on St Stephen's Day, 26 December, to solicit for money; hence the English holiday of Boxing Day.

190 *double Flaggon*: a flagon was a drinking vessel, larger than a wine bottle, here used for beer.

196 *Turnip Tops*: Gay parodies the usual crown of laurel or bays.

205 *Temper*: mix.

214 *Charing-cross*: one of the busiest intersections of early eighteenth-century London.

215 *Meuse*: the Royal Mews occupied part of what is now Trafalgar Square.

216 *White-hall*: a road, a palace, and a metonym for the seat of government. The palace of Whitehall, largely destroyed by fire in 1698, had a walled garden with a Tudor gatehouse into Whitehall (the road), in which Gay lived from 1724 to 1729.

222 *Clasp'd in the Board*: perjury was punishable (until 1837) by a spell in the pillory, as were sodomy, seditious words, extortion, and forgery. The offender's head and hands were put through holes in the wooden framework, and for a set period he (or occasionally she) had to endure being jeered and pelted—from all sides, since the pillory could be turned. Gay's reference to vegetables and rotten eggs makes the episode relatively light; crowds often threw blood and guts, dead cats and dogs, excrement, bricks and stones, sometimes causing fatalities. There was a pillory at Charing Cross.

227 *Expedition*: here meaning haste rather than excursion.

228 *no rang'd Posts*: Gay means a street with no posts to protect pedestrians from wheeled traffic.

234 *the gen'rous Steed*: although horses and other draft animals were not protected by law from abuse until 1821, many early eighteenth-century writers deplored cruelty to animals. Pope wrote an essay in *The Guardian* (No. 61) in 1713, 'Against Barbarity to Animals', and Hogarth's 1751 series, *The Four Stages of Cruelty*, shows in plate 2 a young man beating a horse, with the lines: 'The generous Steed in hoary Age / Subdu'd by Labour lies, / And mourns a cruel Master's rage / While Nature Strength denies.'

237 *Samian*: the philosopher Pythagoras, born on the island of Samos. Gay uses Pythagoras's doctrine of metempsychosis, or the transmigration of souls, for imaginative purposes.

240 *Hackney Horse*: a riding horse for hire. Possibly etymologically from Hackney in Middlesex where many horses destined for London were bred and pastured. The seventeenth-century contraction 'hack', for both riding horse and drudge, was applied in the early eighteenth century to writers—hence the expression hack writers.

243–7 *Watling-street . . . Tow'rs*: Gay moves the action back to a geographically specific district, east of Whitehall, Charing Cross, and the Strand, to the area between the City and the Tower of London. Cheapside, whose name means a marketplace, was an especially busy street.

247–53 *mix'd Fumes*: many early modern writers complained about the smell of manufactories in London, including, as here, butchery, fishmongering, and candle-making, or chandlery. Those trades were related since fat from cows and blubber from whales were rendered down into, respectively, tallow and 'trainy Oil', to make candles.

254 *Cornarvian*: at the time of the Roman invasion, the Cornavii inhabited the area now known as Cheshire.

256 *th'unwilling Chaplain*: domestic chaplains were customarily excluded from dessert at the tables of the rich. So too was Gay when employed by the Duchess of Monmouth as secretary and domestic steward 1712–14.

257 *Pell-mell*: the street then, as now, was normally called Pall Mall. Gay may have preferred the topographically strange term to provide a rhyme, or he may have wanted the associations of 'pell-mell' at the time, meaning confusion and disorder.

261 *Lets*: hindrances.

263 *Sashes*: sash-windows, although possibly with a trace of a pun on sash's normal meaning as an article of dress.

269 *crumbled Lime*: in early eighteenth-century London, lime was used both in mortars and in plaster.

277 *spacious Beaver*: a broad-brimmed beaver hat worn by businessmen.

280 *bye Streets*: back ways, the opposite of highways.

282 *fair Recluse*: a secluded prostitute.

284 *Dun*: to demand payment. Just as the prostitute has hidden away, the rake evades creditors pursuing him for payment for his clothes. Gay's ideological grid of gender and class informs even quiet places in the city.

287 *Jugler*: juggler or magician.

289–90 *Dray*: a brewer's cart, with no sides, from which yeast or foam would be blown onto passers-by.

291 *Ludgate-hill*: *The Female Tatler* No. 9 (1709) celebrates Ludgate Hill's mercers' shops, as 'perfect gilded theatres'. Gay stresses the gradient's dangers.

295 *Parthian*: of Parthia, an ancient kingdom of Western Asia, famous for its horsemen and their skill in shooting arrows as they galloped off (as in Parthian shot, a sharp remark or glance given as one leaves).

298 *Tea*: urine.

306 *fence*: keep out.

308 *Wisps of Straw*: the equivalent of modern red and white striped plastic strips around construction sites and scaffolding, straw tied to string alerted pedestrians to building or repair works.

314 *His Horses Foreheads*: meaning unclear. Dearing and Beckwith suggest 'perhaps this means the horses try to warm their heads against the clothes of incautious bystanders'.

319 *nitry*: containing nitre, potassium nitrate, which was believed to cause frost or ice. Compare James Thomson, *Winter* (1726), ll. 301–3: 'Clear Frost succeeds, and thro' the blew Serene, / For Sight too fine, th'Aetherial Nitre flies, / To bake the Glebe, and bind the slippery Flood.'

328 *Pole*: coach-pole.

337 *'Change*: the New Exchange, on the Strand's south side, was a fashionable shopping place for dresses and haberdashery.

338 *The Belgian Stove*: in 1716 Lady Mary Wortley Montagu wrote enthusiastically from Belgium about stoves: 'I am surpriz'd we do not practise in England so usefull an Invention. This refflection naturally leads me to consider our obstinacy in shakeing with cold 6 months in the year rather than make use of Stoves, which are one of the greatest conveniencys of Life'. *Letters* (ed. Halsband), i. 290.

339 *half-whipt*: to whip is to sew with overhand stitches; the cold makes it impossible for the sempstress to finish her sewing. The Belgian stove, which could be tucked under skirts, implicates her in overheated sexuality; hence 'the danger'rous Flame of Love' arises, not just because she is temporarily idle.

343 *Covent-garden's famous Temple*: St Paul's Church, at the west side of the square, was built by Inigo Jones in 1631, who also designed housing with arcades or 'Porches' for the north and east sides.

348 *Foot-ball*: until the foundation of the Football Association in 1863 and the codification of rules, football was an anarchic affair, often played by whole villages or towns. The point was to get and maintain possession, not score goals.

357 *great Frost*: the Thames froze over in the winters of 1709–10 and 1715–16, solid and long enough for frost fairs to take place.

359 *Oziers*: osiers are shoots of a species of willow.

368 *Steer*: an ox, being roasted as part of the fun of the fair.

376 *Elegiac Lay*: Gay adds mock-elegy to mock-heroic here, using crepuscular clichés and conventional reflections on mortality.

380 *Philomela*: in mythology, Philomela was raped by her sister's husband, Tereus, who cut her tongue out and imprisoned her in a remote place.

There she wove a tapestry showing her wrongs which she sent to her sister, who then fed her own young son to its father. All three were changed into birds. Ovid tells the story in *Metamorphoses* Book VI. Etymologically the name Philomela means a lover of song, hence its figurative use for poetic expression.

391 *Pippins she cry'd*: Doll sold apples on the streets.

393 *Thracian Furies Orpheus tore*: Orpheus, having failed to bring back Eurydice from the underworld, wandered the world. The Thracian maidens or Maenads, devotees of Dionysus, grew angry at his indifference—to them or to the god Orpheus had abandoned, depending on which version you read. They tore him limb from limb and threw his head and lyre into the River Hebrus. The Muses buried Orpheus' remains; his lyre was set among the stars and his shade reunited with Eurydice. The story is told by Ovid, *Metamorphoses*, in Books X and XI, and Virgil, *Georgics* IV 454–527. Gay echoes the latter.

405–24 *Days of the Week*: Virgil gives an account of lucky days of the month in *Georgics* I 276–86. Gay borrows, comically, the idea of reading natural signs as prognostications.

410 *Hockley-hole*: at Hockley-in-the-Hole, on what is now Ray Street, just north of where Faringdon and Clerkenwell Streets intersect, there was a bear garden. Here bears and bulls on chains were matched against fighting dogs. 'You should go to Hockley-in-the-Hole . . . to learn Valour' says Mrs Peachum to Filch in *The Beggar's Opera* (Act I scene VI).

414 *broad-finn'd Maid*: probably one or more species of shad, which live in coastal waters and return to rivers to spawn.

415 *Joul*: head and shoulders.

416 *unscaly Soale*: Dover sole, sometimes known as slime sole, are especially soft and slippery to handle.

418 *Zealots*: fervent believers. Fasting practices were becoming more relaxed in Gay's time, but it was still common to abstain from meat on designated days and periods.

419 *Wednesdays and Fridays*: Judas arranged for Christ's arrest on a Wednesday; Jesus was crucified on a Friday.

429 *Elders early Bud*: the elder, *Sambucus niger*, was usually in flower at the end of May.

432 *Mackrell Cries*: mackerel in season were cheap—six for fourpence in Laroon's Cryes (1711).

433 *Wallnutts . . . stain*: when first picked, walnuts are green and have staining juices.

435–6 *Oranges . . . Dice*: for penny stakes, children customarily threw dice for oranges, especially on Shrove Tuesday.

437 *Rosemary, and Bays*: long-lasting and aromatic, these plants were used as Christmas decorations. Compare Robert Herrick, poem for Candlemas Eve (1 Feb.), beginning 'Down with the Rosemary and Bays . . .'

442 *sacred Mistletoe*: in his *Natural History*, Pliny reported mistletoe was sacred to Druids. An influential plate in Aylett Sammes's *Britannia Antiqua Illustrata* (1676) showed a Druid with mistletoe.

458 *palsy'd*: paralysed. Anglican ideas of charity placed great emphasis on the giving hand.

461 *Farthing*: a small coin worth a quarter of a penny.

463 *Rail*: railings running round the square, and separating off rich from poor.

465 *cheaply wipes his Score*: pays his debts.

467–8 *Flannel Band*: door knockers were muffled when someone inside the house was dying. Compare Pope, *Epistle to Dr Arbuthnot* (1735), ll. 1–2, pretending to be not at home: 'Shut, shut the door, good John! fatigu'd, I said, / Tie up the knocker, say I'm sick, I'm dead'.

469 *Upholder*: undertaker. A harbinger is one who announces the approach of someone or something.

475 *F****: William Fortescue, an attorney, as indicated by the next line's reference to his briefs (a brief is a summary of facts and law points relevant to a case). He was a friend of Gay's from childhood and a cousin by marriage; Pope dedicated to him the first of his *Imitations of Horace*. In invoking a friend notionally accompanying the poet on a walk, Gay echoes Virgil, *Georgics* II 39–41: 'And draw thou near, O Maecenas, and with me traverse the toilsome course I have essayed' (Fairclough).

477 *Temple*: there were four Inns of Court, of which Middle and Inner Temple were two.

479 *Strand*: the long, busy thoroughfare that connects Charing Cross to Fleet Street, so called because it ran parallel with the strand or shore of the Thames.

480 *With thee conversing*: as Williams notes, an echo of Eve to Adam in Milton, *Paradise Lost* IV 639, 'With thee conversing I forget all time'.

481 *that narrow Street*: Arundel Street, built in 1678. Dearing and Beckwith note that the embankment of the Thames made it less steep.

483 *Arundell*: Arundel House, which housed the art collection of the second Earl of Arundel, Thomas Howard (1585–1646), connoisseur,

collector, and promoter of artists including Inigo Jones, van Dyck and Rubens. Gay contrasts Renaissance masterpieces of colour and beauty by the painters Titian and Raphael with topical ephemera on paper.

487 *the Bell-man's Song*: either verses about the bellman, or, like the Cries of London, a representation of the bellman's various announcements.

488 *Overton*: probably Philip Overton (*c.*1680–1745), one of two print-selling brothers, whose shop was nearby in Fleet Street.

Phidias: the most acclaimed sculptor of antiquity, Phidias (*c.*490–430 BCE) was famous for two monumental works in particular, a gold ivory statue of Zeus at Olympia and Athena Parthenos at Athens. He oversaw the design and sculptures of the Acropolis. The conceit of breathing statues is used by Virgil.

490 *Pump . . . Watch-house*: the watch-house, now surrounded by King's College London buildings on the Strand, still survives; the adjacent pump has gone.

Essex: Gay takes us westwards down the Strand, in elegiac evocation of aristocratic palaces along the river bank. Essex House, home of Elizabeth I's favourites Robert Dudley and Robert Devereux, was largely demolished in 1675–6.

491 *Cecil's, Bedford's, Villers'*: Cecil House, on the north side of the Strand, once the residence of Elizabeth I's chief minister William Cecil, Lord Burleigh, was in Gay's time occupied by millinery and home furnishings. Bedford House, built by the first Earl of Bedford on what is now Southampton Street, was torn down in 1704. York House belonged to James I's favourite George Villiers, first Duke of Buckingham; it also housed his fine collection of Italian paintings. The site's associations survive in street names marking the site: York, Villiers, Duke, and Buckingham Streets still exist.

493 *Burlington's fair Palace*: the mansion in Piccadilly, a mile west of the Strand, turned by the third Earl of Burlington, Richard Boyle, into a Palladian mansion. Both Gay and Pope addressed poems to Burlington as a patron of the arts. In 1854 the government purchased Burlington House as a home for the Royal Academy of Arts and other learned societies.

494 *without*: outside. Gay's elegant line means, beauty reigns on the inside of Burlington's palace, proportion reigns on its outside.

497 *Hendel*: Georg Friederich Händel, German composer who settled in England from 1712. By 1716 he used an Anglicized spelling of his name—George Frederick Handel; up to that date, Hendel was what appeared on his music. He lived at Burlington House 1712–16; he also knew Burlington through the Royal Academy of Music.

501 *The Happiness of Walkers*: a parody of Virgil's *Georgics* II 458–74, on the happiness of husbandmen.

506 *Saffron*: true jaundice gives a yellow pigment to the eyes, from bilirubin, a by-product of old red blood cells.

510 *burning Gout*: gout, caused by a build-up of uric acid crystals in body joints, painfully impedes mobility. On its traditional association with the rich, see Roy Porter and George S. Rousseau, *Gout: The Patrician Malady* (New Haven, 1998); for general views of eighteenth-century medicine, see Roy Porter, *Disease, Medicine and Society in England, 1550–1860* (Basingstoke, 1987). Gay links ailments to inactivity for poetic purposes; his description of jaundice as 'lazy' has no basis in medical ideas then or now.

521 *the Coach's various Harms*: Gay comically exaggerates the dangers of travelling by methods involving the labour of others. Nonetheless, coach accidents were common, and often injurious.

529 *Dustman*: as Dearing and Beckwith note, an Act of 1671 provided for clearance of sewer grates at least once a week; those who drove carts of muck away were to proceed at walking pace, which Gay's dustman comically does not.

535 *Son of Phoebus*: Phaeton, headstrong son of Phoebus Apollo, the sun god, took his father's chariot, much to Jove's displeasure, who hurled a thunderbolt to stop him burning up the earth. Unable to control the horses, Phaeton crashed and was killed. Gay parodies Ovid's description in *Metamorphoses* II 1–328, especially 311–15. A fresh translation of Ovid by Dryden, Pope, Congreve, and others was published in 1713. In the 1740s, a light, four-wheeled open carriage called a phaeton continued the association.

541 *the seventh-born Doctor*: folk wisdom had it that the seventh son of a seventh son was a born physician. On quackery, see Roy Porter, *Health for Sale: Quackery in England 1660–1850* (Manchester, 1989).

544–8 *Such . . . Suits*: the markets Gay names sold general goods as well as particular specialities. The passage parallels Virgil, *Georgics* I 56–9, on commodities.

552 *Science*: in its general sense, from the Latin *scientia*, knowledge.

553 *Scholiasts*: commentators, especially those writing on classics or theology.

555 *Bee*: the trope of learning as honey distilled from flowers was an old one.

559 *Plutarch*: Greek biographer, historian, essayist (46AD–*c.*122AD). His *Moralia*, containing essays, speeches, and other works, was still influential in the eighteenth century.

560 *Bacon*: Sir Francis Bacon (1561–1626), Renaissance essayist and philosopher; his essays (1597) were widely admired in the eighteenth century.

Stagyra's Sage: Aristotle, born at Stagirus, a Greek colony and seaport in Thrace.

561 *o'er Otway weep*: Thomas Otway (1652–85) dramatist; his blank verse tragedy *The Orphan* (1680) regularly moved eighteenth-century audiences to tears; *Venice Preserv'd* (1682) found Europe-wide success. In 1712 his *Works* were published, with an account of his life and writings.

562 *Congreve*: William Congreve (1670–1729), playwright best known for his comedy *The Way of the World* (1700).

D***: John Dennis (1657–1734), author of plays, poems, and criticism, now almost all forgotten except for their ill-nature. Dennis quarrelled with Pope, *inter alia*, who devoted a 1713 work to him, *The Narrative of Dr Robert Norris*, and satirized him notably in *The Dunciad*. In 1712 in a parodic dedication to his play *The Mohocks*, Gay poked fun at Dennis's choleric criticism.

563 *the Lock's fam'd Rape*: Pope's *The Rape of the Lock* had been published in a two-canto version in 1712, and five cantos in 1714.

564 *Garth*: Sir Samuel Garth (1661–1719), a friend of Gay and Pope. His satirical poem *The Dispensary* (1699), about rivalries between physicians and apothecaries in London, took up a quarrel about physicians prescribing medicines for free to the poor. An apozem is a deconcoction or infusion made from boiling.

565 *Lintott*: Bernard Lintot (1675–1836), the bookseller who published *Trivia*: his emblem of crossed keys, which adorns *Trivia*'s title-page, imaged the location of his shop, at the Cross Keys between the Temple Gates on Fleet Street.

567 *gratis*: free. To open-air browsers, yes; otherwise, 1716 purchasers paid a shilling for Gay's poem. A 1795 edition sold for sixpence.

570 *vain Virgin*: it was increasingly a cliché in the early eighteenth century that women were too inclined to marry for money and over-attracted by the status symbols of retinue, especially a fine coach.

574 *Flanders Mares*: grey mares whose elegant trot made them fashionable among the aristocracy.

575–86 Gay's gallery of ostentatious, talentless types echoes Juvenal's list of despicables in *Satires* I 22–80.

575 *Equipage*: here, the trappings of rank.

Place: a post at court or in government.

blazon: formal language of description for a coat-of-arms, here, also echoing 'blaze' or visibility.

577 *Scutcheon*: escutcheon or coat-of arms, originally on a shield; here, painted arms on the side of a coach.

578 *Coxcomb*: a shallow, showy fellow, a conceited type. From cock's comb, imitated by a jester's badge, hence a fool.

581 *begirt with tinselled Slaves*: surrounded by servants dressed in gold or silver-ornamented livery.

583 *clustering Train*: a long trailing part of a robe; it can also mean a large retinue. Both evoke extravagant ostentation.

586 *The Publick rifles*: metaphors of plunder were commonplace in eighteenth-century discussions of corruption.

590 *Wrapt in my Vertue*: an echo of Horace, wrapped in his virtue in *Odes* III xxix 54–5, and providing a light internal rhyme for surtout, an overcoat.

BOOK III

4 *Cynthia*: one of the epithets for Artemis, goddess of the moon, from her birthplace of Mount Cynthos on Delos. Dearing and Beckwith note 'The Romans identified Trivia with Diana (Cynthia), and Diana with Luna.'

10 *Vest*: here, in the sense of loose outer garment (not waistcoat, as the term usually means in this period, nor the nineteenth-century term for a thin undergarment worn next to the skin on the upper body).

12 *Shop-Windows*: wooden shutters hinged at the top, raised during opening hours and let down at closing time.

13 *Lab'rers*: labourers.

16 *Passes*: restricted passages.

18 *Saint Clement*: in full, St Clement Danes, rebuilt by Sir Christopher Wren in 1680. The spire, built by Gibbs, was added in 1719–20. In Gay's time St Clement's was hemmed in by houses and small streets running into the Strand that became wider beyond the church.

25 *steep Lanes*: Essex Street and Milford Lane, which connected the Strand to the Thames; the *Collier's Steeds* are horses hauling coal from barges on the river below.

27 *Team*: of horses, the number depending on the weight of the load. More would be added to haul heavier loads, as in line 31.

35–44 This section echoes Juvenal, *Satires* III 236–7 on drovers, and Virgil, *Georgics* III 220–41 on bulls fighting; it also plays with the mock element of mock-heroic, because coachmen with whips could and did injure people.

45 *Ytene*: '[place] of the Jutes', who inhabited the area before the Norman
    Conquest. Gilbert White's *Natural History and Antiquities of Selbourne,
    in the County of Southampton* (1789) devotes Letters XXXII and
    XXXIII to characterful local boars; he also describes New Forest fauna
    as it was in Queen Anne's day.

46 *Westphalia*: an independent duchy on the North Rhine (after 1815,
    part of Prussia). Its chestnuts are still famous.

51 *Of Pick-Pockets*: Gay's account imparts more sleight-of-hand to pick-
    pockets than was often the case in practice, to stress the middle part
    of the legal definition of pickpocketing, which was to steal from the
    person of another, without their knowledge, goods worth more than a
    shilling.

53 *Silver Hilt*: in February 1716, Joseph Hutton was tried for stealing a
    silver hilt sword, value 52 shillings, from a Captain James Cox, on
    Fleet Street, also a silver watch, value 4 pounds, from a young man.
    The month before Hutton had stolen a periwig worth 15 shillings.
    The crimes were aggravated by violence; he was sentenced to death.
    See *The Proceedings of the Old Bailey*, **oldbaileyonline.org**, case ref.
    t 17160222–7.

55 *Flaxen Wigg*: a wig (the word is a shortened form of periwig) could
    be various colours; fair shades cost as much as 30 guineas (according to
    The Guardian No. 97) Theft cases tried at the Old Bailey in 1715–16
    involved wigs ranging in value from £8 to 15 shillings. Drunken fracas
    in which wigs came off seem more common than Gay's hidden pur-
    loiner. On the significance of wigs, see Lynn Festa, 'Personal Effects:
    Wigs and Individualism in the Long Eighteenth Century', *Eighteenth-
    Century Life*, 29 (2005).

58 *Rapine*: literally, seizing by force (from the Latin *rapere*, to seize.) Pope's
    The Rape of the Lock (1714) uses this sense as well as its more usual
    meaning of sexual violence.

59 *Slight*: acts of dexterous practice and trickery. Both this spelling and
    'sleight' were accepted usage (thus in Johnson's *Dictionary*, 1755).

64 *scudding Lurcher*: a characteristically ingeniously layered allusion. A
    lurcher is a crossbreed dog, usually part greyhound (hence swift, like
    scudding clouds), used in hunting small prey. Gay may have known a
    fable of 1710, *The History of Reynard the Fox and Reynardine his Son*,
    which pits a Lurcher against a Fox (in a political allegory). The allusion
    is more probably to John Fletcher's play (1633, with James Shirley
    but usually printed among the plays Fletcher wrote with Francis
    Beaumont) *The Nightwalker; or, The Little Thief*, its title apt for the
    setting of Book III, in which a thief called Tom Lurcher collaborates

with a small boy to steal valuables from a household in an uproar over a tragi-comic wedding. Fletcher's mix of heroics and farce informs Gay's fusion of the ordinary and the allegorical, myth and satire, the topical and timeless.

68 *callow*: unfledged. The word comes from the Latin for bald, *calvus*, an etymology made witty in the light of the wig-snatching scene previous.

73 *Rout*: disorderly company, though the word was increasingly used in the eighteenth century to describe a fashionable gathering.

74 *Pump*: petty thieves caught by onlookers were often roughly punished by being held under pumps or dragged through ponds.

79 *Syrens*: the Sirens lured men to their deaths by their irresistible songs. Odysseus sailed past them safely by heeding Circe's advice to plug his crew's ears with wax and lash himself to the mast. Homer, *Odyssey*, Book XII 33–55.

80 *diving*: dart out of sight; also slang for pick-pocketing.

82 *Cambrick*: fine white linen, from Cambrai, a town in northern France famous for fabrics.

95 *the Trojan*: Aeneas; his lost bride was Creusa, eldest daughter of Prima and Hecuba. Compare Dryden's translation of Virgil's *Aeneid* Book II (1697): 'For, while thro' winding ways I took my flight, / and sought the shelter of the gloomy night, / Alas! I lost Creusa . . .'

97 *Nisus*: having escaped the vengeful forces of the Greek Turnus, Nisus went back to look for his friend Euryalus, only to see him killed and be himself killed. Virgil, *Aeneid* Book IX, 367.

114 *th'officious Link-Boy's smoaky Light*: a link was a torch of tow or pitch (from medieval Latin, *linchinus*, a wick or match). To keep links burning, the charred parts had to be rubbed away; hence link-slabs or stones in doorways, on which links could be rubbed without damaging brickwork.

124 *Huckster*: a peddlar, hawker, or trader of small goods.

131 *impervious*: literally, not affording passage to.

133 *Lincoln's Inn*: north of the Strand, east of Holborn, Lincoln's Inn is one of the four Inns of Court (named for the third Earl of Lincoln, d. 1311, who had an estate there). Development in the 1630s included twelve acres of land, known as Lincoln's Inn Fields, laid out by Inigo Jones and others, to remain a green space in perpetuity. It was fenced off by wooden rails.

141 *quench the flaming Brand*: neither link-men nor beggars are much represented in street robbery records of the time, suggesting poetic licence in this episode.

145 *Augusta*: in the fourth century AD, London was given the honorary
name Augusta, according to the historian Arminius Marcellinus. The
name didn't stick, but poets used it for variety, to evoke the grandeur of
Augustus's Rome, and to summon up an association with Augustus's
chief poet, Virgil. Gay's contemporaries played with variations, including Thomas D'Urfey's *The Trophies, or Augusta's Glory* (1707); Elkanah
Settle's *Augusta Triumphans* (1707) and *Augusta Lacrimans* (1709),
and Daniel Defoe's *Augusta Triumphant: or, the Way to Make London
the Most Flourishing City in the Universe* (answer: establish a university.)

145–52 *Happy Augusta . . . made*: the comparisons are standard ones: compare
Settle, *Augusta Triumphans*, on '*Rome's* Tyrannick Sons of *Blood*'.

151 *Bravos*: hired assassins.

153–4 *Let not the Chairman . . . side*: Dearing and Beckwith cite Swift,
Journal to Stella, 22 February 1710/11: 'the chairmen that carried me
squeezed a great fellow against a wall, who wisely turned his back, and
broke one of the side glasses in a thousand pieces.'

158 *Flambeau*: a torch made of wicks dipped in wax, which gave a cleaner,
stronger light than a link and was mostly carried by footmen.
Sashes: sash windows. Vertically sliding, usually with the upper half
fixed until both halves were adapted to slide *c*.mid-century, they
became a staple of Georgian architecture after their adoption in 1681
(the word comes from the French for frame, 'chassis'.)

Pell-Mell: better known as Pall Mall, this fashionable street laid out
in 1661 took its name from *pallamaglio*, Italian for a game, popular
among the nobility, in which one hits a wooden ball with a wooden
stick through an iron hoop.

183–4 *Charybdis*: the daughter of Poseidon and Gaia, turned by Zeus into
a savage monster who sucked waters in and out three times a day, in
a whirlpool off Sicily, opposite the rock of Scylla. Scylla, loved by
Glaucus, was jealously transformed by Circe into a monster who
terrorized ships. She ate some of Odysseus' companions as he passed
between her and Charybdis. Gay's comedy of the dangers of crossing
the road uses mock-epic jokes lightly here.

185 *Ostrea*: an oyster-woman. The native oyster, *ostrea edulis*, sometimes
called the brown oyster, had been prized since Roman times. Many
were harvested from Essex estuaries; Wallfleet oysters were thought to
be among the finest. Until the nineteenth century when over-fishing
put an end to abundance and turned oysters into food for the rich, they
were affordable to the poor: as Dickens wrote in *Pickwick Papers*,
'Poverty and oysters always seem to go together.' In Gay's time a barrel
of oysters cost between one and three shillings, depending on size.
Samuel Johnson bought them to feed his cat.

195–8   *The Man . . . Throat*: a parody of Horace, *Odes* I. iii. 9–10 on the first man to venture on the ocean.

201   *Blood stuff'd in Skins*: blood was an ingredient of black pudding, a kind of sausage.

202   *the croaking Brood*: frogs. A nice example of periphrasis, a roundabout way of describing that invites the reader to enjoy the difference between a simple definition and a poetic one.

203   *Morells*: a rich-tasting fungus, a kind of mushroom. A ragout is a stew. British writers were contemptuous of the liquidity of French cuisine, thought to disguise the inferiority of their meat, as opposed to the solid virtues of, say, roast beef.

211   *Shed*: penthouse.

215–24   *Œdipus . . . Way*: Laius, king of the Thebes, married Jocasta. Years passed; the couple were childless. Laius consulted an oracle at Delphi which advised him to remain without an heir because his own child would kill him, marry his mother, and bring disaster on the city. Jocasta then bore a son, whom Laius sent away to be exposed on Mount Citheron. A shepherd took pity on him and gave him to the childless king of Corinth. The child, Oedipus, grew up and in pursuit of his true parentage, consulted the Delphi oracle which told him he would kill his father and marry his mother. To prevent this, Oedipus wandered the world. At a crossroads he met with Laius and his entourage. A quarrel about rights-of-way ensued; Oedipus killed Laius and went on his way. He met the Sphinx, who tore to pieces everyone who failed to answer a riddle. Laius's successor, Creon, offered his queen and his kingdom to anyone who could solve it. Oedipus did, and thereby married his mother, producing several children. When the city of Thebes was afflicted by a plague, the Delphi oracle declared it could only be ended if Laius's murderer was driven out. By various means the truth was discovered and Oedipus, distraught, discovered he was guilty of incest too. He blinded himself and left Thebes, accompanied by his daughter Antigone.

227   *sable*: the heraldic (and poetic) term for black.

239   *colour'd Oil*: eighteenth-century paints were made from white lead, pigment, linseed oil, and turpentine. The last two ingredients create a distinctive smell.

249   *Guinea-Dropper*: a form of cheat, in which the perpetrator pretends to find money on the street and offers a passer-by a share, who thereby becomes susceptible to more ruses, such as being relieved of money by card games.

252 *Sham-Quarrel*: a particular phase of the Guinea-Dropping, in which the perpetrator and confederate pretend to quarrel so as to reassure the victim they are not confederates.

260 *Drury's mazy Courts*: the area around Drury Lane was well known for prostitutes. Drury Lane runs north–south next to Covent Garden.

268 *Stays*: an underbodice stiffened with whalebone. Where the nineteenth-century corset emphasized a waist and separated breasts, eighteenth-century stays created a flattened front and breasts pushed upwards.

270 *new-scower'd Manteau*: her loose gown is newly cleaned, but Gay implies a need to scour, rather than (moral) spotlessness.

271 *High-draggled*: though the prostitute has tucked up her clothes behind to stop them trailing in mud, they are immodest and muddy.

272 *hollow Cheeks*: loss of teeth from venereal disease (rather than poverty) explains the prostitute's hollow cheeks; the use of rouge ('artful Blushes') manifests her artifice.

276 *muffled Pinners*: a pinner is a small cap, pinned to the head, sometimes with long flaps or strings, often with a ruffle at the front and sides— here big enough to shade her face.

277–9 *empty Bandbox . . . Quaker's Hood*: the empty bandbox—Gay's sexual innuendo—implies the prostitute is carrying something legitimately bought (rather than illicitly sold); by pretending she comes from the Exchange (either Exeter Exchange or the New Exchange, both a little farther down off the Strand) she avoids her profession being immediately identified. Quaker hoods had particularly deep sides, for modesty, which the prostitute's business inverts or profanes.

281 *Sarsnet*: fine soft silk.

296 *Hanger*: a short sword, originally one hung from a belt.

297 *Round-House*: where the watchmen kept suspects.

300 *nauseous Pills*: the yeoman faces treatment for venereal disease. John Marten, *A Treatise of all the Degrees and Symptoms of the Venereal Disease, in both Sexes* (6th edition, 1708, 120), gives a recipe for such pills, prescribed by Samuel Smith, surgeon at St Thomas's Hospital, which induced both vomit and purge.

302 *the Surgeon's fees*: it was commonplace to believe medical practitioners usually cared more about payment than effecting cures.

304 *ruin'd Nose*: syphilis induces rottenness of nasal bones. 'Ruin' was a word constantly applied to unchasity in women. Dearing and Beckwith detect an allusion to Girolamo Fracastoro's poem *Syphilis* (1530).

306 *Mug*: a colloquialism for face.

314 *scow'ring Crew*: here, to scour is to go along hastily, especially in search or pursuit.

326 *Mohocks*: in 1712 Gay published *The Mohocks: A Tragi-Comical Farce. As it was Acted near the Watch-house in Covent Garden.* 'The Subject of it is *Horrid* and *Tremendous*', Gay wrote, and his Mohocks sing in chorus 'We will scower the Town, / Knock the Constable down, / Put the Watch and the Beadle to flight' (Prologue and p. 4). The Mohocks, so-called after a Mohawk chief visited London in 1710, had a reputation in part exaggerated by literature, although *The Town Rakes, or the Frolicks of the Mohocks* (1712) also alleges they had rolled an old woman in a tub down Snow Hill, and several sources say they enjoyed slashing the noses and legs of passers-by, to which Gay refers in 'new-invented Wounds'.

330 *Snow-hill*: a steep and busy street, south of Smithfield and west of Holborn. Snow Hill ends just opposite Newgate, hence symbolic for Gay's purposes.

334 *Regulus*: Marcus Atilius Regulus, Roman general in the first Punic War, was captured by the Carthaginians and sent back to Rome to sue for peace. Instead he advised the Senate to resist, returned to Carthage, and was tortured to death (*c.*250 BCE). According to Diocassius, his eyelids were cut off and he was placed in a barrel of spikes in the sun until he died. Gay's comic contrast of patriot hero and harmless women is also a parallel of sadism.

335 *paly*: a poeticism for pale.

345 *Eddystone*: the Eddystone lighthouse, England's most famous lighthouse, marks a dangerous reef off Rame Head in Cornwall. First built by Henry Winstanley in 1698, it was rebuilt in 1699, then replaced by John Rudyerd in 1703 after a great storm. Rudyerd's version lasted forty-seven years until destroyed by fire; it was succeeded in 1759 by John Smeaton's design, which set a worldwide standard, then redesigned again in 1882.

354 *Fire*: the most famous conflagration in London, the Great Fire of 1666, supposedly began at a baker's shop in Pudding Lane and spread to destroy much of the City of London, which was then redesigned by Sir Christopher Wren. But the nature of eighteenth-century life was flammable: tradestuffs and timber led to frequent fires, and Gay's description is generalized, though previous editors note parallels with Virgil, *Georgics* II 303–11, and with Dryden's *Annus Mirabilis* (1667) on the Great Fire. Survivals of the period's fire-fighting equipment, including fire-engines and firemens' uniforms, can be seen at Blazes, The Fire Museum, near Taunton in Somerset.

362   *crooked Arms*: probably from steadying yokes used to carry two buckets
of water.

363   *Casque*: helmet.

368   *Dardan hero*: Aeneas, who was descended from Dardan, Zeus's son.
Virgil, *Aeneid* II, tells how Aeneas carried his old father Anchises away
from burning Troy.

376   *sanguine*: blood-red.

377   *such a Light*: before Julius Caesar's assassination, portents were
reported, including fires in the sky. See Virgil, *Georgics* I 461–8.

382–6   One way to slow the spread of fire was to destroy houses in its path,
either by pulling them down, or by blowing them up with gunpowder
(the 'nitrous Store'). During the Great Fire, this was done, but late in
the fire's progress.

388   *Naples' Fate*: volcanic activity around Naples had increased after major
eruptions of Vesuvius in 1631, and Etna in 1669. In 1712–15 there
were annual eruptions of Vesuvius; in 1702, an eruption of Etna had
smothered Catania, Sicily's second-largest city. Though Gay's progno-
sis owes something to Virgil, *Georgics* I 471–3, it also follows contemporary descriptions which saw eruptions as coming from subterranean
bowels and entrails—Gay's more sexualized 'womb' is less usual. For an
account of eighteenth-century vulcanology, or the study of volcanoes,
see Davis A. Young, *Mind over Magma: The Story of Igneous Petrology*
(Princeton: Princeton University Press, 2003), ch. 1.

401   *barb'rous Arabs*: although the cruelty of Arabs was an eighteenth-
century cliché, here it is conflated with Barbary, the name given to the
north coast of Africa.

405   *Journals*: first-person accounts of travels—some, like Gulliver's, wildly
fictional—were becoming increasingly popular among eighteenth-
century readers.

407   *Finish'd . . . Immortality*: Williams notes an allusion to Horace, Odes
III. xxx. 1: 'I have finished a monument more lasting than bronze'.

411   *W* and G***: Ned Ward, author of *The London Spy* (1698–1700) and
Charles Gildon, author of *The New Rehearsal* (1714), which mocks
Pope and Gay. Like Pope in *The Dunciad*, Gay takes the opportunity
to retaliate, here by associating unashamedly topical writers with transience and worthlessness.

412   *Chelsea . . . Custards*: Chelsea was then a village on the west of London,
noted for its baked goods, including open pies. The anxiety aired by
Horace in *Epistles* II I 269–70, that his works would be used to wrap
purchases made on the street, was recycled by early eighteenth-century

writers. Commonest forms were that sheets of poetry would end up being used in boghouses, or to wrap food. Gay's playful fantasy of literature wrapping fireworks is uncommon.

415 *Fleetstreet Posts*: advertisements for new books were posted upon walls and in the doorways of booksellers along Fleet Street. Thus *Trivia* ends, topographically neat, at one possible place of its purchase.

Select Bibliography

Addison, Joseph, and Steele, Richard, *The Spectator, 1711–14*, ed. Donald F. Bond, 5 vols. (Oxford, 1965; 1987).

Ames, Diane S., 'Gay's *Trivia* and the Art of Allusion', *Studies in Philology*, 75 (1978), 199–222.

Anonymous, *A Walk from St. James's to Covent-Garden, the Back-Way through the Meuse* (1717).

Armens, Sven M., *John Gay: Social Critic* (New York, 1966).

Bahlman, Dudley, *The Moral Revolution of 1688* (Hamden, Conn., 1968).

[Bancks, John], *A Description of London* (1751).

Borden, Iain, et al. (eds.), *The Unknown City* (Cambridge, Mass., 2001).

Boswell, James, *Boswell's London Journal, 1762–1763*, ed. Frederick A. Pottle (1951).

Boulton, Jeremy, *Neighbourhood and Society* (Cambridge, 1987).

Boyer, C. M., *The City of Collective Memory: Its Historical Imagery and Architectural Entertainments* (Cambridge, Mass., 1994).

Braund, Susanna Morton, 'City and Country in Roman Satire', in Susanna Morton Braund (ed.), *Satire and Society in Ancient Rome* (Exeter, 1989), 23–47.

Breval, John D., *The Art of Dress* (1717).

—— *The Petticoat: An Heroi-Comical Poem* (1716).

Brosseau, Marc, 'The City in Textual Form: *Manhattan Transfer's* New York', *Ecumene*, 2 (1995), 89–114.

Brown, Thomas, *Amusements Serious and Comical*, ed. Arthur L. Hayward (1700; 1927).

Canetti, Elias, *Crowds and Power*, trans. C. Stewart (1984).

Carnochan, Bliss, 'Gay's *Trivia* and the Ways of Walking', in Peter E. Firchow and Hermann J. Real (eds.), *Perennial Satirist: Essays in Honour of Bernfried Nugel* (Münster, 2005).

Clifford, James, 'Traveling Cultures', in Lawrence Grossberg, Cary Nelson, and Paula A. Treichler (eds.), *Cultural Studies* (1992), 96–116.

Copley, Stephen and Haywood, Ian, 'Luxury, Refuse, and Poetry: John Gay's *Trivia*' in Peter Lewis and Nigel Wood (eds.), *John Gay and the Scriblerians* (1988), 62–82.

Corfield, Penelope, 'Walking the City Streets: The Urban Odyssey in Eighteenth-Century England', *Journal of Urban History*, 16 (1990), 132–74.

Crang, Mike, *Cultural Geography* (2004).

de Certeau, Michel, *The Practice of Everyday Life*, trans. Steven Randall (Berkeley, 1988).

Defoe, Daniel, *The Complete English Tradesman* (1726).

—— *A Tour through the Whole Island of Great Britain*, ed. P. N. Furbank and W. R. Owens (New Haven, 1991).

Draper, William, *The Morning Walk, or City Encompass'd* (1751).

Dugaw, Diane, *'Deep Play': John Gay and the Invention of Modernity* (2001).

Earle, Peter, *A City Full of People: Men and Women of London 1650–1750* (1994).

Fielding, John, *A Description of the Cities of London and Westminster* (1776).

Forsgren, Adina, *John Gay, Poet 'of a Lower Order': Comments on His Urban and Narrative Poetry* (Stockholm, 1971).

Gay, John, *The Fan* (1714).

—— *Letters of John Gay*, ed. C. F. Burgess (Oxford, 1966).

—— *Poetry and Prose*, ed. Vinton A. Dearing and Charles E. Beckwith, 2 vols. (Oxford, 1974).

George, M. Dorothy, *London Life in the Eighteenth Century* (Harmondsworth, 1965).

Gregory, Derek, *Geographical Imaginations* (Cambridge, Mass., 1994).

Griffiths, Paul, and Jenner, Mark S. R. (eds.), *Londinopolis: Essays in the Cultural and Social History of Early Modern London* (Manchester, 2000).

Hammond, Brean, 'The City in Eighteenth-Century Poetry', in John Sitter (ed.), *The Cambridge Companion to Eighteenth-Century Poetry* (Cambridge, 2001).

Harte, Negley B., 'The Economics of Clothing in the Late Seventeenth Century', in Negley B. Harte (ed.), *Fabrics and Fashions: Studies in the Economic and Social History of Dress, Textile History* (1991), 277–96.

Hitchcock, Tim, *Down and Out in Eighteenth-Century London* (2004).

—— and Shore, Heather (eds.), *The Streets of London from the Great Fire to the Great Stink* (2003).

Holme, Randle, *An Academy of Armory* (Chester, 1688).

Hunt, Margaret R., *The Middling Sort: Commerce, Gender, and the Family in England 1680–1780* (Berkeley and Los Angeles, 1996).

Jacobs, Jane, *The Death and Life of Great American Cities* (2000).

—— 'The Use of Sidewalks: Safety', in Richard T. Le Gates and Frederic Stout (eds.), *The City Reader*, 2nd edn. (2000), 107–11.

Jenks, Chris, 'Watching your Step: The History and Practice of the Flâneur', in Chris Jenks (ed.), *Visual Culture* (2002), 142–60.

Johnson, Samuel, *Lives of the English Poets,* 2 vols. (Oxford, 1905).

—— *The Yale Edition of the Works of Samuel Johnson*, eds. W. J. Bate and Albrecht B. Strauss, 16 vols. (New Haven, 1958–90).

Kernan, Alvin B., *The Plot of Satire* (New Haven, 1965).

Kirk, Eugene, 'Gay's "Roving Muse": Problems of Genre and Intention in *Trivia*', *English Studies*, 62 (1981), 259–70.

Klein, Bernhard, *Maps and the Writing of Space in Early Modern England and Ireland* (Basingstoke, 2001).

Kneale, James, 'Secondary Worlds: Reading Novels as Geographical Research', in Alison Blunt et al. (eds.), *Cultural Geography in Practice* (2003), 39–51.

Lambert, Sam (ed.), *London Night and Day* (1952).

Lees, Lynn Hollen, *The Solidarities of Strangers: The English Poor Laws and the People, 1700–1948* (Cambridge, 1998).

McDowell, Paula, *The Women of Grub Street: Press, Politics, and Gender in the London Literary Marketplace, 1678–1730* (Oxford, 1998).

Macky, John, *A Journey through England* (1714).

McWhir, Anne, 'The Wolf in the Fold: John Gay in *The Shepherd's Week* and *Trivia*', *Studies in English Literature, 1500–1900*, 23 (1983), 413–23.

Mandeville, Bernard, *The Fable of the Bees, or Private Vices, Publick Benefits* (1714).

Melville, Lewis, *Life and Letters of John Gay* (1921).

Miller, William I., *The Anatomy of Disgust* (Cambridge, Mass., 1997).

Mitchell, Don, *Cultural Geography: A Critical Introduction* (Oxford, 2000).

Morgan, Fidelis (ed.), *The Female Tatler* (1992).

Mumford, Lewis, 'What is a City?' (1937), in Richard T. Le Gates and Frederic Stout (eds.), *The City Reader*, 2nd edn. (2000), 92–106.

Nokes, David, *John Gay: A Profession of Friendship* (Oxford, 1995).

Nussbaum, Felicity, *The Brink of All We Hate: English Satires on Women, 1660–1750* (Lexington, Ky., 1984).

Ogborn, Miles, *Spaces of Modernity: London's Geographies 1680–1780* (1998).

Paulson, Ronald, *Don Quixote in England: The Aesthetics of Laughter* (Baltimore, 1998).

Picard, Liza, *Dr. Johnson's London* (2001).

Ribeiro, Aileen, 'Men and Umbrellas in the Eighteenth Century', *Journal of the Royal Society of Arts*, 5362 (Sept. 1986), 653–6.

—— 'Provision of Ready-Made and Second-Hand Clothing in the Eighteenth Century in England', in *Per una Storia della Moda Pronta: Problemi e Ricerche* (Florence, 1990), 85–94.

Robinson, Howard, *The British Post Office* (Princeton, 1948).

Rogers, Katharine M., *Feminism in Eighteenth-Century England* (Urbana, Ill., 1982).

Rogers, Pat, *The Augustan Vision* (1978).

—— *Grub Street: Studies in a Subculture* (1972).

—— *Literature and Popular Culture in Eighteenth-Century England* (1985).

—— 'Why *Trivia*? Myth, Etymology, and Topography', *Arion*, 3rd series, 12 (2005), 4–5.

Rojek, Chris, and Urry, John (eds.), *Routes: Travel and Translation in the Late Twentieth Century* (Cambridge, Mass., 1997).

Ryder, Dudley, *The Diary of Dudley Ryder, 1715–1716*, ed. W. Matthews (1932).

Sennett, Richard (ed.), *Classic Essays on the Culture of Cities* (Englewood Cliffs, NJ, 1969).

—— *The Fall of Public Man* (1977).

—— *Flesh and Stone: The Body and the City in Western Civilization* (2002).

Shesgreen, Sean (ed.), *The Criers and Hawkers of London: Engravings and Drawings by Marcellus Laroon* (Palo Alto, Calif., 1990).

—— *Images of the Outcast: The Urban Poor in the Cries of London* (Manchester, 2002).

Simmel, Georg, *On Individuality and Social Forms: Selected Writings*, ed. Donald Levine (Chicago, 1971).

Sinclair, Iain, *London Orbital: A Walk around the M25* (2002).

Soja, Edward, *Postmodern Geographies: The Reassertion of Space in Critical Social Theory* (1989).

Spacks, Patricia, *John Gay* (New York, 1965).

Stephen, Leslie, 'In Praise of Walking', *Studies of a Biographer*, 3 vols. (1902), iii. 254–85.

Stevenson, Deborah, *Cities and Urban Cultures* (Maidenhead, 2003).

Summerson, John, *Georgian London*, ed. Howard Colvin (New Haven, 2003).

Sutherland, John, 'John Gay', in James Clifford and Louis Landa (eds.), *Pope and His Contemporaries: Essays Presented to George Sherburn* (Oxford, 1949).

Tieken-Boon van Ostade, Ingrid, 'Of Formulas and Friends: Expressions of Politeness in John Gay's Letters' in Guy A. J. Tops et al. (eds.), *Thinking English Grammar: To Honour Xavier Dekeyser* (Leuven, 1999), 99–112.

Wilson, A. N. (ed.), *The Faber Book of London* (1993).

Wilson, Elizabeth, *The Contradictions of Culture: Cities, Culture, Women* (2001).

Winton, Calhoun, *John Gay and the London Theatre* (Lexington, Ky., 1993).

Zukin, Sharon, *The Cultures of Cities* (Cambridge, Mass., 1995).

Index

Bold figure numbers are references to illustrations